Antoine de Saint-Exupéry

BY THE SAME AUTHOR

Pétain's Crime

Antoine de Saint-Exupéry

THE LIFE AND DEATH
OF
THE LITTLE PRINCE

PAUL WEBSTER

MACMILLAN
LONDON

First published 1993 by Macmillan London Limited

a division of Pan Macmillan Publishers Limited
Cavaye Place London SW10 9PG
and Basingstoke

Associated companies throughout the world

ISBN 0–333–54872–8

1 3 5 7 9 8 6 4 2

A CIP catalogue record for this book is available from
the British Library

Phototypeset by Intype, London
Printed by Mackays of Chatham Plc

Contents

ACKNOWLEDGEMENTS
ix

LIST OF ILLUSTRATIONS
xi

PROLOGUE
The Last Flight
3

PART ONE 1900–1930

CHAPTER ONE
Five Children in a Garden
11

CHAPTER TWO
Looking Death in the Face
27

CHAPTER THREE
'A nous les airs'
47

CHAPTER FOUR
A Battle Missed
62

CHAPTER FIVE
The Disposable Fiancé
73

CHAPTER SIX
A Precise Idea of Nothingness
92

CHAPTER SEVEN
The Lost Navigator
111

PART TWO 1931–1939

CHAPTER EIGHT
Gomez Carrillo's Widow
129

CHAPTER NINE
Happiness, Freedom and Duty
141

CHAPTER TEN
Wadi Natroun
164

CHAPTER ELEVEN
Terre des Hommes
181

PART THREE 1939–1944

CHAPTER TWELVE
Flight to Arras
201

CHAPTER THIRTEEN
The Man Who Didn't Believe
220

CHAPTER FOURTEEN
Le Petit Prince
243

CHAPTER FIFTEEN
Heaven's Pilgrim
253

EPILOGUE
The Search
266

BIBLIOGRAPHY
268

INDEX
270

Acknowledgements

THIS biography could not have been written without the help and advice of relatives and friends of Antoine de Saint-Exupéry and his wife, Consuelo. Mr Frédéric d'Agay, the literary executor, kindly gave permission to use letters and other material, including Simone de Saint-Exupéry's unpublished *Five Children in a Garden* and Marie de Saint-Exupéry's *I Listen to My Tree Singing*. He also drew up the family tree and provided invaluable photographs from the family album. Mr Jean d'Agay, Antoine's nephew, gave considerable guidance. Mr André de Fonscolombe, Antoine's cousin, provided both a fund of anecdotes and photographs.

My wife, Marcelle, was brought up in the Bugey region near Antoine's childhood home and found many of the original stories concerning Ambérieu and Saint-Maurice-de-Rémens as well as discovering previously unexploited archive material and personal recollections. Sources for other passages are usually acknowledged in the text but I would particularly like to express my gratitude to Mr and Mrs Claude Werth, Mr and Mrs Henri Claudel, Mr and Mrs Edmond Petit, Mr Jean Israel, Madame Andrée de Vilmorin, Mr Bernard Dupérier, Mr Daniel Decot, Mr Manuel Sorto, the mayor and councillors of Saint-Maurice-de-Rémens, staff and pupils at the Notre-Dame-de-Sainte-Croix college at Le Mans and Bossuet school in Paris as well as the curators of the Musée d'Air France and the Musée de l'Armée de l'Air. Gallimard gave permission to publish extracts from Pierre Chevrier's 1949 biography while the French civilian pilots' magazine, *Icare*, edited by Jean Lasserre, allowed me to quote from Jean Dutertre's account of the flight to Arras. *Icare*'s eight-part series on Antoine de Saint-Exupéry, with its unique photographs and first-hand accounts of pioneer and wartime flight, was an indispensable guide in locating original sources.

This book owes a great deal to the research, interviews and revision of Patricia Dawson-Boccadoro whose help and encouragement, as well as her admiration for Saint-Exupéry's writing, are gratefully recognized by the author.

List of Illustrations

BETWEEN PAGES
116–117

1. Saint-Exupéry's father, Jean

2. Saint-Exupéry's mother, Marie

3. Marie and Jean's wedding

4. Saint-Maurice-de-Rémens

5. Maria with Saint-Exupéry and François

6. Saint-Exupéry with Tante Madeleine, Marie's sister

7. Gabriel Salvez-Wroblewski with his brother Pierre, 1912

8. Father Auguste Launay's class in 1913

9. Studio portrait of Saint-Exupéry aged twenty-two

10. Saint-Exupéry's sister Gabrielle's wedding to Pierre d'Agay
in October 1923

11. Louise de Vilmorin, Saint-Exupéry's first fiancée

12. Didier Daurat, Aeropostale's operations manager

13. An aerial view of Cape Juby

14. Saint-Exupéry and his best friend, Henri Guillaumet

15. Consuelo Suncin, Saint-Exupéry's wife

16. Saint-Exupéry and Consuelo on their wedding day, April 1931

BETWEEN PAGES
212–213

17. *Consuelo with family friends*

18. *Saint-Exupéry and Consuelo in Nice*

19. *Léon Werth*

20. *Saint-Exupéry and Consuelo at a ski resort in 1931*

21. *Saint-Exupéry with Claude and Léon Werth*

22. *Saint-Exupéry in Toulouse, 1933*

23. *An illustration done for Marie-Sygne Claudel*

24. *Saint-Exupéry aged about thirty-eight*

25. *Saint-Exupéry's drawings for Marie-Sygne Claudel*

26 & 27. *Saint-Exupéry with colleagues during the War*

28. *A Lockheed P–38 Lightning similar to the one in which Saint-Exupéry died*

29. *Consuelo with her bust of Saint-Exupéry*

Antoine de Saint-Exupéry

The Last Flight

By noon on the last day of July 1944, high summer had settled along the Riviera and a cloudless sky spread across a still, azure sea stretching southwards to the island of Corsica. These were the last few days of deceptive peace as Allied troops waited to be shipped across the Mediterranean to liberate Provence from German occupation. The glorious weather was a final benediction before the battle began, a blessing for everyone except a lone airman returning to Corsica from a long-distance reconnaissance flight along the Rhône Valley. Air force weathermen had forecast cloud cover over the coast which would hide him from German fighters. Instead, the empty sky became an ideal setting for an aerial ambush.

The solitary pilot was Antoine de Saint-Exupéry, who had suffered enough injuries in more than twenty years of flying to give an unexpected advantage to an attacker. A tall and heavy man restricted by a bulky flying-suit, he barely fitted into the cramped cockpit. Old wounds made it painful to turn round and watch the dangerous skies and prevented him from using a parachute in an emergency. Under attack, Saint-Exupéry either had to make the most of the exceptional speed and high-altitude abilities of his unarmed P–38 Lightning or go down with his aircraft.

A few minutes after midday, the distinctive twin-boom Lightning roared into view at a low altitude to the west of Nice, twisted towards the sea and disappeared in the Baie des Anges between Nice and Monaco. Behind the Lightning, German fighters pulled out of a dive and returned to report the 'kill' to their base.

Saint-Exupéry might have escaped the ambush if he had not given in to compulsive nostalgia, a characteristic theme of his best-known books. The photographic mission along the Rhône Valley, starting from Bastia in northern Corsica at 8.45 a.m. on 31 July, took him east of Lyon and only 60 kilometres from the family castle at Saint-Maurice-de-Rémens which had provided the happiest moments of his childhood. Almost every metre of the southern French coastline was familiar territory which he had covered many times in pre-war years by road, rail or air. After a similar observation flight on 29 June, Saint-Exupéry had been reprimanded for deviating from his flight plan to overfly his sister's château at Agay, near Saint-Raphaël. The temptation to take another look at places he loved may also have proved irresistible on 31 July.

Just before he plunged into the sea, Saint-Exupéry was slightly off course and flying well below his safe height of 6000 metres. Three places could have drawn him a minute or two westwards from his planned route once he reached Provence, his favourite part of France. His mother's house was at Cabris, above Grasse, which he had last visited in December 1940 before leaving for more than two years' exile in the United States. Further westwards was the château at La Môle, near Saint-Tropez, where his father had been taken on the night he died when Antoine was only three years old. And between these two villages there was the church at Agay where he was married in 1931 to his South American wife, Consuelo Suncin.

In terms of flying time, the detour was of little apparent importance and by swinging eastwards back to Nice along the coastline, Saint-Exupéry might also have spotted the villa where he spent some of the most idyllic moments of his life with his wife when writing *Night Flight*, the novel which recalled his pioneer flying days in Argentina. On 31 July 1944, the villa's vine-covered *terrasse* overlooking the Baie des Anges would have been a privileged vantage-point to witness the final moments of Saint-Exupéry's last mission.

ANTOINE de Saint-Exupéry was forty-four years old when his plane crashed into the sea. His reputation as a writer was well established although he had published only five short books amounting to hardly 1000 printed pages in the original French. However, fame in his lifetime fell far short of his posthumous popularity. He never knew that his best-known story, *Le Petit Prince*, published the year before he died, would one day become the most translated work in the French language with more than eighty foreign editions. Along with this childhood fable, two of his other books, the novel *Vol de nuit* (*Night Flight*) and the non-fictional *Terre des hommes* (*Wind, Sand and Stars*) remain among the ten best-selling French books of the century. All the works released when he was alive, including *Courrier sud* (*Southern Mail*) and *Pilote de guerre* (*Flight to Arras*), were inspired by his flying experiences as a pioneer civilian pilot or during the Battle of France. When his complete works were published as an anthology it outsold similar collections by almost every other French author, contemporary or classical.

The anthology is also evidence of an astonishing versatility. Only Saint-Exupéry's first two books, *Southern Mail* and *Night Flight*, were novels while the other three fit into no identifiable category. It is too easy to say that *Wind, Sand and Stars* is a travel book, that *Flight to Arras* is a war memoir or that *The Little Prince* is written for children. Each is a development of philosophical and moral ideas that he intended refining in his last work, a collection of parables called *Citadelle* or *Wisdom of the Sands*, published after his death from unfinished notes.

Because Saint-Exupéry's adventurous life, ethical observations and mysticism are so present in his books, one of the most important qualities of his work is often overlooked or taken for granted. He is, quite simply, an exceptional writer with a professional and artistic fascination for the use and impact of written language. The conciseness of his books, except for the posthumous *Wisdom of the Sands*, reflected a precision with words which enhanced their beauty and emotional power. Behind Saint-Exupéry's quest for perfection was a laborious process of editing and rewriting which reduced original drafts by as much as two-thirds of their length.

This patient literary craftsmanship, which he compared to releasing a gem from the matrix, was to make him the equal of the greatest names in a golden era of French writing. Even critics who felt ill at ease with Saint-Exupéry's emphasis on duty and sacrifice in *Night Flight* and *Flight to Arras* or resented the sweet idealism of *The Little Prince* became enthralled by some of the most evocative prose in the French language.

Saint-Exupéry was often at pains to say that his personal problems were his own affair, yet his books read like thinly disguised messages to the people who knew him best, containing the essence of his disappointments, joys and moral confusion. Most of the enigmatic sequences should become clear in this biography which will also try to explain the hidden language in *The Little Prince*, a story in which Saint-Exupéry is his own model for both the child and the marooned pilot, full of regret that age has separated him from the absolute truths of his Catholic aristocratic boyhood.

None of his books says more about Saint-Exupéry's inner dilemmas than *The Little Prince*, written during a period of deep melancholy and self-criticism at his inability to make a success of the most adult of challenges, his marriage. This mystical fable about the loss of innocence was in large measure a love letter to his wife, Consuelo, after a union which was nearly destroyed by mutually excessive emotional needs and infidelity.

There is no mystery why Saint-Exupéry turned to a childlike fable to write about his relationship with his wife, the little prince's rose, and his recognition that their destinies were irrevocably bound together by the pain and joy they had shared. In all his writing, Saint-Exupéry drew heavily on childhood sensations as a protection against despair or events beyond his understanding. In *The Little Prince* he went even further and let the voice of innocence speak for him.

The book was completed during a depressing phase in 1942 when he was exiled in the United States between periods of service in the French air force. At the time, he was torn between obligations to his wife and his desire to return to battle in a spirit of patriotic sacrifice. His letters during the months that followed contained a fascination with a purifying death-wish and a yearning for a spiritual rebirth. Later, the little prince's disappearance and the sentence that he 'will appear to be dead but it will not be true' sounded like a self-fulfilling prophecy because Saint-Exupéry's body was never found.

This mythical death may have been the end that he wished for himself after admitting in *The Little Prince* that personal disarray caused by the dissolution of childhood certainties had been the price of entry into an adulthood world where 'everything was a great mystery'.

This desperate note of bewildered resentment echoed the recognition in *Wind, Sand and Stars* that he would never again recapture the dreams and romantic adventures of summer days spent in the house at Saint-Maurice-de-Rémens, near Lyon, not far from the airstrip where he was given his first joy-ride at the age of twelve. The house was sold when Antoine was thirty-two, putting the 'provisions of gentleness' which surrounded him in childhood out of bounds.

Saint-Exupéry made no secret of the sentimental deprivation which followed the sale and desecration of his lost past. Just before the war, he returned to Saint-Maurice and walked along the grey wall around the castle garden 'full of the shadows of childhood'. He wrote of his sadness in a handful of words which were more full of insight into the solitude of adult man than volumes of philosophy.

Struck by a 'form of despair', he was astonished to find that the infinite perspectives he had seen as a boy had narrowed. His playground paradise was gone, shrunken by grown-up eyes, and it pained him that he would 'never again enter this infinity'. Manhood had shut him out of the fairy-tale garden with its alleyways of linden trees and copses of fir and excluded him from innocent games for all time.

'I am not sure that I have lived since childhood,' he wrote to his mother long after he had discovered the apparently exhilarating compensation of flying. For Saint-Exupéry, growing up was the unpardonable sin.

PART ONE

1900–1930

CHAPTER ONE

Five Children in a Garden

THE bedroom at Saint-Maurice-de-Rémens, which Antoine de Saint-Exupéry shared with his younger brother François, looks eastwards across the château's huge garden to the dark green Monts du Bugey among the foothills of the Jura Mountains. This is scenery filled with natural magic, where thick forests are half hidden by autumn mist or summer haze, and sometimes deep in snow. In the crystal-clear air of early spring, the rocky granite valley of the narrow, fast-running Albarine river seems within touching-distance.

Through a child's eye the shadowy hills were a foreign land with its own mysteries and secrets. From his window, Antoine looked over gentle, vine-covered landscape just beyond the protective walled garden of his family château to distant harsh escarpments where battles had been fought for 2000 years both against nature and man. Almost in line with the château, he contemplated the forbidding Saint-Denis tower standing like a lonely sentinel over the entrance to limestone gorges and the ancient Roman road from Lyon to Geneva. More hidden, yet more impressive, was an immense square fortress known as Les Allymes, which made a sand-coloured imprint on the surrounding forest.

From this mighty stronghold, medieval lords once controlled the approaches to the Ain, the most picturesque river in this south-eastern corner of France. Around them, they imposed order, ceremony and religious codes that had crumbled even before the battlements began falling into ruin. Images of this chivalrous world, maintained by a balance between arms and wisdom, accompanied Saint-Exupéry throughout his life, inspiring his last, posthumously published book *Citadelle*, released in English as *Wisdom of the Sands*.

Into this biblical epic, where Christian and Muslim ethics stand side by side in a mythical desert palace, he meditated the lessons of a long journey which had led into the bewildering world beyond the grounds at Saint-Maurice.

Saint-Exupéry called the château grounds 'the country of my childhood'. He was first taken there through the wide iron gates and along the alleyway of four ranks of linden-trees at the age of six weeks for his baptism in the family chapel. He had been born on 29 June 1900 in his parents' apartment at 8 rue Alphonse-Fochier in Lyon, later renamed rue de Peyrat, near the central place Bellecour.

Because of the family's strong religious convictions, they were given permission by the Archbishop of Lyon for a provisional christening within a day of his birth. This allowed time to summon relatives to a solemn ceremony in honour of the heir apparent to the Saint-Exupéry title which dated back to the thirteenth century. His father's family had to make a day-long journey from the western city of Le Mans and his mother's relatives had to travel from Provence, while time was needed to prepare a garden party which many of the 300 villagers would attend either as guests or servants. On 15 August 1900, the feast of the Assumption, the parish priest, François Montessuy, gave the baby his five Christian names, Antoine Jean-Baptiste Marie Roger Pierre. The baptismal certificate was covered with the signatures of family and friends including that of his uncle and godfather, Roger de Saint-Exupéry, an infantry captain.

The godmother, Alice Boyer de Fonscolombe, Antoine's maternal grandmother, was unable to travel from her castle at La Mole near Saint-Tropez and was represented by Antoine's spinster aunt, Madeleine, his mother's younger sister. The first signature was that of Antoine's father, Jean, Vicomte de Saint-Exupéry, who died less than four years later leaving his wife, Marie, to look after five children under eight years of age. The two eldest, Marie-Madeleine and Simone, then three and two years old, were present at the baptism. François was born two years later and the last, Gabrielle, in 1904. Together with Antoine, they were the *Five Children in a Garden*, the title of unpublished memories by Simone which provide the most authentic detail on Saint-Exupéry's early childhood.

[12]

THE first notes for this book were written on the solid oval table in the big dining-room of the eighteenth-century château, the only part still furnished as it was when Antoine's baptism took place. Although his home was sold to Lyon city council in 1932 to become a children's holiday centre, the dining-room has remained for ever fixed in a self-assured aristocratic world. An imposing Italianate dresser covered with carvings of grapes and wheatsheaves stands with the original red leather chairs on a floor of black and white marble tiles. A heavy chandelier is reflected in a huge mirror above an ornate fireplace.

There is not much grace about the setting but there is a feeling of permanence. This is a temple of tradition where the widowed chatelaine, Gabrielle, Comtesse de Tricaud, née de Lestrange, presided over the unspoken hierarchy of a noble family, their guests and the servants.

The area was usually out of bounds for children during their early years when they were looked after by a housekeeper or governess and given their meals near the kitchens. Saint-Exupéry gave the impression that much of the downstairs of the château was a forbidding area peopled by a severe race of grown-ups who had been set above the young to admonish, judge and punish. In *Flight to Arras*, in which he recounted childhood memories that resurfaced during a mission over the 1940 battlefront, he recaptured this fear of adults. When he was five or six years old, he had hidden in terror in the corridor outside the dining-room, listening to snatches of conversation between two of his uncles. One of them, Hubert de Fonscolombe, 'the very image of severity', had threatened to import a whipping-machine from the United States.

From this same panelled hallway, where toys were kept in four long wooden boxes, the five children sometimes listened to the buzz of adult chatter around the dinner-table while they schemed amongst themselves in whispers. In Antoine's recollection, the daunting atmosphere was enhanced after dark by narrow pools of light from paraffin lamps, throwing shadows across a concealed passage to the chapel and from the staircase leading to the bedrooms.

The seeds of Saint-Exupéry's impatience with the obscurity of the adult mind were planted by this mutual incomprehension of the young and the old. The children sought their own refuges that they embellished with fanciful imagination and an atmosphere of juvenile conspiracy. In his first novel, *Southern Mail*, Saint-Exupéry remembered how they watched the stars through the cracks in the tiles above the château's attics, while conscious of the murmur of grown-up conversation from far below. The attics were a playground to be filled with dreams and nightmares. The children were convinced that a great treasure was hidden among the stored family relics, but the strangest hoard was a wardrobe full of their father's civilian clothes and uniforms. It was probably there where Saint-Exupéry found the first book that he read from cover to cover when he was only four years old. Among a pile of magazines in an old trunk, he discovered an instruction book on wine-making. Forty years later he remembered how he had read every word although he barely understood the sense.

If the great, heavily furnished rooms of the château were essentially an adult domain, the children's kingdom was the garden. Saint-Maurice was occupied only during the spring, summer and early autumn so that Antoine's nostalgia for his childhood often seemed bathed in the eternal sunshine of the pre-Great-War years. The three eldest children, Marie-Madeleine, Simone and Antoine, all wrote at length about their realm, an expanse of lawns, kitchen gardens, pine-copses and hidden corners, so big that it was never fully explored.

For Antoine, this vast terrain became his first workshop for mechanical experiments in which he tried to build a plane and set up a motor-powered irrigation scheme for a vegetable plantation. It was also the playground for heroic adventures inspired by story-books. In *Flight to Arras*, Saint-Exupéry compared the sensation of dodging German anti-aircraft fire to one of his early games in which the children tried to avoid the raindrops in a summer storm. The last one to escape being hit was dubbed 'Chevalier Aklin' until the next sudden shower.

This garden paradise was peopled by pets, many of them belonging to Antoine's eldest sister Marie-Madeleine, known as the doe. She was so gentle that she would not pick flowers in case she hurt them. Simone, much more robust and self-assertive, remembered long hours of embroidery in the open air perfumed with the scent of sweet peas, flowering laurels and geraniums. Often their mother would read to them or watch them playing as she painted water-colours. Blossoms on the linden trees, which have long since been cut down, were the only enemy here. They gave Antoine hay fever, forcing him to creep back to the house to read in the library.

The thrill of returning to this immense wonderland where adult supervision could be shrugged off began with a 50-kilometre steam-train journey from Lyon to the main-line halt at Leyment, 3 kilo-metres from the château. A horse and trap waited to carry the family along a narrow, unpaved track through vines and dairy farms to the large iron gates and the driveway under the lindens. Because the main approach to the château was through the garden, the village of Saint-Maurice was avoided. The long driveway gave direct access to most of the downstairs rooms, increasing the feeling of arriving in an enclave isolated from the outside world.

The dining-room windows give on to a rear courtyard where the well is a reminder that there was no running water or bathroom until the century was well advanced. Today, this yard provides the main access to the château and its nineteenth-century chapel. A gateway gives directly on to the streets of Saint-Maurice-de-Rémens, a village which has changed only superficially in the past hundred years.

A conspicuous recent addition is the plaque on the war memorial where Saint-Exupéry's name is inscribed. The stone cross overlooks the disorderly central square, named place de Saint-Exupéry in 1991, where plane-trees provide shade for a café *terrasse*. The narrow, dusty streets around the square have long since been paved, but most of the houses are still models of the dark grey, steep-roofed homes of the Jura foothills where snow is often heavy and prolonged.

The real changes in the village are invisible. Saint-Maurice no longer lives at the rhythm of the ruling landlords at the château and the sense of community which Saint-Exupéry knew has been dissipated by the rural drift and the arrival of townspeople seeking country homes.

In Antoine's childhood, unreliable transportation made visiting the nearby market town of Ambérieu-en-Bugey something of an expedition. The villagers lived as they had for centuries, turned in upon themselves. Noblemen in the castle and the day-labourers in the village shared memories that stretched back for generations and unquestioningly assumed the social ranking that God had designated. The poignancy of Antoine's references to his childhood is increased by the knowledge that this apparently unchanging world was already doomed and that aristocratic self-assurance and privilege was soon to be consumed by the Great War.

His elder sister Simone kept a diary of this period from which she took some of the main incidents for her *Five Children in a Garden*. Her account was dominated by one of the most formidable adults in Antoine's life, the chatelaine, the Comtesse de Tricaud, usually known as *'Tante'*. She was sixty-seven at Antoine's baptism and had been widowed for fifteen years. Her married life was marked by the death of her only daughter from diphtheria at the age of three, leaving her with a mission to rule over a family network in a château and a Lyon flat inherited from her diplomat husband.

The central figure in her adopted family was Antoine's mother, Marie, her great-niece, and it was Gabrielle de Tricaud who presided over the matchmaking that led to Marie's marriage to Antoine's father in 1896.

An aristocratic background provided more than social advantage. It was a voluntary welfare system based on loyalty and property, and the whole of Saint-Exupéry's family was absorbed into Tante Gabrielle's environment after Antoine's father died in 1904. They were to live largely off the revenues from the Tricaud farmland, of which 250 hectares surrounded the château. The family accepted the comtesse as head of a household ruled by women and servants.

Gabrielle de Tricaud was a character made for a novel. Dressed in black and carrying a cane, she was both a generous relative and a tyrannical great-aunt. She was born in an age when girls did not even brush their own hair and was looked after by a lady's maid, another young widow. Guests were summoned to entertain her at regular domino and bridge evenings held under the light of paraffin lamps at Saint-Maurice or to attend Wednesday-night musical evenings at the Lyon flat when the household moved to the city in the winter.

Father Montessuy, the parish priest at Saint-Maurice, was treated as her personal confessor, called on to bless her peremptory method of leading Latin prayers in the private chapel after dinner. He had to listen to her lectures on the way he should treat the villagers, a community she governed by divine right, knowing all her subjects by name.

Although Gabrielle de Tricaud adored Antoine's elder sister Marie-Madeleine, she had no time for small boys or animals. Antoine and François had to be seen and not heard, and the children's many pets were banned from the house with the exception of Madeleine's tame birds.

In Simone's accounts of her domineering aunt, there is affection for the singularity that sometimes obscured a warm heart. Part of the admiration was inspired by the comtesse's ability to choose servants as eccentric as herself. As many as eight were in full-time employment at Saint-Maurice. Often treated like children themselves, the staff acted as intermediaries between the brothers and sisters and the patronizing grown-ups. Sometimes the children had to console the servants, especially the cook who would be roundly scolded in public by Tante Gabrielle if the meal was a few minutes late or not considered good enough for the constantly changing stream of house-guests.

Of the strange figures who stalked the shadows of the château, the most appealing was the butler Cyprien, a lugubrious Swiss dressed in a black uniform. A bachelor, he had been rejected by Tante's personal maid, Noémi, and turned to drink for consolation. He was so emotional that he sometimes served dinner with tears streaming down his cheeks because of his broken heart.

Both Simone and Antoine wrote at length about Marguerite Chapays, known as Moisy, short for Mademoiselle, who appears 'trotting like a rat' through Saint-Exupéry's memory in *Wind, Sand and Stars*. '*Ah, mon Dieu. Quel malheur*,' she says in despair as she examines the worn family linen. The contents of her four linen cupboards became a persistent theme in Saint-Exupéry's adult writing. From *Southern Mail* onwards, there are abundant references to the soothing qualities of white bedsheets and metaphorical references to table-cloths.

Moisy was the boys' ally in their struggle with uncomprehending grown-ups, hiding Antoine under the bed to save him from a smacking. She was more of a nanny than a housekeeper, and in the evening

Antoine used to sneak into her room for a *'canard'* – a lump of sugar soaked in wine. When the other children found out, she bought a hoard of sugar to satisfy them all, but her little store of drink was sometimes restocked by altar wine from the parish priest.

She was an ageless country child, with apple-red cheeks, who took refuge at Saint-Maurice as a maid after a chastening period working ten hours a day in a textile mill in Lyon. While the children's uncles and aunts talked of finance, property and religion, Moisy taught them the names of wild flowers and took them to pick fruit for bottling.

Over the years, she was promoted from maid to housekeeper. The linen cupboards she possessively surveyed, constantly rearranging the sheets and table-cloths to avoid uneven wear, were as much her secret kingdom and playground as the children's garden and attics. A frail and tiny woman, she was soon outgrown by Antoine who could pick her up easily and swing her in his arms while cajoling her to arrange his favourite meals. The guardian-angel role changed hands when he grew up and she had achieved her lifelong dream, a little house of her own in her native village in the southern *département* of the Drôme. Saint-Exupéry sent her money for the house's upkeep and visited her as often as he could until mobilized in 1939, sharing the nostalgia of the little box of photographs from Saint-Maurice which she kept in her bedroom.

A spontaneous relationship between employer and servants was a mark of a confident aristocrat, but Gabrielle de Tricaud was also a caricature of a dying past. Although the Revolution had taken place more than a century before, she treated republicanism as a mood rather than a sea change.

Arranged marriages, with the inbuilt protection of property and titles, had steadily restocked noble lineage nearly ruined by the Terror. Fortunes were restored by absorbing the newly rich industrialist class, who could afford to trade money for an aristocratic alliance. Since the Revolution, France had lived through periods of Bourbon and Orléanist kings and a Napoleonic empire that had each contributed a share of newly ennobled families.

When the pretender, the Comte de Chambord, ended a corrosive

rift between the legitimist and Orléanist factions, provincial aristo-
crats thought it was only a matter of time before the return of the
monarchy. When Antoine was born, the Republic was cutting itself
to pieces in the wake of an apparently irrelevant controversy over a
Jewish army captain called Alfred Dreyfus. To the rejected hereditary
ruling classes, backed by the Catholic Church, the scandal was proof
that a popular national assembly was self-destructive and the emanci-
pation of Jews in 1791 was, for them, part of the slow poison of
liberalism. Enough time had passed for the excesses of the *ancien
régime* to be forgotten and only its glories remembered.

Saint-Maurice's chatelaine was a born reactionary, proud of her
attachment to the deposed royal house, and she chose friends of
like mind. She refused to take the local paper, the *Progrès de Lyon*,
considering it too avant-garde, and read the pro-monarchy *La Nouvel-
liste* instead, thus indirectly giving her great-great-nephews and
nieces a taste for royalist politics that Simone and Gabrielle kept all
their lives.

She had total assurance in her hereditary right to rule, an opinion
shared by most villagers who depended on the château for day-
labouring jobs, domestic work or farm tenancies. Few refused to
uncover their heads or make a bow as the chatelaine toured her little
domain. Tante Gabrielle also took the support of the Catholic Church
for granted, comforted by Father Montessuy, who became an honor-
ary member of the household. The two ideals of the Catholic faith
and the monarchy came together in her own chapel where the marble
floors were covered with the royal fleur-de-lis.

If Antoine had little reason to turn against religion until the
confusion of early adulthood, much of the credit went to François
Montessuy, the first of a number of priests who influenced his choices
in life. Montessuy might have been mistaken for a family retainer
because so much of his time was spent at the castle. His real charge
was the parish church at Saint-Maurice where the Saint-Exupérys
reserved the front seats and where Antoine's mother played the
harmonium and trained the all-girl choir.

Because the family were close friends of the nearby Bishop of
Belley, they probably had a say in the appointment of Father Montessuy, who did not resemble the average rustic *curé*. A former math-

ematics teacher from a middle-class family, he was transferred from the Ain *département*'s largest town, Bourg-en-Bresse, because of ill health. He had a lively fund of culture, picked up while he studied in Paris where he had been caught up in the 1870 siege, and he mixed happily with the children, playing the role of an indulgent uncle. Like Antoine and François, he often had to suffer Tante's bullying and was once mortally offended when the chatelaine told him that he visited the château only for the abundant home-grown food or to drink her special eau-de-vie. He refused to come back until Tante sent an emissary to the parish priest's house.

The priest endeared himself to the children through a repertoire of billiard tricks which he demonstrated on the big table in a library dominated by glass-fronted bookcases. He was their companion on horse-and-trap rides through the country to the Dombes lakes and other nearby beauty spots while cheerfully putting up with frequent practical jokes. Oblivious to the children's uncontrolled giggling, he once ate his way through a roasted crow which Antoine had pretended was a chicken dinner.

During a crippling drought in 1911, the most brilliant of a series of pre-Great War summers, the parish priest became an early target for Antoine's fantasies. Accompanied by two servants, the children were sent to amuse themselves on the mudbanks of the Ain river. They used the wet earth to model the heads of the multitudinous world that packed the castle during the three-month school vacation. Simone recalled that most of the mud heads were recognizable except for Antoine's model of the parish priest whose face was disguised by an invented beard.

He told his sister it was not lack of observation. Montessuy's mouth was too difficult to shape.

I Listen to my Tree Singing

IF the priest's usually florid and long-winded sermons were considered a minor weekly torture for the Saint-Exupéry children, they were the bread of life for their widowed mother, Marie, to whom the Catholic faith was her inspiration until she died in 1972 at the age of 97. Marie's resolute devotion to God made her seem like a lay nun in the priest's eyes and they shared the spiritual complicity of a couple vowed to celibacy; by choice for the priest and by circumstances for Marie.

Tante Gabrielle believed that the *curé* had more influence on her great-niece than she did herself and once opened her heart to him about the dangers to Marie's health caused by her tireless spirit of self-sacrifice. Village children were invited to the château at least once a week for tea and games, but Tante believed that Marie was going too far in planning to take her choirgirls for a country picnic. What the château needed was a man, she told Father Montessuy.

Marie's interest in contemporary music and painting was another attraction for a priest who was brought up in an urban, educated environment but found himself dealing with the superstitions, prejudices and petty rivalries of an isolated rural community. Providing spiritual comfort for a courageous widow, determined to see her children inherit her Christian beliefs, made sense of his priestly mission, at least from April to October when the château was occupied.

Marie de Saint-Exupéry was widowed after only eight years of marriage. She was pregnant with a fifth child and her husband's death was the first of a series of personal trials that strengthened her Catholic faith in which the guidance of the New Testament and the certainty of God's love were accepted without question. She was the guiding force in Antoine's life and his abandoning of religion must have tormented her even more than the risks he took as a pilot.

Nothing can be understood about Saint-Exupéry's often misplaced choices or hesitations without reference to his mother's influence which he tried to bend without ever breaking. He must have recognized that she was a finer person than himself, living close to an understanding God that he failed to find.

Even though he ignored her justifiable opposition to his dangerous career, rejected her attempts at family matchmaking and pressed her for money even when her fortune ran low, their closeness never diminished. Her only fault was unwittingly to set standards of feminine perfection, sympathy and devotion that Saint-Exupéry failed to find with any other woman.

She was revered even for her autocratic tendencies and

occasional sarcasm. Neither she nor Antoine cared much for the careful money management of families more concerned with husbanding resources for their descendants than meeting present desires. Whenever she had a little extra money she spent it on fashionable new clothes, preferring her children's admiration to the tut-tutting of pennypinching relatives.

Maternal love was supplemented by maternal pride. Antoine led the independent life that she was denied as a noblewoman born in the nineteenth century when family interests had the first and last say. A woman's destiny was an arranged marriage for the sake of property, prestige and posterity.

Antoine's published letters to his mother are the best indication of how much he needed her love and encouragement until his dying day, not least because of the memories of the long summer holidays at Saint-Maurice and the visits to her own château among the scented hills behind Saint-Tropez. His last message, written days before he died, and which she received a year after his final flight, ended with the appeal: 'Maman, embrassez-moi comme je vous embrasse du fond de mon coeur'; kiss me as I kiss you from the bottom of my heart.'

The letter contained a forty-year-old echo of Antoine's worst punishment for his constant unruliness when he was sent to sleep without a good-night kiss. His persistent and heart-rending pleas for reconciliation never went unanswered.

His lifelong need for the affection of his 'petite maman' owed much to their mutual attachment to the joys of childhood and their gift for sharing a sacred past in simple terms. In 1964, when more than eighty years old, Marie de Saint-Exupéry published reminiscences of her own early youth at the Fonscolombe family château at La Mole in a book of essays and poems called J'écoute chanter mon arbre, 'I listen to my tree singing'. Her love of music, nature and literature, evident in the recounting of her own idyllic girlhood with her three brothers and younger sister, were passed on to her son.

OF the many photographs that exist of Antoine's immediate family, the most nostalgic were taken on the summer lawns at Saint-Maurice. Marie, tall, elegant and coquette, is surrounded by her five small children, each with a singular character. The family group was most closely united when their mother read them stories from the Bible and other morally uplifting books under the linden-tree. Most of the time they were split into little clans reflecting their characters and interests. The eldest, Marie-Madeleine, known as Biche, fled company, especially adults, by hiding in the attic in an area called her Chinese room where she read, assembled jigsaw puzzles or catalogued her collection of postcards depicting flowers and animals.

Simone, her younger sister, was the acknowledged story-teller, a gift which became a lifelong frustration because most of her novels and stories were rejected by publishers despite her brother's fame. Like her elder sister, she was educated at home, either in the Tricaud flat in Lyon or at Saint-Maurice. Good-humoured but overbearing, she was Antoine's ally in expeditions into the country around Saint-Maurice where she escaped her long-suffering German tutor, remembered only as 'Fraülein'.

The second son, François, had much of the gentle character of his sister Marie-Madeleine, and lived in the shadow of Antoine, putting up with his domineering and demanding leadership until an argument would bring them to blows. Finally there was Gabrielle, a pretty child who was either the sacrificial victim of sibling torment or the heroine of their romantic games. Only Gabrielle would one day have children of her own, around whom she recreated the indulgent atmosphere of Saint-Maurice in her Mediterranean family home at Agay, which became Antoine's favourite grown-up refuge. Gabrielle's children were the last to appreciate Marie's sensitivity to innocent pleasure. They looked forward to their grandmother's visits so much that they fought to carry her suitcase until she brought empty bags to satisfy them all.

By far the most striking portrait in the family photographs was that of Antoine himself. His cheeky look and strong features were evident from an early age, but his hair was abundant and golden, earning him the nickname of 'the Sun King'. Forty years later the crown of blonde hair would be romanticized in his naïve drawings of the Little Prince, when he could reflect on the irony of being progressively robbed of so much beauty as a punishment for growing up.

[23]

The family group was most closely united when their mother read them stories from the Bible and other morally uplifting books under the linden-trees. Most of the time they were split into little clans reflecting their characters and interests.

All the traits that made Antoine a captivating or exigent companion in later years were evident from infancy. He expected to be the centre of attention, as if he assumed he was the favourite child. He gave his mother little rest, following her around carrying a small armchair so that he could sit beside her when she painted or embroidered, demanding to hear the same Bible stories over and over again.

In adulthood, his friends had to accept telephone calls at any time of the day or night when he sought an opinion on his writing or wanted to relate an adventure. The habit had begun in boyhood when he used to wake up his brother and sisters in the early hours and make them come to his mother's bedroom to hear a new poem or a story. There was no resisting his demands. Stubbornness was another of Antoine's lifelong characteristics.

A natural gentleness compensated for this demanding side. His mother recalled that as a small boy he used to step off the path to avoid walking on caterpillars and climbed the fir-trees around the château to try and make friends with the turtle-doves.

From the age of reason, Antoine was made aware that inheriting the family title also marked him down as the *chef de famille*, a role that complicated an exaggerated awareness of responsibility. Simone recalled losing her communion watch while on an exhausting walk with Antoine on nearby hills in the high summer of 1912. With the obstinate resolution that marked much of his adult behaviour, her young brother set out alone, walking miles in a vain quest. He returned exhausted and dirty late at night, angry and ashamed at letting his sister down.

SAINT-EXUPÉRY'S precocious fascination for mechanics and flying from the age of nine will be the subject of a later chapter, but his passion for creative writing went even further back. As long as anyone could remember he wrote at every opportunity, stuffing notes into a little box, in a habit that foreshadowed a grown-up need to jot down his thoughts in leather-bound books.

The constant note-taking contributed to another lifelong characteristic – untidiness. Memories of his disorderly desks went back to pre-adolescence. At Saint-Maurice only Gabrielle was allowed to put some order into his sacred territory when it became too cluttered.

His early poems and stories, derived from heroic literature or popular entertainment, were to give way to ever more ambitious projects until he scripted an operetta in his early adolescence. Behind this creativity there was a compelling need for immediate praise from his family circle, a need that was later fulfilled by close acquaintances who learnt that criticism had to be ladled out with care if they were to stay in Saint-Exupéry's favour.

This thirst for instant adulation was never satisfactorily replaced by the loyalty of an anonymous general public even when his books were rewarded with literary prizes. His published work was only a minor contribution in comparison with correspondence made up of hundreds of letters to friends and family, often accompanied by humorous or sentimental drawings. It is doubtful if anything ever lived up to the pure pleasure of presenting work to family and guests when evening drew in around the château. One play is still remembered, an outrageous melodrama called 'Le Téléphone' in which an absent husband rings home and overhears his entire family being murdered by intruders.

There were more spontaneous moments of invention in charades. The mimes were neutral ground where the children were allowed to mock the grown-up world without being considered impudent. One of the best-remembered was when Antoine sat snoring in an armchair wearing a dressing-gown inside-out to show the red lining. The allusion to the Bishop of Belley and his boring sermons was quickly recognized.

Another charade showed that the older children were kept informed of national and international news. Among the most successful mimes was a representation of the 1912 Turkish-Bulgarian conflict, the first combat in which planes were used as weapons of war.

ANTOINE's first and most loyal admirer in his search for self-expression and individuality was his mother. Marie de Saint-Exupéry ignored family pressures on her children to treat life with less fantasy, encouraging them to break some of the more suffocating rules of aristocratic rigidity that Antoine would eventually throw off in his bid for 'non-conformity'.

Nothing in Marie de Saint-Exupéry's writing indicated bitterness at her own life which was to be marred by many tragedies, the greatest shock being the death of her husband in a railway station in Provence during a visit to her parents' home at La Mole in March 1904. The tragedy robbed her of a companion and a provider, while leaving Antoine, then only three years old, without a male hero-figure.

CHAPTER TWO

Looking Death in the Face

La Croix du Littoral, 20 March 1904

Accident in La Foux station

On Monday evening, Monsieur de Fonscolombe's son-in-law, who was travelling with his wife, collapsed suddenly in the station at La Foux as a result of a stroke. Urgent first aid was immediately given to him in the waiting-room. The doctor who had been summoned rapidly was there almost immediately but, alas, all was in vain. The unfortunate patient died in the arms of his grief-stricken wife after receiving the blessing of a priest and the last sacraments. The body was taken to La Môle where the funeral took place.

This accident seriously upset travellers arriving at La Foux station from several directions – Saint-Raphaël, Hyères, Saint-Tropez and Cogolin.

Death's cruel surprises! We send our respectful condolences to the families who have been plunged into mourning by this fatal accident.

LA CROIX, a national pro-royalist Catholic newspaper with local editions for the Mediterranean region, was the only newspaper to report the death of Antoine's father on 14 March 1904. The most striking irony was that the father's name was not mentioned although the reporter presumed that readers knew the father-in-law, Charles de Fonscolombe, one of the most influential landowners among the arid Maure Hills of Provence.

Even though the anonymous reporter added confusion by calling the tragedy at La Foux 'an accident', the article's intention was clear enough. It cut short gossip by insisting on the fact that Jean de Saint-Exupéry received the last sacraments and was attended by his wife. The sudden death in such undignified circumstances of a man of only forty-one, whose wife was pregnant with a fifth child, was bound to cause speculation.

The article did not say if any of the children were present when Jean de Saint-Exupéry collapsed at seven in the evening although this was not unlikely. They frequently visited La Môle with their parents and Antoine's first conscious memories as a child, which he recorded in *Flight to Arras*, were of the château's frightening shadows and the disturbing sounds of the mistral. Whether or not he was at La Foux station or present at the burial, conducted by Father Montessuy at Saint-Maurice four days later, Antoine must have been perturbed by the sudden onset of mourning ritual and the disappearance of the central male figure in his family.

Saint-Exupéry's lifelong discretion concerning aspects of his private life wiped out any direct reference to his father and this was only partly compensated in his philosophical work *Wisdom of the Sands*, where there are enigmatic references to the death of the Berber chief's father which conclude: 'It was he who taught me about death and forced me when I was young to look at it straight in the face because he never lowered his eyes.'

In failing to identify Jean de Saint-Exupéry by name, *La Croix*'s journalist unintentionally summarized the general family view that he was not a man of much distinction. There was nothing remarkable in his bachelor past before he married at the age of thirty-three, probably under family pressure to make something of an aimless life.

Jean de Saint-Exupéry was an officer in the dragoons, like his younger brother Roger, before accepting a job as an insurance agent in his father's firm. On his wedding certificate he described himself as '*sans-profession*', the equivalent of gentleman. Before marriage, Jean had enjoyed the advantages of a titled bachelor officer in provincial garrison towns and it would have taken a strong character to cope with being uprooted from this easygoing environment and set down in a rural household dominated by women and soon to be transformed into an ever growing nursery. He took little or no part in running the Tricaud estate and seems to have been a figure of no great influence. The only real legacy he left was the aristocratic family name and title. *'J'ai un beau nom,'* Antoine told a friend, Jean Escot, during his national service in the air force in 1921. At the time, he was unable to make up his mind whether to impress his companions with his title or try to play down his privileged background.

Some of the subconscious effects of the father's early death became apparent later in life when Saint-Exupéry became increasingly hypochondriac as he approached the age when his father died. To be left fatherless at an early age was not an uncommon fate among Antoine's contemporaries. Saint-Exupéry's name is often grouped with those of three other twentieth-century authors whose writings analysed ethical attitudes in modern society. Two of these fellow humanists, Jean-Paul Sartre and Albert Camus, also lost their fathers when young. Sartre was only a year old and Camus three years old. André Malraux was also three when his father deserted him. Although Saint-Exupéry, Camus, Malraux and Sartre were brought up in female-run households, each developed very personal views on moral, social and emotional questions.

SAINT-EXUPÉRY did not exaggerate when claiming a *'beau nom'*. In 1991 his great-nephew, Frédéric d'Agay, drew up a summary of the family trees of Antoine's four grandparents, all of whom claimed impressive ancestors. The contradictory sides of Saint-Exupéry's character as both man of action and man of literature reflect the fusion of cultural and military influences from the past.

A common determination to maintain aristocratic lineage by carefully arranged Catholic marriages either for social rank or enrichment ran through all four genealogical streams. Antoine's marriage to Consuelo Suncin, who grew up in an obscure Latin American family, was considered by some of his family to be as heretical as giving up religion. Rejecting the advantages of a *'beau nom'*, with its inbuilt privileges and promise of inter-family support, needed a special sort of courage. Until the financial value of Saint-Exupéry's writing became apparent after his death, most of his relatives considered him a wasted asset and a poor example.

One of the documents that Frédéric d'Agay drew on was Fernand de Saint-Exupéry's *'Notice sur la famille Saint-Exupéry'* in which Antoine's grandfather traced origins back to the Crusades. When Antoine was at school at Le Mans his grandfather's book must have fired his imagination, although he was too young to understand why the descendant of such a noble line was living in a modest town house instead of an imposing castle. The grandfather, despite his role as director of the Compagnie du Soleil, an insurance firm, had not shown much business acumen and was blamed for bad investments that reduced the family fortune.

The true wealth was the genealogical tree going back to the first recorded Saint-Exupéry, Raymond, ruling his fief in the Limousin area of central France in 1235. The name originated from a village called Saint-Exupéry-des-Roches, near Ussel, in the Corrèze *département*. Royal blood was added in the sixteenth century when one Madeleine de Saint-Exupéry married a Bourbon, born on the wrong side of the blanket, who was appointed the king's chamberlain. In the seventeenth century, loyalty to the crown earned Jean-Antoine de Saint-Exupéry, an army captain, the personal recognition of Louis XIV and each subsequent generation produced its military heroes. Most were soldiers and some served during the American War of Independence or fought against Napoleon as monarchist *émigrés* after the Revolution.

Royalist military links were strengthened during the Restoration and the Second Empire, whose collapse in 1870 also ended Fernand de Saint-Exupéry's provincial administrative career as a *sous-préfet*, representing the national government in the provinces. His loyalty to the Bourbons made it impossible for him to serve a republic.

ANTOINE's grandfather was born in 1833 near Bordeaux at Château Malescot in the Margaux wine area. Fernand's mother was the daughter of a wine-dealer and it was due to some misguided investments in wine-growing and the phylloxera plague that their wealth dwindled. Finances were partially restored by Fernand's marriage to Antoine's paternal grandmother, Alix Blouquier de Trélan, who came from the royal town of Tours.

Again his forebears were strongly connected to royal military causes that pitted the Trélans against Napoleon's revolutionary army in the Vendée. Not surprisingly, both of Antoine's paternal grandparents were fervent supporters of the legitimate Bourbon monarchy and made enemies among republicans by campaigning for another restoration. Their involvement in the royalist cause became a strong influence on Saint-Exupéry in his adolescence.

King Francis's Lover and Other Stories

WHILE Saint-Exupéry discovered much of his paternal ancestry from his grandfather's own research, contact with his mother's side of the family was more personal and was embellished by Marie's skill at story-telling. The dominant military characteristic of the father's side was countered by an artistic streak among the ancestors of his mother whose full name was Boyer de Fonscolombe.

Noble from the eighteenth century, the family left a lasting cultural and artistic legacy in Aix-en-Provence. Descendants included painters, musicians, writers, art collectors and scientists. Marie was encouraged to paint and write from childhood and her children grew up in an environment where their sharpest recollections included listening to their mother telling them stories while she painted their portraits.

Saint-Exupéry's links with Le Mans in the Sarthe *département* of western France never had the seduction of the generous and sun-filled atmosphere of the south. After being widowed, Marie first took refuge with her children in a relative's castle at Aix. Forty years later, Provence would be Antoine's last sight of France before his plane disappeared in the Mediterranean.

The Provençal château at La Môle, near Saint-Tropez, where Marie was brought up, was bought in 1770. Nearly 100 years later, Napoleon III made Marie's grandfather, Emmanuel de Fonscolombe, Baron de la Môle. He married the daughter of a Marseille shipowner and became mayor of the village while spending some of his time composing music.

Fonscolombe royalist pretensions were more impressive than

those on the Saint-Exupéry side. Marie's uncle, Baron Fernand, who married into a Marseille banking family, was the senior aide-de-camp to the Comte de Paris, pretender to the French throne. Uncle Fernand's castle at Aix was one of the aristocratic homes where Antoine spent part of his holidays.

Marie's mother was born Romanet de Lestrange, a feudal family with many branches. One of her ancestors was reputed to have been a lover of the sixteenth-century king Francis I, while another was superior-general of the Trappist order during the First Empire and persuaded Napoleon to take a more benign attitude towards religious orders.

The future Marie de Saint-Exupéry's move to Saint-Maurice-de-Rémens was due to the matchmaking skills of Gabrielle de Tricaud, who had married into a family that owned other castles near by. Marie had only a relatively small dowry, which meant that Tante Gabrielle had to make an exhaustive search for a potential suitor among her own relatives. Among her forebears was a marquis, Joseph de Lestrange, who was made a baron by Napoleon in 1814. The marquis married a noblewoman called Adelaïde Green de Saint-Marsault. In 1790, Adelaïde's cousin, Victoire Green de Saint-Marsault, was wedded to a country gentleman, Georges de Saint-Exupéry, comte de Saint-Amans. This distant link was enough to start marriage negotiations with the Saint-Exupérys. The potential husband, Jean de Saint-Exupéry, was sent to Lyon to represent the Compagnie du Soleil as an insurance agent. Marie, then only seventeen, was introduced at Tante's regular Wednesday-night dinners and musical evenings at the flat on the place Bellecour in Lyon.

A century after her wedding, Marie was still considered lucky to have married such a 'beau nom', despite her own family's standing and Jean de Saint-Exupéry's meagre fortune. However, Tante de Tricaud's matchmaking skill was not enough to find a husband for Marie's sister, Madeleine de Fonscolombe, who sacrificed her chances of marriage to look after her widowed mother.

Madeleine became part of the protective feminine entourage at Saint-Maurice. A photograph of her in profile looking at Antoine as a child reveals part of the physical Fonscolombe heritage. Antoine's upturned nose, which annoyed him during years of schoolboy and adult teasing, came from the Fonscolombe side.

OBSCURE political forces also played their part in Saint-Exupéry's early years. Viewed from the inside, the aristocracy's common identity was not as clear-cut as might be supposed. Fernand de Saint-Exupéry's legitimist royalist clan was suspicious of the Orléanist Fonscolombes. According to André de Fonscolombe, a retired diplomat and Antoine's favourite cousin, his family was suspected of being tainted by dangerous socialist ideas dating back to the eighteenth-century composer Emmanuel de Fonscolombe.

At that time enlightened nobles came under the influence of Comte Claude de Saint-Simon, a precursor of democratic campaigners for the equality of man and the sharing of property. Emmanuel was a friend of the composer Félicien David, a disciple of Saint-Simon. When the Saint-Exupéry and Fonscolombe families were united in marriage in 1896, the legacy of Claude de Saint-Simon's ideas was still considered treacherous by many royalists.

To Ferdinand de Saint-Exupéry's military caste, the composer Emmanuel de Fonscolombe, Antoine's great-grandfather, was effete into the bargain. He was a member of the Academy of Saint Cecilia in Rome and chapel-master at Aix-en-Provence where he composed masses and motets and wrote a study of the Venetian musician Carissimi. Marie's father, Charles de Fonscolombe, was also a composer; he insisted that both his daughters learnt the piano and they continued to take lessons at Saint-Maurice. All Marie's children were taught to play an instrument while their mother later added the composition of sacred music, with words in Provençal, to her other talents.

André de Fonscolombe often went to Saint-Maurice and remembered hearing music by Hahn, Fauré, Schumann, Schubert and Massenet being played in the château under the guidance of professional music teachers. Antoine learnt the violin, but his main talent was a memory for folk-songs with which he entertained his friends as a schoolboy and as a pilot. His appreciation for his mother's interest in contemporary piano music, notably Debussy, was not always respectful. Throughout his life, he often repeated his favourite musical joke, rolling oranges up and down the keyboard and challenging friends to say that the result was less entertaining than a Debussy score.

Marie de Saint-Exupéry's open mind on modern culture was just

[33]

as marked in painting, where she was an excellent pastellist. An ancestor, Jean-Baptiste de Fonscolombe, was a member of the Marseilles Académie des Beaux-Arts and the Del Disegno academy in Italy. Her inspiration was more modern and her later portraits resembled the work of Marie Laurencin.

With the insidious Saint-Simon philosophy in the background, Fernand de Saint-Exupéry was unlikely to have been impressed by his daughter-in-law's encouragement of individualism and tolerance and the elevation of culture to much the same level as religion. In a family argument, though, she had only limited authority over the children's upbringing.

French law supported the view that women were incapable of exercising independent decisions and were subject to men. Emotional needs did not count. Antoine and his younger brother François lived under the *de facto* tutelage of a family council headed by the paternal grandfather, Fernand de Saint-Exupéry. On spiritual matters, Antoine depended on the guidance of his uncle and godfather, Roger de Saint-Exupéry, who in the absence of a father was honour-bound to encourage a strong religious vocation.

When Antoine was nine, it was felt that he should prepare for his future role as *chef de famille* and a military career. Overnight, he was taken from the indulgent, female-run environment of Saint-Maurice and thrust into the stark and virile world of a Jesuit college at Le Mans where his father and uncle had once been students.

The Indoctrination Centre

THE Collège de Notre-Dame-de-Sainte-Croix now stands in the rue Antoine-de-Saint-Exupéry, a narrow street in the centre of Le Mans which used to be called rue des Vignes. The material connection with the author, who entered the Jesuit School on 7 October 1909, is tenuous. The school moved twice before he left in June 1915 and its original Gothic building was confiscated by the state in 1911 and turned into a barracks. The most tangible link with Saint-Exupéry is the present-day central building, previously used for classrooms at an earlier site in the rue Prémartine where Antoine was taught.

The priests who surrounded him were missionaries devoted to fundamental Catholicism, administering a daily regime of religious sacrifice and military discipline. Today the regimentation has gone. Notre-Dame-de-Saint-Croix is still a Catholic private high school associated with the Society of Jesus, but the head teacher is a layman and the classes are mixed. Boys and girls work within a tolerant programme in which religion is a subject, rather than a crusade.

The navy-blue cadet-style uniform that Saint-Exupéry wore has long since disappeared. Students dress as casually as the average French adolescent and have as little respect for bigoted authority. The interior of the central building has changed too much to catch even a faint echo of the fierce routine of the pre-Great-War years although there is a clue on the war memorial outside. Many of the boys went to the college as preparation for a military academy. More than fifty career officers who died in the brief battles of 1940 and the few months after the Liberation are remembered on the memorial, one of the highest proportions of old boys at any school in France.

While the Jesuits of Notre-Dame-de-Sainte-Croix are still in the forefront of a battle to maintain religious education against the indifference of a secular republic, there is no common measure with the Catholic struggle against the lay republican state that followed the defeat by Bismarck's Prussia. The college had a national vocation to recruit acolytes in a crusade to defend the old faith threatened by a government ban on religious teaching. Jesuit schools deliberately set out to train young men for the civil-service and military academies, known as *grandes écoles*, which had become anticlerical bastions after the Revolution. Noble and bourgeois families backed the campaign with vigour and finance, and by 1939 the academies were full of conservatives.

When Antoine arrived at Le Mans, his uncle, Roger de Saint-Exupéry, was a valuable source of information on what amounted to a holy war against a godless state. Roger had entered the school in 1876, four years after Antoine's father Jean. The Saint-Exupérys were among several noble families who sponsored the college which had been a centre of resistance to the German invasion in 1870. Housed at the time in a grand, abbey-like building, the school was turned into a garrison for French troops, many of whom were later cared for in the same buildings when they became a military hospital. Before the college was again used as a school, Bismarck's troops had moved in, using the classrooms as stables. The occupation left bitter memories that later convinced Antoine's family to move him to the safety of a school in Switzerland during the First World War.

The Jesuits took control of the college from another religious order after the war with Prussia. From then on, it was more of an indoctrination centre than an educational institution as priests fought republicanism with the fanaticism that they later turned against communists. Ugly memories of the 1871 Commune, when religious leaders were executed by the rebellious people's government, were kept alive, just as the communards remembered massacres perpetrated by the army with the backing of royalists and the Church.

Until he went to Le Mans, Antoine's formal education had been limited to two years in a Catholic preparatory school in Lyon. As well as dragging him unwittingly into a bigoted religious camp, the college was a cruel initiation into premature adulthood. In 1909 the school was still in its original Gothic buildings, but the struggle between the Jesuits and the state was at its height. The quarrel over private religious education spilled over into even more spiteful divisions following the Dreyfus affair when the school became a recruiting-ground for Charles Maurras's royalist, anti-Semitic Action Française.

The atmosphere at Notre-Dame-de-Sainte-Croix was spartan. Privately contributed finance was so tight that there was no heating in the refectory where the 250 boys wore their overcoats while eating their meagre ration of tepid broth in silence except for the background of Bible readings.

Most of Antoine's schoolmates came from large families with strong royalist traditions. It was common for ten or twelve boys from the same titled or bourgeois clan to be spread among the classes, with the record being held by the de Romanets and the de Maurys with nineteen each. About the only important change in teaching since Antoine's father attended Le Mans was that Latin was no longer obligatory as the main classroom language. Otherwise, the college timetable was medieval in its demands, although Antoine, as a day-boy, had a slightly less rigorous schedule than the boarders who had to get up at 5.30 a.m. His mother had registered him at the school and she lived for part of the year with Antoine and François, who otherwise lodged with grandfather Fernand in a grey, bourgeois town house at 39 rue Pierre-Bellon, a half-hour walk from the college.

Fernand's home was spacious in comparison to the house at 21 rue Clos-Margot which was rented for Marie de Saint-Exupéry and her boys whenever she came to Le Mans. Both the interior and the garden were depressingly cramped. When absent from Le Mans, Marie joined the girls at Lyon or Saint-Maurice while Antoine and François were looked after by an aunt, Anaïs de Saint-Exupéry, lady-in-waiting to the Duchesse de Vendôme, a member of the French royal house.

The impact of being forcibly transferred so far from the joyous atmosphere of Saint-Maurice is evident in a first-form class portrait which shows Antoine standing with a stoical expression among fellow pupils who appear to be in a state of shock over the sacrifices expected of nine-year-old boys. Another day-pupil, Paul Gaultier, Antoine's class-mate and a future journalist, recalled the hardships in the school's centenary magazine in 1971. All boys had to attend mass at 7.30 a.m. six days of the week and high mass at 8.30 a.m. on Sunday. Weekday study ended at 7 p.m. and only Sunday afternoon could be spent at home. The constant fight against the cold, with the water in the lunch-time carafes often frozen and the boys complaining of chilblains, was worsened by the fear of punishment.

The most insufferable was *la colle*, or detention, which usually had to be served during recreation periods on Thursday and Sunday afternoons. The morning of the Lord's Day was already prolonged by an hour's religious instruction after high mass, but the chance of a break was often replaced by extra classroom study to make up for rowdiness, inattention during lessons or sloppiness in religious instruction.

Playground activity was also strictly supervised and immediate punishment handed out by priests for minor offences. Boys were made to run five or six times around the big recreation field or told to stand beside a tree throughout playtime. The worst behaviour was punished by a whipping administered by a priest.

Individuality was not encouraged. Outings were in large groups

[37]

and most of them were pilgrimages to sacred sites. One of these early summer excursions in crowded horse-drawn buses to the Benedictine abbey of Notre-Dame-du-Chêne at Solesmes was described in a 1910 letter to Antoine's mother. The tone was humorous and uncomplaining and it was not until many years later that Antoine recalled the misery of Le Mans when his mother was away in Lyon and unable to protect him.

'I remember when you used to go and see the father prefect [priest] to ask for the "*colles*" to be dropped,' he wrote. 'I used to come back home with my big satchel on my back, sobbing because I had been punished – you remember Le Mans – and you would make me forget everything by kissing and hugging me. You were an all-powerful support against the supervisors and the father prefects and we felt secure in your house; we were nothing except yours. It was good.'

Discipline was relaxed only in the days just before the summer holidays when the boys were allowed to bathe in a nearby river. Otherwise, sport was a vigorous and violent team effort. André Dunant, another former student, remembered that games were usually 'very virile'. Football matches were played fifty a side with two balls and few rules.

Most games had an element of military tactics, notably '*le jeu des boucliers*', the shield game. Classes were divided into two sides who fought with balls while manoeuvring to capture the flag in the enemy camp.

'There was no resentment over the discipline because most of the boys were destined to go to *grande écoles* like the Polytechnique and the Centrale which trained military and civilian engineers,' André Dunant recalled. 'I went to the army cadet officers' academy at Saint-Cyr after leaving the college and I saw no difference between military discipline and the education at Notre-Dame-de-Sainte-Croix.'

The severe regime and intense religious study also prepared many pupils for a life of self-sacrifice in the priesthood and one of Saint-Exupéry's senior fellow students became Bishop of Le Mans.

APART from letters to his mother, Saint-Exupéry made little reference to Le Mans in his writings, although he later told friends that he was rarely happy there. For a boy of such sensitivity, the intolerant atmosphere, particularly when combined with separation from his mother, was torture and his response was often sullen acceptance.

His marks for general conduct, tidiness and assiduity were usually poor. The first months were probably the most distressing but the worst school years were 1913 and 1914. Until then he suffered in well-mannered silence and early school reports showed his politeness as beyond reproach. Between 1913 and 1914, the assessment of his manners, noted on a descending alphabetic scale, plunged to E along with what were described as 'very bad marks' – EI – for behaviour in general. There was more to this rebellion than the usual adolescent insolence because Antoine came close to expulsion.

Every E was punished with two hours of detention. Antoine earned seven EIs and six Is, which were far worse, in the last three months before the 1914 summer holidays, meaning that he sacrificed most of his free time for long periods of detention. He did not attend the 1914 autumn term and when he returned for the first six months of 1915, his conduct was hardly any better, but at least he was no longer rebuked for rudeness.

The heart of the problem was a clash with his grandfather, Fernand. As a young boy, Antoine had accepted this white-bearded figure as an unquestioned authority, and his juvenile wonder at the imposing patriarch sitting behind an enormous desk was later captured in *The Little Prince*, where Fernand was caricatured as the geographer. Although the grandfather's house in the rue Pierre-Bellon may have been dull in comparison with the château at Saint-Maurice, it had an extraordinary library with a collection of rare volumes started by Fernand's father. Antoine was shown some of the precious books, notably a leather-bound volume of astronomy that impressed him enough to give the news priority when he returned to Saint-Maurice for the 1911 summer holidays.

As Antoine grew older, the relationship with his grandfather became tense. Fernand's authority as president of the family council cut across Marie de Saint-Exupéry's liberal attitudes. There was a clash of personalities and priorities in which Antoine was firmly on his mother's side. Helen Crane, an American academic, was told by one of Antoine's cousins, Charlotte Churchill, that Antoine and his grandfather were often at odds. She put it down to their voluble southern French temperaments, saying that both liked to talk a lot. Antoine had been encouraged to speak out while Fernand de Saint-Exupéry believed that little boys were there only to listen.

In Fernand de Saint-Exupéry's harsh view, Antoine would have been seen as over-protected and in need of toughening up by strict physical discipline. During a conversation with Simone, recorded in 1912, Saint-Exupéry revealed that even his aunt Anaïs used to whip him when he was insolent.

The most valuable lesson Saint-Exupéry learnt at Le Mans was the consolation of comradeship in adversity. At the same time, he had to accept his share of teasing over his appearance. At home he was known as Tonio. At Le Mans he had put up with two nicknames that annoyed him even when grown up.

The first, 'Tatane', was aimed at his big feet which caused amusement all his life, so much so that they were the most striking memory of a sixteen-year-old girl who danced with him at a night-club on the evening before his death in 1944. Tatane gave way to the even more irritating 'Pique-la-lune', an allusion to his odd, turned-up nose as well as to an air of distraction which would one day plague his flying career.

Academically, Saint-Exupéry rarely made a favourable impression on his teachers although many of his poor marks can be put down to passive resistance to authority. The largest class he ever attended had nineteen pupils and the smallest only eleven, but he rarely rose above the bottom ranks. His worst placings were for history, geography, German, Latin and spelling. His best were in French although he was considered poor in grammar.

His interest in subjects where he failed at Le Mans, such as mathematics and geography, was awakened only when he applied them in practice as an airman and an inventor. In adulthood, the boredom of maths at Le Mans was replaced by a passion for geometry. The only subject which had a consistent hold on him at college was writing, his personal measure of self-esteem and a refuge in times of distress. Antoine's highest marks for composition – the main French studies were called narration – were between the ages of twelve and fourteen, the period which coincided with his indiscipline and rudeness.

The credit for encouraging his literary talent does not go to an intellectual Jesuit. In 1900 the order had been expelled from France and was not allowed to teach. At Le Mans, and in many other colleges, Jesuits defied the government by leaving some fathers in place behind the scenes and entrusted teaching to priests recruited from outside the established religious orders.

These diocesan priests from small rural towns and villages around Le Mans promised to follow Jesuit principles to the letter, a task they did so well that Notre-Dame-de-Sainte-Croix remained a sanctuary for reactionary conservatism and royalism up to the Second World War. While their courage in defending the faith against state harassment deserved admiration, the sad result of their efforts was that many old boys made wrong decisions after the Fall of France and associated with the extremism of Philippe Pétain's Vichy regime and the divisive ideals of Action Française.

Fortunately, the priests each had their own personalities and were not blind to natural talent. One of them, Abbé Auguste Launay, deserves credit for first recognizing that Antoine's grasp of story-telling was unique. The priest was the central figure in one of the most striking class-group photographs of Antoine's stay at Le Mans, portraying seventeen solemn thirteen-year-olds standing or sitting around a grim, broad-faced man with cropped hair. The apparently severe Auguste Launay, with his inevitable nickname of 'Caesar', was an instinctive literary critic. By the time Antoine reached the third grade, his writing ability had already been spotted by other masters, but only Abbé Launay saw beyond the natural creativity and used Saint-Exupéry's essays as models long before he was a published writer.

Auguste Launay was born and died in the nearby small market town of Sillé-le-Guillaume where his father was a carpenter. There were no state schools when he was brought up and his education was ensured by a religious vocation that he fulfilled a thousandfold during his thirty-four years of teaching at Le Mans. The austere image in the group photograph was confirmed by pupils' recollections of a distant figure in an impeccable soutane who, during lessons, rarely left his desk on a podium. He refused to touch chalk, making his pupils write for him on the blackboard while he tormented them with relentless questions on Latin grammar.

His subjects included Latin, Greek and religion, all of which Antoine balked at in his fourteenth year. There was a much better understanding in French classes, despite Saint-Exupéry's low marks for grammar. The priest was so impressed by Antoine's essays that he used two of them as examples for French lessons until his retirement from the school at the beginning of the Second World War.

The better-known of the essays was 'The Odyssey of a Hat', telling of the sad decline of a top hat which ends up as a battered covering for a distant African chief. At the beginning of the tale, which runs to more than 1000 words, the hat tells of its own birth in a hat factory where 'I endured all sorts of torture'.

After being cut up, stretched and varnished, the hat is sent to a Paris shop where it is one of the most handsome on display. 'I was so glossy that the ladies passing by could not resist admiring their reflection in my brilliance. I was so elegant that no distinguished gentleman could look at me without a covetous glance.' After being bought by a rich man, the hat is admired by the man's friends at his club, then kept and dusted with great care for several months of 'delightful existence.'

'A faithful manservant especially entrusted with Monsieur's wardrobe looked after me with flattering kindness. I was polished every evening and repolished every morning.'

The hat dates the decline of its fortunes from the day it is given as a present to a coachman who is about to be married. On the first day, it is rolled in the mud and dust three times without being wiped and then, 'filled with a righteous desire for revenge', the hat shrinks and is sold to an old-clothes dealer for 30 centimes.

'This man was a frightful Jew, his slightly hooked nose setting off a shifty, ill-tempered face. After having been cleaned, I was once again placed in the window but this time I was exposed to public mockery, dangling carelessly from a dirty piece of string.'

A brief period of happiness follows when the hat is bought by a young couple. 'But one day when Caroline and Matthew were walking by the Seine, a violent gust of wind turned me into a bird. After several seconds of dreadful anguish I landed on the river and drifted peacefully along in the company of the fish who looked in fear at this new kind of boat.'

A ragman rescues the hat and, after new tortures to repair the damage, it is parcelled up and sent to Africa.

Then one fine morning, I opened my eyes to the light and I was horrified to see dark people in front of me, most of whose faces were taken up by their lips, and whose only clothing was a pair of old-fashioned bathing-trunks and rings in their noses and ears. Seated apart on a crate of biscuits, one of these strange men held a sceptre in his hand made of a feather duster which had lost its feathers and wearing the skin of a lion which he had once slain with courage equal to his huge size.

Two black hands grabbed hold of me admiringly. I started in fear and was only reassured when I saw that the dye did not come off. Then I was deposited on the top of the black mass which made up the king. And here I still am, spending happy days. Sometimes my varnish is almost melted by the burning sun and at times my master's practical sense has caused me to be used as a saucepan . . . But I live peacefully enough, adorning the head of the terrible Bam-Boum, most powerful prince in the land.

I write these lines in my declining days hoping they will reach the French, telling them that I live in a country where headgear will always be fashionable and, in fact, when I am worn out, I really hope to be venerated as a relic for having once graced the head of my illustrious owner, Bam-Boum II, King of the Niger.

Antoine de Saint-Exupéry, aged thirteen

THE original handwritten text contradicted fellow pupils' claims that Saint-Exupéry was a messy student, who covered his copy with blots. That was possibly true for subjects that did not interest him, but the 'Hat's Odyssey', which earned Saint-Exupéry a rare end-of-term prize, was written with an assurance and maturity shown in the neat, almost adult, handwriting.

Unfortunately, Abbé Launay's other model essay, based on the

[43]

funeral of an ant, has been lost, but the outline was remembered by several pupils. Supposedly, the ant's funeral was observed by the writer, Jean de La Fontaine, who was describing it to a friend. The high point of Antoine's version reflected his interest in mechanical invention. The funeral cortège was held up by a trickle of water and he described how the worker ants used their mandibles to build a bridge with fresh grass.

It would be pleasant to add that Antoine returned to Le Mans after winning his first literary prize in 1931 (for *Night Flight*) to thank his old teacher for his insight and encouragement, but his memories were not happy ones and he does not appear to have gone back after he left in 1915. Auguste Launay did not live long enough to see his own intuition confirmed when Saint-Exupéry's books, particularly *Night Flight* and *Wind, Sand and Stars*, became standard national teaching-aids in primary and secondary schools.

ABBÉ Launay awarded Saint-Exupéry 12 out of 20 for his story about the top hat. A mark was taken away for spelling mistakes but there was no comment on Antoine's harsh and racist description of one of the hat's owners, the second-hand clothes dealer, the horrible Jew with a deceitful and bitter face. The sentence cannot be dismissed as nothing more than the confused view of a boy of nearly fourteen years of age who had probably never met a Jew. The image reflected the environment in which he lived and where most of his relatives were uncomfortable in the company of a community they called Israelites.

Saint-Exupéry's juvenile attachment, shared by his schoolmates, to the royalist, anti-Semitic Action Française had brought him into contact with the vicious caricatures and slanders that one day would be used by Vichy as an excuse to persecute an ethnic minority. In the summer holidays before he wrote his 'Odyssey', Antoine told Simone that he sympathized with the movement and that he was founding a royalist secret society, of which he would be chairman, to distribute propaganda. The following term, his classmates put together a newspaper called *L'Écho du troisième* in which humour obscured any political ambitions. During its passage from hand to hand, the laughter provoked by its articles attracted the attention of one of the priests and the paper was confiscated and destroyed. Whether there was any support for Action Française in *L'Écho du troisième* is not known.

The passage in his schoolboy essay and his flirtation with Action Française are less interesting as an indication of youthful misguidance than striking examples of how he unravelled the pernicious influence of Le Mans in later life. No one could accuse Saint Exupéry of being anti-Semitic in adulthood. His tolerance went far beyond an easy relationship with Jews and he wrote a powerful parable in defence of persecuted minorities in *Wisdom of the Sands* at a time when Vichy had introduced a witch-hunt.

Personal experience influenced Saint-Exupéry's opinions and writing far more than the social and religious theories which kept many of his classmates in thrall throughout their lives. Only a few of the lessons he learnt at Le Mans, such as the value of loyal friendship and the ability to suffer hardship without complaint, were retained. Others, like the rigid image of God and faith, were modified and then discarded when confronted with the realities of life. Ethnic, class and religious bigotry eventually vanished in adulthood when he formed his belief that mankind had a common cause that transcended the divisions and absolute truths that the priests of Le Mans were dedicated to maintaining.

AT the same time as announcing his secret society in 1912, Antoine also told his brother and sisters on his return to Saint-Maurice-de-Rémens for the summer holidays that he might one day become a priest; but neither confidence caused the sensation provoked by his new companion, a white rat.

According to his class-mate Paul Gaultier, the rat was one of a pair given to him by Aunt Anaïs de Saint-Exupéry. As the animals were said to have belonged originally to the royal Duchesse de Vendôme, they may have given strength to Antoine's monarchist politics, which led him to sign his fellow students' autograph books with the inscription *For my God, my king and my lady*.

The rodent was housed in a cage beside the children's pet rabbits and much of the first evening was spent planning its diet for the next day. In the morning the cage was found open and the creature had disappeared. Rightly or not, it was thought that Tante Gabrielle had ordered the servants to do away with it.

Within days, the mystery of the vanishing rat and Antoine's ephemeral priestly vocation were relegated to the background by the most important single event since the death of his father. A passion for flying was ignited by his first joy-ride in a plane over an airfield near the château, the initial step on a dangerous path which would eventually lead to a violent and lonely death.

CHAPTER THREE

'A nous les airs'

In the early summer of 1909, just before Saint-Exupéry was sent to
Le Mans, the first trial flights were made by pioneer pilots on the
Bellièvre plain at Ambérieu-en-Bugey. By taking a short cut through
the hamlet of Château-Gaillard, the landing-area was hardly three
kilometres from the château at Saint-Maurice-de-Rémens. The news
caused great excitement. At the time, the whole country was talking
of Louis Blériot's cross-Channel flight in July 1909, an event that had
a far greater impact on French imagination than Orville Wright's first
flight in the United States nearly six years before.

One of Saint-Exupéry's fellow pupils in the first form at Notre-
Dame-de-Sainte-Croix, Jean-Marie Lelièvre, lived near the Auvours
landing-field at Le Mans, and in 1908 had watched Wilbur Wright
and other pioneer pilots give demonstrations which attracted thousands of people. Although Antoine did not cycle to the airfield until
much later, his fellow pupil's descriptions ensured that a passion for
flying was established well before Saint-Exupéry returned to Saint-
Maurice for the 1910 Easter holidays.

Antoine was not unique in being a young flying fanatic. There
were few sporting heroes at the beginning of the century, but their
absence was more than filled by pilots and racing motorists. The
smallest aviation exploit was front-page news, with national and
provincial papers even reporting the progress of pilots in training. A
national magazine, *L'Aérophile*, was first published in 1893 to report
on the many experiments in powered flight that started in 1890 with
a steam-powered, bat-like contraption invented by the Frenchman
Clément Ader.

The daily *Progrès de Lyon* and the *Journal de l'Ain*, which Saint-

Exupéry's mother read, had some solid news to report at the beginning of 1910. A local cycling champion, Louis Mouthier, had bought a copy of Blériot's cross-Channel plane for 10,000 francs and had decided to set up a flying-school at Ambérieu. From these modest beginnings, the Base d'Aviation 278 developed into one of the most important civilian and military training-grounds in the country. Between the wars, Saint-Exupéry often landed at the aerodrome in his private plane either for visits to his family or to his fellow writer, Léon Werth, who had a country house in the Jura. Ambérieu's Café de l'Aviation, where his hosts waited with a car, was still in the hands of the same family in 1993, although the original building was blown up by the Germans.

Among Ambérieu's future pupils was the Great War air ace, George Guynemer, as well as many of the pilots who served with Saint-Exupéry in the Second World War. More recently, the base was transformed into a French air force repair centre, sprawling across an industrialized plateau around the main rail line.

In 1910 there were no sentry-posts or fences to stop the public entering the rustic airstrip. An early photograph showed Louis Mouthier, a small man with a flamboyant moustache, standing beside his primitive Blériot and surrounded by a crowd made up mostly of schoolboys. Mouthier was one of the last of a disappearing breed. He had received no education since leaving school at thirteen and had to teach himself to fly with the aid of Blériot's manual. On 9 August 1910, after intensive practice watched by hundreds of local inhabitants, he became the 157th pilot that year to be given a flying-licence. On 5 February 1911 he founded his own school.

In the many published glimpses that Saint-Exupéry gives of his childhood, there is no information on his early passion for aviation. However, his sister Simone recalls in her unpublished writings how he told stories of his project to build an aeroplane which would take him and his sister above Saint-Maurice while the crowd shouted, 'Vive Antoine de Saint-Exupéry.'

Antoine's dream of flight was accompanied by a passion for engines, and Simone remembered how he and François acquired a small motor for a planned irrigation scheme during the 1911 drought. While François was playing with it, the petrol engine exploded. Antoine thought his brother had been killed when he found him covered with blood from a head wound. The exploding motor may explain why Father Montessuy discouraged Antoine's plan to build an engine of his own design to drive a home-built plane derived from his bicycle. Instead, the priest asked the village carpenter, who was also the château's odd-job man, to make wings for a sail-powered plane – the sails came from Moisy's linen cupboard – that never had the remotest chance of taking off, however hard Antoine pedalled.

His bicycle still played a part in Antoine's initiation into flying, taking him on almost daily visits to the Ambérieu airstrip set among vegetable fields and paddocks. Mouthier's flying-school attracted other pioneers and Ambérieu acquired more and more hangars where planes were built as well as parked. The pilots who flew in and out of Ambérieu were young, some of them barely out of their adolescence, and they were kind to their schoolboy admirers. Most of Antoine's early mechanical knowledge came from watching engines being designed and assembled, while he kept up a flow of questions which he transformed into lessons on mechanics for his brother and sisters.

Visits to the new aerodrome, which would soon be brought into a business partnership with the far more important civilian base at Lyon-Bron, were also a social education. Antoine's aristocratic ancestral heroes were replaced by men of modest and mixed background, for whom success was measured by invention, hard work and daring. The spirit of classless comradeship which Saint-Exupéry revered as an adult was already present at the Hôtel du Lion d'Or in Ambérieu where experienced and trainee pilots lodged in the easygoing atmosphere of a club. To the villagers they were as glamorous as any stage or sporting star. When planes flew over the town, crowds came out in the streets to applaud.

The nationwide craze for aviation took a sharp upward curve from 1909 after Blériot's flight across the Channel. By 1912 it was the central focus of life in Ambérieu. The *Journal de l'Ain* carried a daily serial called '*Les Hommes de l'Air*' which mixed romance and daring. Later in the year, the Grand Guignol theatre at Lyon responded to the flying craze by putting on a play called *Le Grand Oiseau*, full of melodramatic treachery and heroism, in which a plane crash was simulated on stage.

At Easter a three-day festival was organized to inaugurate the Ambérieu military and civilian pilots' school. Antoine usually went to Saint-Maurice for the spring holidays and was probably among the crowd of 10,000 which saw flying displays by Mouthier, René Vidart, a recent winner of the Paris-Rome race, Jules Védrines, the world speed record-holder, and Marius Lacrouze, chief pilot for the Deperdussin flying-school.

The occasion left a vivid memory in the mind of Annette Flamand, who was born in Saint-Maurice in the same year as Antoine. Her parents kept a café and transport business in a house she still lived in eighty years later, but it was not the huge crowd and the aerobatics that left a lasting mark. Just before the fête, she was given her new spring outfit, a grey dress and matching bonnet with black ribbons. At noon on the first day, Saturday 27 April 1912, she remembered a thunderstorm and violent north wind spoilt her new hat. Flying was interrupted and the rest of the weekend was affected by rain. But the pilots took off even in heavy mist. One of them could not find the airstrip and landed 20 kilometres away.

Local shopkeepers sponsored a cavalcade led by a life-size imitation wooden aeroplane drawn by a horse. Behind the 'pilot', the passengers, four young boys in pink flying-costumes and caps, escorted a local beauty queen. Streets were bedecked with flags while the band of the 23rd Regiment of the line played marches for spectators who included local MPs and a former war minister. Several people were given their first joy-rides, among them pretty village girls who hung around the pilots like pit-stop fans.

Profits from the 50-centime programme were used to finance military aviation, a patriotic gesture that echoed the sentiments of a march called '*A nous les airs*', written by the regimental bandmaster. The words became a popular local ballad, especially for the many aspiring pilots of Antoine's age-group. There was more than an innocent dream of flight contained in the opening lines:

The time has come for the dreams of Icarus

Man has conquered the empire of the birds.

At a national level, aviation was seen as the way to challenge the British Empire, a sentiment shown in the second verse which began

> *The Englishman, who wants to remain ruler of the waves,*
> *Will he get tired of launching his ships?*

This prophetic vision of air-power threatening Britain's maritime domination was already being translated into reality. Frenchmen led the world in aviation. By 1912, nearly 1000 flying-licences had been issued by the Aéroclub de France, nearly three times more than in Britain or Germany, while in the United States there were fewer than 200 registered pilots.

Ambérieu's fête was an unintended farewell to the amateur spirit of flying. The heroic days were giving way to professionalism while the ideal of emulating Icarus had been overtaken by the development of fighting-machines already being used in wars in south-eastern Europe. The plane that took Antoine de Saint-Exupéry on his first voyage above the earth was a military prototype. The two young men who built and flew it were to become premature casualties of the race to give France a master-weapon in the battle for European dominance.

The Berlin Conspiracy

THE exact date of Antoine's aerial baptism is unknown, although an eyewitness, Alfred Thénoz, narrowed probabilities to the second half of July 1912. More precision would show whether Antoine had his mother's permission or whether he lied and was punished as another eyewitness, Georges Thibaut, affirmed. Despite the joy-riding at Ambérieu, the dangers were extremely great and permission would not have been given lightly. Every week, newspapers carried reports of flying accidents wherever they occurred in the world, but an event much nearer home had plunged the whole Ambérieu region into consternation a few days before Antoine's first flight.

Many of the aviation fanatics at the Ambérieu fête were also present at a flying display at nearby Bourg-en-Bresse, the Ain *département*'s biggest town, during the 14 July weekend. Gaston Olivarès, a speed and altitude record-breaker, was the star attraction. His aerobatics only 70 metres above the crowd provided the thrills on the first day, when stormy weather should have encouraged caution. On the second day the air was still unstable. In the middle of a manoeuvre, Olivarès' plane hit an air-pocket and fell to earth, killing the pilot.

The meeting was immediately stopped. The accident dominated local newspapers for days and marked the decline of popular air rallies in the region. The trend accelerated the following year when France's youngest professional flyer, Eugène Mercier, only six years older than Antoine, died in a crash during a demonstration at Ambérieu.

ANTOINE was taken for his first flight by a twenty-three-year-old pioneer called Gabriel Wroblewski, who hid his Polish name behind the pseudonym Salvez. With his elder brother Pierre he built four monoplanes between 1909 and 1914. Because the Salvez brothers were killed in their last aircraft, their names were better known in Poland than in France until a mechanic, Alfred Thénoz, remembered Antoine's first joy-ride after reading sixty years later that the credit had been wrongly given to Jules Védrines.

Thénoz's version might have been doubted if he had not met Saint-Exupéry in the late thirties when the writer dedicated a post-card of the Salvez brothers sitting in one of their machines and added a note recalling that both he and Thénoz took their first flights in the same plane. According to Thénoz, Saint-Exupéry was given two low laps over Ambérieu's primitive aerodrome.

The other eyewitness, Georges Thibaut, was only eight years old and had been one of the four pink-clad passengers in the mock aeroplane which led the inauguration parade at Easter. Like most of his class-mates, he spent breaks from school on Thursday afternoons and Sundays at the airfield, often carrying messages from the flyers to his two elder sisters. Thibaut, a future professional photographer, was given a joy-ride by Gabriel Salvez, whose plane was one of the few with two seats.

Later, Thibaut claimed that he acted as a go-between for Antoine in persuading the brothers to take him as a passenger. Perhaps Antoine was just being kind in letting little Georges think he had such influence, because Saint-Exupéry was well known at the landing-ground where even his mother had met the Wroblewski-Salvez brothers.

They belonged to a breed of fanatical aviation pioneers who would have taken their place alongside Great War manufacturers like Fokker or Sopwith, had they lived. Their father, a Polish doctor, went to work in Chile, leaving them in the care of their mother, who owned a dye factory in Lyon. Her sons' flying projects drained much of her money because their first plane crashed in 1910. But in 1911, when Gabriel Salvez earned his licence by flying the brothers' second plane 25 metres above the Ambérieu airstrip, their technical innovations were putting them well ahead of most of their competitors.

Antoine flew in their third model, built in a hangar at Ambérieu under the guidance of Pierre Salvez, the engineering genius, who was a less dashing figure than his slim, elegant brother. The 70-horsepower Gnome-engined aircraft, with a revolutionary all-metal frame and a 14-metre wing-span, was well in advance of most constructions of that year. An identical model, powered by a 130-horsepower Laviator engine, was built soon afterwards to show to war ministry officials in March 1914. The day before the demonstration, both brothers were killed when the plane, equipped to carry a machine-gun, crashed into a quarry on the edges of the Ambérieu airstrip.

Saint-Exupéry was at school in Le Mans when the deaths were reported in national and provincial newspapers. His mother wrote a letter of sympathy to Madame Wroblewski, saying she had asked for masses to be said for the brothers, who 'were so good to my little Antoine who was upset by the terrible news'. A letter of sympathy signed Antoine de Saint-Exupéry was also sent, but the writing did not resemble other samples of his work that year and was possibly written on his behalf by his mother.

By the time Antoine returned to Saint-Maurice for the 1914 Easter holidays, the death of the Wroblewski/Salvez brothers had developed into a sombre mystery. Their brother, Édouard, who became a Great War test pilot in secrecy because his distraught mother had forbidden him to fly, carried out an inquiry and decided that the plane had been sabotaged when experts discovered a hidden hair-line crack in a wing-strut. He remembered that a week before the accident, the hangar door at Ambérieu had been forced and a stranger had been spotted making drawings of the crashed plane.

Later in the year, the Wroblewski family took in a German lodger at their Lyon flat where blueprints of the aeroplane were kept. Just before war broke out, the man left without warning and was later identified as a spy by a local police chief. Military engineers who studied the Salvez prototype were later struck by the similarity to the Dutch-designed Fokker that gave the German air force the edge in 1914. In a letter to the *Progrès de Lyon* in 1914 Édouard Wroblewski said that the Fokker was a copy of his brothers' design.

An undated fragment of a poem by Antoine was the only written souvenir of his first flight, but his dream of astonishing the local population was fulfilled by the Salvez brothers. Their epitaph was written prematurely by an anonymous *Progrès de Lyon* reporter who, a few days before their death, watched them fly together above Ambérieu to the medieval Saint-Denis tower before returning to the town centre after an hour's flight.

> Turning lazily over the town in magnificent flying patterns of rare daring, the display over the church steeple was truly marvellous. The public massed in the roads below to follow the impressive curves and dips of this majestic bird with emotion, applauding the pilot for the absolute mastery of his machine.

The reporter should have added: '*Vive les frères Salvez.*'

A White Villa Under the Pines

THE happiest photographs of Saint-Exupéry during his adolescence were taken at his new school, the Collège de la Villa Saint-Jean at Fribourg in Switzerland, where he was a boarder for two years from 1915 to 1917. The sulky, withdrawn look of group pictures at Le Mans was replaced by that of a contented student. Several pictures were taken in the open air where he wore a Tyrolean-style suit and hat instead of a uniform.

He was already much taller than most of his contemporaries and would eventually measure 1 metre 84. His stay at Le Mans had ended in June 1915 after he fell ill with anaemia, but concern over his health was only one of the reasons for sending him to an experimental school with emphasis on sport and other outside activities.

The outbreak of war had been traumatic for Fernand de Saint-Exupéry whose surviving son, Roger, Antoine's godfather, was killed leading his infantry company in the opening weeks of fighting. Although Roger left seven children, only one was male. Le Mans's unhappy experiences under Prussian occupation in 1870 were still vivid for grand-père Fernand and he was easily persuaded that his grandson should be sent to safety to protect the 700-year-old lineage. The main condition, that it should be a religious education, was fulfilled at Saint-Jean, a Catholic school run by priests and laymen who were members of the Marist order dedicated to the mother of God.

The school, situated on the boundary of German and French cantons, was not chosen by chance. Marie de Saint-Exupéry sounded out friends and family. One of their neighbours in Lyon, Louis de Bonnevie, was already a pupil. Advice was also given by the Sallès family who lived on the other side of the valley from Saint-Maurice. Louis de Bonnevie and Charles Sallès were Antoine's class-mates and became his closest friends at Fribourg, where his brother François was in a lower form.

The school was set in hilly scenery which recalled the familiar Jura foothills around Saint-Maurice and was staffed by the most enlightened teachers Saint-Exupéry ever met. The forbidding aspect of the school buildings at Le Mans was replaced by chalets that served as classrooms and dormitories. Although he never showed much interest in sport, except swimming, Antoine was encouraged to take part in open-air activities including football, tennis, tobogganing and ice-skating when the local river, the Sarine, froze over. Walks among the pine-forests and along the lakes were frequent while the war was a distant affair, recalled only by daily bulletins pinned on the school notice-board or when Swiss regiments camped in the college grounds.

More than seventy years later Charles Sallès, who spent most of his life running a family estate in Provence, was still enthusiastic about the teaching methods at Saint-Jean, which contrasted with the severity of French religious schools. The relationship between staff and pupils was based on trust, he recalled. Most teachers were of Alsatian origin and were inspired by a tolerant version of British public-school methods complemented by relaxed German classroom schedules.

Religion was not force-fed. The priests and lay teachers preached more by example than stricture, a lead being given by the headmaster, Father François-Joseph Keiffer, who took refuge in neutral Switzerland rather than stay in Alsace under German rule.

One figure stood out among the other teachers, Antoine Wahl, who taught German, geography and natural sciences. He was believed to have spent his personal fortune founding the school in 1903. The kindness of this small, strictly dressed Austrian with a goatee beard left a lasting memory on all the boys long after he died while still a master in 1933. His past, in Sallès words, was 'quite mysterious' and the boys decided that he had turned to education to mend his broken heart.

There was an emphasis on German language and culture which Marie de Saint-Exupéry had always encouraged at Saint-Maurice, especially for the girls. Antoine was taught German at Fribourg as if it were a first language, although this did not stop him writing patriotic, anti-Kaiser poems in which he often expressed a frustration at being kept out of the fighting.

The college at Fribourg was the only school Saint-Exupéry wrote of with nostalgia in his published writings and yet he often gave the impression while he was there that he was a resentful dunce. Although his school records have been lost, teachers noted that most of the time he was near the bottom of the class and did not even try very hard in French composition.

He saved his creativity for private projects, such as the libretto for an operetta called *Le Parapluie*. The script was sent to his violin teacher, Anne-Marie Poncet, in Lyon, but she was unenthusiastic about a tale in which a woman's umbrella, abandoned in a café, becomes the centre of a young man's romantic dreams until the ugly owner arrives to reclaim it.

At Le Mans, Saint-Exupéry's disrespect and refusal to shine in class had been severely punished. At the Villa Saint-Jean, the priests were more understanding and never lost hope of winning over their hyper-sensitive and undisciplined pupil by patience. Their efforts were rewarded many years later by a sympathetic passage in Saint-Exupéry's first novel, *Southern Mail*. In the guise of his romantic pilot hero, Jacques Bernis, Saint-Exupéry evokes 'a white villa under the pines' in a long, nostalgic episode in which Bernis, a mail pilot on the Africa run, takes a friend on a 'melancholy visit to our childhood'.

The passage was inspired by a trip to Saint-Jean more than ten years after Antoine left, and contained a note of deep affection and gratitude for his ageing 'gay and charming' schoolmasters. In *Southern Mail*, the teachers press their visitors with questions on a life of action while the book's narrator compares the dangerous reality of pioneer flying with philosophy lessons on Pascal, Taine and Nietzsche which give only a theoretical preparation for life. Speaking of the gap in experience between the existence of the men he admired when young and his own life of calculated risk, the author remarks: 'Suddenly, we understood that we [Bernis and his friend, another pilot] already knew another flesh. Old boys have the habit of coming back with a hard step to take their revenge.'

To avoid saddening these idols of his youth, who bring out a rare bottle of wine at dinner to honour the former pupil, Bernis/Saint-Exupéry prefers to stress the disappointments of a life of action and let the most senior teacher continue to dream that the truth lies in the peace that comes from books.

If this was the summary of a real conversation between Saint-

Exupéry and his teachers, the passage amounted to a subtle form of apology for withholding the constructive side of his intelligence and character at the college where these dedicated men had sought nothing except the satisfaction of serving others.

THE benign atmosphere at the Villa Saint-Jean helped Saint-Exupéry to shake off Jesuit influence and Fernand de Saint-Exupéry's prejudices. By the time he had taken his *baccalauréat* in 1917, in preparation for an eventual naval career, other foundations of his early youth had been put in question.

Some changes were far-reaching. His mother was a member of the Red Cross which had provided an outlet for the consciences of the rich and titled in pre-war years. Within months of the outbreak of fighting, she was confronted with harsh and pitiless inhumanity. Maimed and disfigured French prisoners were sent home from German PoW camps through Switzerland, and the first stop in France for ambulance trains was at Ambérieu. Marie was in charge of their reception. The grim, darkened trains, full of dying and crippled men crying out for small comfort, left a lasting memory in the small town.

Marie had a state nursing diploma and was among the first civilians to see the terrible consequences of a war in which several of her relatives were killed. From then on, she accelerated her detachment from materialism and devoted the greater part of her time to bringing comfort to other people, especially the old and very young.

War service reduced the staff at Saint-Maurice while the shared grief of local families broke down the barriers between château and village. Annette Flamand, whose Easter hat was spoilt by the rain in the 1912 inauguration of the air base, said that before the war there was a distinct social gap. Antoine was the same age, but she would bow when he passed, calling him Monsieur Antoine, while his patent leather shoes were a talking-point for children who usually wore clogs. Annette's father owned the village's first motor taxi. Before the war, a servant used to summon him to the château when the Saint-Exupéry family needed transport. After 1914, the lack of staff meant that Marie de Saint-Exupéry had to walk to the local café herself to ask for a car to take her to her nursing-post.

Children who grew up after 1918 speak of the château with less respect than those of the pre-war years, even though Marie continued to train the church choir and teach embroidery to the village girls. Rather than referring to Antoine as a remote figure glimpsed playing behind the château's iron gates, the post-war generation remembered him as their first Père Noël, dressed in red gown and white beard, and distributing presents.

The mood at Saint-Maurice was a reflection of changes on a national scale which masked divisions in society. More than one and a half million Frenchmen were killed in four years of fighting, but their blood sealed a fragile faith in republicanism, ending hopes of a royalist revival. While there was no apparent causal link, two of the lifelong monarchists in Antoine's life died soon after the 1918 victory; Fernand de Saint-Exupéry in 1919 and Gabrielle de Tricaud in 1920.

The Death of François

IN July 1917, François de Saint-Exupéry died at the age of fourteen, just after Antoine's seventeenth birthday. Saint-Exupéry published nothing about his distress over François's death until more than twenty years later. He had been given little time to prepare for the loss and spent most of his life trying to come to terms with it.

Marie de Saint-Exupéry usually visited the brothers once a week at Fribourg, even though war conditions made the 200-kilometre rail journey difficult. In the spring of 1917, François caught a chill during a school visit to Divonne-les-Bains when he lost his overcoat and was reluctant to tell the supervisors. His mother brought him back to Saint-Maurice where rheumatic fever was diagnosed. Antoine made only casual references to the illness in his letters home as if he had been reassured that his brother would be cured before the summer holidays.

When Saint-Exupéry returned to the château in July, François's health deteriorated rapidly. At 4 a.m. on 10 July a nurse woke Antoine and said his brother wanted to talk to him. Twenty minutes later François was dead.

What happened in those twenty minutes resurfaced during Saint-Exupéry's tale of the near-fatal reconnaissance flight to Arras in 1940. As the author tells it, François announced in a matter-of-fact voice that he was going to die but said he was not suffering. In the few minutes left he made his will, leaving a steam-engine, a bicycle and a rifle to Antoine, asking him to write down his words.

A biographer, Nelly de Vogüé, in a book written under her *nom-de-plume* of Pierre Chevrier, said that François then sent Antoine to call his mother, and told her he would be happier where he was going, because 'certain things I have seen or guessed at are too ugly to bear'.

Watching his brother die was another lesson in accepting fate which Antoine outlines in *Wisdom of the Sands* when the Berber chief learns at an early age to look death in the face. Under anti-aircraft fire in 1940, Saint-Exupéry recalls one of François's last sentences in which he said he could not help dying. The decision to die was not his own. 'It's my body'. Remembering those words in *Flight to Arras*, Antoine suddenly realizes that for all the attention he has given to his own body over the years, he does not care about his physical being. By then, like his brother, he has also seen or guessed at things that are too ugly to bear.

François's calm detachment as his end approached was at the heart of Antoine's fatalism throughout his flying career, when fear of death was replaced by a sentiment close to that of awaiting the arrival of a familiar companion. Before Saint-Exupéry's final crash, he told friends that he was not only ready to die but that he was willing to die.

This fatalism did nothing to lessen his grief at losing relatives and friends, as his private letters showed. The death of François, a child with an almost saintly look, was probably the worst emotional shock Saint-Exupéry ever received. He took a photograph of his brother after death and had several copies run off, one of which he always kept with him. For the rest of his life, he would search for a close fraternal relationship to replace that of his gentle friend.

The benefit of two years at Fribourg was swept away by François's death and the family became worried about Antoine's health. Accompanied by his school-friend Louis de Bonnevie, Saint-Exupéry was sent for a holiday at Carnac in Brittany. One of Antoine's aunts from Le Mans, Amicie de Saint-Exupéry, was married to a soldier of English descent, Major Sydney Churchill, whose summer house had much of the easygoing atmosphere of Saint-Maurice.

Louis de Bonnevie acted as nurse as much as confidant, looking after Antoine when he sprained his ankle. Gradually, Saint-Exupéry recovered from a deep depression and accepted family plans for a naval career, although, because of his brother's death, he was forbidden to go sailing off the Brittany coast.

There had already been one scare when he swam too far out into the Atlantic and had to be rescued, but the ban on sailing did not seem to trouble him because he waited more than ten years before making his first pleasure-trip on a yacht. A friend took him sailing at Dakar, Senegal, but the boat overturned after hitting the tidal bar and Antoine nearly drowned.

CHAPTER FOUR

A Battle Missed

IN 1917, Germany had recovered the advantage in the Great War and the fighting seemed likely to go on for much longer than expected. A young man of seventeen was almost certain to fight and many of Saint-Exupéry's class-mates at Le Mans and Fribourg had already been called up.

After the massacres on the Marne and at Verdun, the choice of arms was no longer a theoretical consideration but a question of survival. The predominant links with the army on both sides of Antoine's family predestined him to follow his godfather Roger into the infantry. Instead, the parental council preferred the navy. Apart from the fact that it was the service with the lowest casualty rate, the navy was a monarchist stronghold and known as *la royale*. The same motives which inspired royalist Catholic families to send their children to Jesuit schools like Le Mans were evident in the choice of military service.

There was enough inherited glory to justify a naval career. In Fernand de Saint-Exupéry's book on his family's past, which Antoine saw in the house at Le Mans, one of the most colourful forebears was Fernand's grandfather, Georges de Saint-Exupéry, an infantry officer who wrote of his experiences in the American War of Independence when he was present at the British surrender. Part of his service was aboard ship where he saw action against the Royal Navy. His wife, Victoire Green de Saint-Marsault, was the daughter of a naval officer and niece of a naval lieutenant who died aboard *La Belle Poule* in an engagement with the British warship *Arethusa* in 1778.

To prepare the entrance examination for the naval academy, Saint-Exupéry was sent on a cramming course in Paris at the Lycée

Saint-Louis on the boulevard Saint-Michel. His fellow senior pupils were preparing entrance examinations to *grandes écoles* or academies and were divided into four clans. As a navy candidate, Antoine was a *'flottard'* and his letters showed a profound contempt for the other groups: *'pistons'* who hoped to enter the Centrale civil engineering school, *'taupins'* destined for the military engineering establishment, the Polytechnique, and *'cyrards'* who had chosen to enter an army career through the academy of Saint-Cyr.

A roll-call of students showed how successful the Jesuit campaign had been in preparing an aristocratic and bourgeois intake for the national academies. This was most striking among the *flottards*: all the friends Saint-Exupéry mentioned in letters home came from the provincial nobility. Many of Saint-Exupéry's contemporaries at Saint-Louis were destined to become the middle-level civil servants and military officers of the thirties who would be confronted by a choice between Vichy and the Free French in 1940.

The last few months of the 1914–18 war played havoc with discipline at Saint-Louis where most students were on the verge of call-up. Antoine was caught up in the rebellious atmosphere, sharpened by the often physical rivalry among the four streams studying for entrance examinations. Some of Antoine's escapades were puerile, like setting off firecrackers to disturb classes and calling the fire brigade on false alarms, but this was also his first real taste of life in a capital where frivolity was rarely dampened by the dangers of long-distance shelling from the Germans' 'Big Bertha' cannon and attacks by Gotha bombers. At night, the boys broke bounds to visit cafés where soldiers returning from the front mingled with women of easy virtue. Once, Saint-Exupéry was nearly caught when he crept out of the school through a storm drain after telling friends he had a date with a *'mignonne'* – a term he used to describe a casual woman friend.

Throughout his stay in Paris, he was in close contact with aristocratic relatives who acted as moral guardians, sending back reports to the family council. Antoine's first letters to his mother reassured her that he was resisting the temptations of life in a liberated society, reading the Bible regularly and enjoying the *lycée's* strict study programme. In assuring her that there was no immorality in the dormitories, he added: 'Obviously there are a few who make hay at night in the city, but they also respect the moral choices of others and rather admire those who don't go out.'

His respect for convention was rewarded when he was elected *brigadier des gendarmes* in charge of a dozen other pupils responsible for enforcing a students' disciplinary code. But the dominant theme of his letters was his social life, which reflected his undiminished royalist fervour. After lunching with the Duchesse de Vendôme, the Belgian king's sister, he wrote home to say he was 'mad with joy' and that she had invited him to see a play at the Comédie-Française.

Personal worries, such as a lack of his favourite chocolates, a request for money to buy a bowler hat and his disgust at the poor quality of shoelaces, sounded unreal against the background of the central preoccupation: an impatience to join the great battle going on only a few miles away. In 1918, bombing by Zeppelins and Gotha bombers had forced the *lycée* to transfer to the safety of a suburban school and by June Saint-Exupéry was writing home of plans to escape on foot if the Germans reached Paris after a new offensive.

The greater the danger became, the more his letters took on a light-hearted tone about his hopes of going to war, but there were also hints that naval ambitions had faded and that the aviation dream set in flight in 1912 was again obsessing him. Because Charles Sallès, his friend at Fribourg, had been called up into the artillery, Antoine wrote to his mother saying that he would join the same unit while awaiting a transfer to the air force.

In autumn 1918 he was sent to Besançon for a medical examination and was told he was in perfect health. Nothing stood in the way of immediate conscription but he treated the prospect humorously in illustrated letters to Marie from the military base. He assured his mother, who must have been acutely worried after seeing so much mutilation and despair in the hospital trains at Ambérieu, that he was making progress in learning 'boche'.

The war ended almost on the day he should have reported for military duty. Although there were no letters to show how he felt at the time, his exclusion from the Great War battles would later strengthen his determination to take part in the fight against Hitler when he could have claimed exemption because of age. Saint-Exupéry grew up separated in experience and prestige from a generation of young men who were barely older than himself but whose courage had been tested under fire. The heroic aftermath of the Armistice, with its parades and nationalistic war memorials, only accentuated the disappointment of being left out of the most exciting adventure of his life.

Technically, he had been old enough to fight and like many men of his age who just missed the call-up, he had to live with questions about his delay in reaching the front. As the Second World War would show, Antoine was haunted by fears of appearing to run away from the action.

Many of the writers he would meet had fought in the front line during the Great War. Of the authors who combined action and literature, the most striking was Joseph Kessel, who was only two years older than Saint-Exupéry, but had analysed his experiences of flying in battle even before Antoine had finished his peacetime national service.

The anticlimax to years of being prepared for an heroic military role precipitated a decline in Saint-Exupéry's interest in the navy. In June 1919 he failed the entrance exams, in one paper obtaining only 7 out of 20 for his essay recounting the return of a soldier to his village in Alsace after the Armistice in November 1918. Later, Saint-Exupéry sent journalists on false trails when questioned about his dismal failure at the subsequent oral examination, although the explanation for his apathy was obvious. After four years of promised glory, in which the French army won more honour than at any time since Napoleon, a peacetime military career was a let-down. He was frank about the reasons in a letter to his sister Simone, saying he would never be ready for the naval examination because 'I am not studying the programme'.

His decision to give up the navy proved right in time. Most of his fellow *flottards* who joined *la royale* were drawn into one of the saddest episodes of the Second World War when Admiral François Darlan became Philippe Pétain's Prime Minister and obstructed naval ambitions to join the Allies. In November 1942 young officers, brought up like Saint-Exupéry with the ambition of avenging Trafalgar, scuttled the entire fleet at Toulon rather than join the Anglo-Saxon effort to liberate France.

Among the notable exceptions was Antoine's close companion, his cousin Honoré d'Estienne d'Orves, who studied in Paris at the same time as Saint-Exupéry. His personal itinerary as an aristocratic Gaullist naval officer, who became one of the first Resistance heroes, will become more relevant in 1940 when Saint-Exupéry remained loyal to Pétain.

A Carol in the Trenches

DURING his early weeks as a boarder at his Paris *lycée*, Saint-Exupéry did his best to reassure his mother that he was standing by his faith, but his letters insisting that he was moved by the Bible and enthralled by the Song of Solomon have a hollow sound. Although biblical language and style would influence *Wisdom of the Sands* many years later, the guiding principles of his religion slipped away in the excitement of life in the capital.

Many of his fellow students at the *lycée*, especially the day-boys, were hostile to religion and contemptuous of the moralizing attitude of the Catholic intake. They were considered a dangerous influence and, soon after the attempt to escape through the storm drain, Antoine was found a place as a boarder at Bossuet private school near the Luxembourg Gardens. Like many Catholic institutions in the city, Bossuet provided lodgings for provincial students at state-run *lycées*. Several of Antoine's fellow pupils at Saint-Louis were housed there, watched over by senior masters during their nightly or weekend 'prep'.

Bossuet's boarders left the rowdy, overcrowded and undisciplined atmosphere of Saint-Louis after ten hours of study for the calm warmth of an indulgent club for young men. Much of the style was set by Abbé Maurice Sudour, the last priest to play an important part in forming Saint-Exupéry's character.

In 1918 Maurice Sudour was appointed deputy headmaster and later took complete responsibility for the school. He was a legendary hero for boys forced to sit out the war. A tall, elegant man of forty, he earned the Croix de Guerre while serving in the trenches as an army chaplain. His most courageous act was far from belligerent. At Christmas 1917, he stood on the Verdun battlefield and sang a carol, 'Minuit chrétien', to the Germans across the lines. A German chaplain replied in his own language.

Having returned from so much pointless slaughter, Abbé Sudour did not stint his affection for boys whom he considered to be lucky survivors. His big flat at Bossuet was open house for daily conversations over tea and coffee when he was not taking school parties for climbing holidays in the Alps. He had two other claims to popularity of which he was probably not aware. He was considered an excessively indulgent confessor and held the school record for saying mass, once being timed at sixteen minutes for the Latin service which usually took about three-quarters of an hour.

The priest was a provincial, born into a farming family in the central *département* of the Corrèze, not far from the village dedicated to a fifth-century bishop of Toulouse which had given the Saint-Exupéry family its name. As a farmer's son he had an especially easy relationship with boys from a rural background like Antoine, whose struggle with a fading belief in the Church was becoming more and more evident. No record was kept of the long, soul-searching conversations at Bossuet in which Saint-Exupéry revealed his struggle over the contradictions of Christianity and a God who had taken away his brother. But there was a mutual understanding on a spiritual and intellectual level that developed into a lasting friendship. In 1931, more than ten years after leaving Bossuet, Antoine asked Maurice Sudour to bless his marriage to Consuelo Suncin de Sandoval.

In biblical terms, the priest was also an instrument of the Lord because he found Antoine a job as an airline pilot in 1926, the same year that he published his first short story. During the bleak years between leaving school and finding a career that saved him from mediocrity, Saint-Exupéry turned often to his spiritual adviser. Without him he might not have emerged happily from a period of trial which tested his character through contrasting years of exhilaration and despondency.

Taking Wing

MOST of the adventures related in Antoine de Saint-Exupéry's three pre-war books – *Southern Mail, Night Flight* and *Wind, Sand and Stars* – took place between 1926 and 1932 when he flew for the Latécoère airmail line in West Africa and South America. Saint-Exupéry left high school in 1920 without any sure future in mind. He signed on at the École des Beaux-Arts in Paris as an architectural student, more as a whim than an ambition. The moral watchdogs who kept an eye on him at the *lycée* were held back and he was allowed a period to sow his wild oats in the dissipated atmosphere of cafés and cabarets. There seemed no reason why he should not follow in the steps of his ancestors and marry a rich, titled woman before returning to Saint-Maurice to help his mother manage the estate.

During much of 1920 he lodged in the Hôtel de la Louisiane in Saint-Germain-des-Prés, a hotel that would later become famous for two existentialist residents, Simone de Beauvoir and Jean-Paul Sartre. Antoine's first sexual experiences probably dated from his year of architectural study, although in the autobiographical *Southern Mail* he did not disguise contempt for casual encounters at La Coupole in Montparnasse, a café well known for its easy pick-ups.

The liberated student life-style in the immediate post-Great War years was much the same as it would be after 1945, with Saint-Exupéry spending a lot of time writing on café tables or visiting night-clubs. The Bohemian existence, however, was artificial. He received an allowance from his mother and he could stave off hunger by attending formal dinners given by rich relatives or return to the comfort of a grandiose flat on the quai Malaquais, overlooking the Seine and owned by his mother's cousin, Yvonne de Lestrange.

Much of his spare time was spent plotting ways of overcoming family opposition to a pilot's career. His opportunity came with his call-up in 1921 for two years' national service. Antoine de Saint-Exupéry, the descendant of generations of royalist officers, decided to join the air force as a ground-crew mechanic. On 9 April he was assigned to a fighter squadron in Strasbourg with the rank of second-class private.

In order to fly, a recruit was normally expected to sign on for three years at an officers' academy, but Saint-Exupéry had detected a loophole. Even a private soldier could be sent for training if he was a qualified civilian pilot. Within days of arriving at the base he put the first phase of his plans into operation.

On a bright April morning in 1921, Saint-Exupéry went to the Neuhof airport in Strasbourg and asked a civilian pilot of the Trans-aérienne de l'Est airline if he could be taken on a 50-franc joy-ride over Alsace, the territory annexed by Germany between 1870 and 1918. After ten minutes in the air, he asked for a second flip. Two months later he came back to ask for lessons.

The civilian pilot was Robert Aéby, who had learned to fly with the German air force in 1918 just before Germany relinquished Alsace under the terms of the Armistice. A meticulous man, Aéby was able to recall the exact date Saint-Exupéry began pilot training – 18 June 1921 – and the type and registration letters of the plane – a Farman F40, F-CTEB. Unwittingly, the former German air force fighter pilot was drawn into the centre of what was known in the family as 'the Strasbourg plot', in which Saint-Exupéry trained for a 2000-franc fee with the secret approval of his commanding officer. His instructor had to swear not to let anyone know that he was teaching Saint-Exupéry, his first pupil.

Aéby's log-book was confiscated by the Germans in 1940 but he kept a second copy which demolished Saint-Exupéry's own version of his initial solo flight. According to the story repeated to several friends, he took a plane without permission and nearly crashed when flames from the engine set his trousers alight. The anecdote became more detailed with time and ended with the fighter-base major watching the landing and telling the young pilot that he would never die in an air crash because he should have been dead already.

There was a small measure of truth in this account, as Aéby's records showed. Three weeks and eleven lessons after Saint-Exupéry's first training-flight in a dual-control aircraft, the instructor took him on a ten-minute run before landing and telling him to take the plane up by himself. By then, Antoine had transferred to a Sopwith biplane which had its own temperament. On his landing approach he misjudged the height and accelerated away for a second attempt, but his reaction was too brutal and the carburettor backfired, sending a shaft of flame into the cockpit, scorching his gaiters.

Aéby praised him for his coolness, because the aborted landing had been followed by a perfect touchdown. The initial fault on an unfamiliar plane was excusable, he said, and Saint-Exupéry had reacted well afterwards. Aéby assessed his pupil as being very capable, with quick reactions and sure judgement.

However, the instructor did not fall under Saint-Exupéry's spell and felt he was a snob. Although Antoine developed a more classless attitude over the next twenty years, he used his title and social connections to gain advantage in the air force. Aéby addressed him as 'Monsieur le comte' and said that strings were pulled to get round regulations and enable Saint-Exupéry to take time off from routine duties for his lessons. Aéby bore a grudge for another reason. After his solo flight, Antoine did not buy the traditional glass of champagne for his teacher. The two men made up for this initial coldness when they met by chance at a café in Vichy seventeen years later. Saint-Exupéry, who was convalescing after a near-fatal crash in Guatemala, bought a round of drinks. The afternoon ended in laughter, with Saint-Exupéry telling Robert Aéby's wife that he had been so happy during his first unaccompanied flight that if there had been enough petrol he would never have come back to earth.

Apart from his precision on the beginning of Saint-Exupéry's pilot's career, Aéby remembered being surprised by the scruffiness of his recruit; confirmation of Antoine's lifelong inability to find clothes that fitted or flattered him. His untidiness was a subject of amusement but a more important cause for reproach were his begging-letters to his mother asking for money for flying-lessons or to pay for a room in Strasbourg.

However, there was no reason why Saint-Exupéry should think that his mother was hard up. She had just inherited the château at Saint-Maurice-de-Rémens from Tante Gabrielle, who also left a considerable sum of money to Marie-Madeleine. Saint-Exupéry had meanwhile received a small legacy from his grandfather Fernand whose property was sold on his death and shared between his grandchildren. The house in rue Pierre-Bellon in Le Mans, where Antoine stayed as a schoolboy, was kept in the family.

Even without these gifts, Antoine had every reason to feel that his mother's rich relatives were an endless source of financial help and that there was no shame in taking an unearned portion. In Saint-Exupéry's environment, finance was rarely gleaned by effort, but accumulated by arranged marriages and inheritance. The idea that a family was an endless money chain to be tugged whenever necessary was not far-fetched.

A more valid criticism concerns Saint-Exupéry's indifference to his mother's fears that she could lose her only surviving son in an accident. Her anxiety was shown in the ban on sailing after François's death and now Antoine seemed intent on following the dangerous path of the Salvez brothers when she needed him to run Saint-Maurice. This insensitivity to feminine reaction to his pact with danger would later help wreck his first engagement and damage his marriage.

Marie gave in to his wheedling and pleading because she had never disappointed him, but she probably felt she was signing a death-warrant. The money order she reluctantly sent to Strasbourg to pay Robert Aéby bought her more than twenty worrying years which ended in the inevitable loss of her son.

One other persistent problem was confirmed by his months at Strasbourg. Breaking away from privilege was not as easy as it looked and for most of his life Saint-Exupéry hovered uneasily between the advantages of aristocratic connections and his desire to be independent. His demands for an allowance from his mother – he received the equivalent of about 6000 francs a month at today's values – showed his dislike for the rough-and-tumble life of his fellow privates. While they put up with the levelling experience of national service in crowded dormitories, Saint-Exupéry found lodgings in Strasbourg where he could take hot baths, make tea and coffee and get down to his writing. With the flying-lessons, occasional trips as an observer and the home comforts of his town retreat, life in Strasbourg as a second-class private was surprisingly agreeable, especially as it lasted less than four months.

On 2 August 1921, five weeks after coming of age, Saint-Exupéry's military flying career began. Because of his eleven civilian lessons he was considered advanced enough to be transferred to a fighter unit in the French protectorate of Morocco as a trainee corporal pilot, and he earned his wings when he qualified on 23 December 1921. Recruitment rules were looser for overseas territories and he gained enough hours in the air to be sent to an officer-cadet school at Avord in central France. The posting came a year after his first lesson with Robert Aéby but he was admitted only after an examination in which he was sixty-seventh out of sixty-eight candidates.

On 20 October 1922 he was promoted to second-lieutenant and transferred to Paris's main airport, Le Bourget, to fly with the 34th Aviation Regiment. Less than six weeks later, a government decree separated the air force from army control, creating an independent service, but for Saint-Exupéry the most important event occurred in January the following year. His plane crashed on the edge of Le Bourget airfield and he was taken to hospital with a fractured skull.

His mother's anxiety over his safety had been justified. In June 1923 Saint-Exupéry rejected the chance of a career in the new independent air force and took a job as a civilian clerk in a Paris office. Marie de Saint-Exupéry's concern for her son's survival played no part in the decision. He gave up his burning ambition because he was in love.

CHAPTER FIVE

The Disposable Fiancé

ANTOINE was brought up with a romantic view of women. They were virtuous, cultured and gentle creatures like his mother, sisters and provincial cousins. He often said he would have been happiest during the Renaissance when the practice of courtly love matched his own languorous adolescent attempts at seduction. Several virginal young women received carefully penned homage in classical verse. Among them was Odette de Sinéty, a girl two years older than Antoine and sister of a fellow pupil at Le Mans. In *Southern Mail* she was a part of the composite portrait which made up Geneviève, the married lover of the pilot Jacques Bernis. In the book she appears as she did when Antoine met her at her father's castle at Sillé-le-Philippe, a flirtatious, blue-eyed fifteen-year-old with a passion for romantic poetry.

The picture of Saint-Exupéry's fictional Geneviève also contains several references to his youngest and favourite sister Gabrielle, first as a child at Saint-Maurice and then as a mother. Gabrielle married Pierre de Giraud d'Agay, a friend since schooldays, in 1923. Her first child, Melchior, was born at Saint-Maurice. A year later he died at her new home at Agay on the shores of the Mediterranean near Saint-Raphael. A mother's anguish at the loss of her infant son is a central theme of *Southern Mail*. In a letter to Marie in 1924, Saint-Exupéry referred to the death of another relative's baby as a 'horrible thing'.

Although Geneviève is a composite character, the main inspiration for the adult heroine and the sentiments behind the book could easily be identified. *Southern Mail* was published in 1929 after Antoine emerged from a turbulent and unsatisfactory early manhood. The model for Jacques Bernis's disastrous fictional affair was his first fiancée, Louise de Vilmorin, poet and novelist.

The elegant and beautiful Louise bewitched Antoine when he was twenty-two and she was twenty, causing him years of heartbreak. The novel was part of the therapy. As a literary exercise it was an unevenly balanced mixture of emotion and ill-fated adventure, but was the only occasion on which Saint-Exupéry explored his sentimental life in a published novel.

He may have regretted being so open, as his friends could easily unravel the barely disguised plot which makes Bernis a hero in the air and romantically flat-footed on the ground. The appreciation Saint-Exupéry got from Louise de Vilmorin also fell short of what he must have hoped. She was one of several women in his life to set a disconcertingly low material value on his passion. She sold Antoine's sapphire engagement-ring, a family heirloom, to pay a lover's debts and made light of the affair in an article she wrote for a woman's magazine, *Marie-Claire*, more than thirty years later.

Louise also sold his most important gift, the original manuscript of *Southern Mail*, published six years after their engagement ended; an oddly offhand action considering that writing novels and poetry was her own life-long vocation.

Saint-Exupéry learnt little from his self-analysis. What divided Bernis and Geneviève, just as it divided Antoine and Louise, was a contrast in life-styles. Bernis was a man who should never have married anyone except a totally submissive woman. He needed excitement and Geneviève needed security. Bernis flew to the emptiness of the desert and she yearned for the distractions of a worldly social life.

Stung by his reflections on such a hopeless match, Saint-Exupéry ought to have chosen a companion who was ready to tolerate his self-centred ambitions and put up with his long absences. Yet much of Louise's vivaciously independent and capricious character was later evident in Antoine's South American wife Consuelo. Louise de Vilmorin was creative, funny, flighty but selfish; attracting an endless number of admirers by her spontaneous and playful personality. Some of those descriptions could be applied to Consuelo, who also had a strong artistic temperament and was as eccentric as Saint-Exupéry himself.

Louise and Consuelo were the only important feminine exceptions in the otherwise virile literary world created by Saint-Exupéry,
underlining their place as the two great loves of his life. The grown-
up Geneviève/Louise was the heroine of his first work while Consuelo would become the rose in *The Little Prince*, the last book published before his death.

As well as her much-publicized relationship with André Malraux
towards the end of her life, Louise de Vilmorin had suitors ranging
from the Aly Khan to Jean Cocteau, and she married and divorced
twice. From the description given by her sister-in-law Andrée de
Vilmorin, Antoine was just a disposable marriage prospect among
many.

'He was truly in love with her but she was a great flirt and got
engaged on and off all the time,' she said. 'Louise only liked him a
lot, that's all. A fiancé lasted a week or two and then there was
another one. As a woman, she was both the best and worst, black
and white. She was also generous and amusing and, above all, she
made people laugh.'

The first casual meetings with Louise dated back to the days at
Bossuet just after the Great War. Louise was distantly related to
Antoine and was part of the aristocratic social circle that surrounded
him during his years in Paris. One of her brothers boarded at Bossuet
but the credit for a formal introduction was given to another of
Louise de Vilmorin's admirers, Honoré d'Estienne d'Orves.

Her environment was enough in itself to lure Saint-Exupéry away
from artificial poverty during his student days. Louise's family had
two homes, a castle in the Paris suburb of Verrières-le-Buisson and
a mansion in the rue de la Chaise in Paris. With her four brothers
and sister, Louise took full advantage of the prestige of belonging to
a family which claimed an ancestry going back to Joan of Arc and a
fortune founded on a highly successful botanical industry which
supported one of the richest families in the capital.

The castle and mansion became unofficial matchmaking bureaux
for the rich and the titled, especially as Louise's widowed mother
was herself the centre of a court of suitors. Adored and spoilt by her
brothers, Louise was the attraction for a stream of potential husbands, fascinated by her intelligence and brilliant conversation. Many
of them fell under her spell while talking for hours by her sick-bed

where she was confined for three years. Her imagination and general culture developed freely during the long illness which left her with a damaged hip and what was often described as an enticing limp.

Apart from his *'beau nom'*, Saint-Exupéry had little to offer the Vilmorins. His material prospects were pathetic. The small legacy from grandfather Fernand was quickly spent and shrewd heads in Louise's household saw him as a fortune-hunter. His careless attitude to money was especially worrying as Louise was a spendthrift who used any spare cash for expensive clothes and presents for her brothers and suitors.

A common interest in literature was the strongest intellectual attraction, although André Malraux was given the credit for persuading Louise that her work was worth publishing. And there was a musical side that went unmentioned in *Southern Mail*. Even if Antoine and Louise were frowned on as a couple, they were often called upon to sing classical soprano-baritone duets, a custom they renewed when the worst of Antoine's heart-break had healed.

As the years passed, they formed differing perceptions of their courtship. Saint-Exupéry's fictional reminiscences in *Southern Mail* made the affair seem grim and hopeless, ending with a plane crash in the desert. All the gaiety of Louise's character disappeared in Saint-Exupéry's story, based on Geneviève's reluctance to quit her pampered background. Only the basic emotional force remained intact. Bernis, like Saint-Exupéry, falls head over heels in love with a woman who is playing a different game altogether. Antoine reworked the final days of the relationship into a gloomy car excursion in pouring rain when Bernis tried to help his sick lover face a hostile world where hotels close their doors to late-night travellers.

Allegory, self-analysis, fiction and fact all merge in the end. The conclusion to the affair is the same in real life as in the novel: Geneviève/Louise is too attached to her gilded cage to take flight with an adventurer and she ditches him.

In contrast to Antoine's fatalism, Louise de Vilmorin's magazine version made their affair sound frivolous and silly. She described her friendship with Antoine as 'a joke engagement' and, if her article in *Marie-Claire* can be trusted, the high point was a chaperoned August holiday in the Swiss Jura Mountains. Antoine, who had completed his national service at Le Bourget two months before, was forced to sell his camera to pay the fare. They took walks and picked flowers for the feast of Saint-Louis. In a small railway station they kissed as if they were parting lovers 'even though we were cheating'.

The article gave a glimpse into Antoine's preoccupation with approaching baldness although he was only just twenty-three. Louise said they both worried about his hair and made an unplanned detour to Geneva in search of a patent hair-lotion.

Two months later, she slipped off to Biarritz without a word and would not even answer his desperate letters.

BETWEEN leaving Antoine in the lurch in autumn 1923 and writing her article in October 1955, Louise de Vilmorin squeezed in a tumultuous married life with different husbands in Las Vegas and Budapest, but she did not forget to mention one of the fundamental reasons why Antoine was unsuitable as a husband. In Switzerland, her ardent suitor could not stop talking about flying and of the 'terrifying and sublime moments between heaven and earth'. All she wanted to talk about were home comforts, sitting on a new sofa by a winter fire.

Saint-Exupéry's morbid delight in describing hair-raising adventures was a warning that he might not be serious in bowing to a Vilmorin demand which would have removed the last obstacle to marrying Louise. After he recovered from the Le Bourget plane crash of January 1923, he was told that he had to choose between a flying career and his fiancée. At the time, he was tempted to sign on as a professional officer. Instead he chose to ground himself but soon lost Louise as well as his planes when adventure and freedom were replaced by the confinement and boredom of a tile-manufacturer's office in central Paris.

Before leaving the air force, the one advantage Saint-Exupéry had over his stereotyped noble rivals was his reckless glamour, which he traded in for stifling routine in the hope of saving his doomed engagement. Although Louise possibly loved the penniless, aristocratic daredevil more than she cared to admit, she found herself stuck with a poor office-worker and went in search of someone more suitable.

[77]

In a postscript to the engagement, six years later when he took the first draft of *Southern Mail* to Louise's house in Paris, Saint-Exupéry admitted he had given a poor impression of himself. Because she was out, he sent her a letter the same evening regretting that she had seen him as 'a weak child' during their engagement. He wrote of his despair at projecting a false image of himself as a shy and melancholic person, but even in this message he still seemed intimidated by Louise's self-assurance. Referring to *Southern Mail*, he added almost apologetically: 'I wanted to write it a bit for you and wanted to talk about it, and perhaps dedicate it to you if you can see some way of doing it.'

His love for her seemed undiminished. 'As for me, you can ask for anything, as you know. No matter the sacrifice and no matter when. I don't ask you to think of this as a great gift because you will never really need me, but it could mean a little less loneliness in moments of solitude. And I will always forgive you everything even if you hurt me sometimes.' Later, he told her: 'I was a child. You were a woman.'

The Silver Ship

THE months between autumn 1923, when Louise ran away, and November 1926 when Saint-Exupéry began a full-time civilian pilot's job, were not as pointless as they first seemed. During this apparently aimless period as an office-clerk and then as a travelling salesman he served his apprenticeship as a writer. The utter boredom of humdrum work and the struggle to live in some sort of style on a workman's wage were compensated by the opportunity and the motivation to discuss literature with his friends and put his thoughts down on paper.

Since ending his national service, Saint-Exupéry had often made references to a novel he was working on. By the time the outline for what was later to become *Southern Mail* appeared as a short story in April 1926, he had come to the conclusion that he detested writers who strove for abstract effect. It was only worth putting pen to paper if there was 'something to say', he wrote to a friend. Romantic poetry was abandoned and vacuous student theories on style were replaced by a desire to observe and interpret real life.

His main outlet was a flow of letters to his mother and sisters, many of them written on scraps of paper, including a tailor's bill. The content and style were extraordinary and nearly all were covered with drawings, some of which previewed illustrations in *The Little Prince*, while others were caricatures of people he had met.

Saint-Exupéry adopts a special tone and even different hand-writing for each letter, evoking the characters of the recipients. His elder sister Marie-Madeleine is addressed with a special tenderness, while Simone is treated more like a *copine* or chum. Most of the correspondence reads like a continuing conversation from their child-hood at Saint-Maurice.

He also deluged friends outside the family with details of his boring office life which he treated with hilarity. His two most appreci-ative correspondents were Charles Sallès and Renée de Saussine, the sister of a youth he had met at Bossuet. Sallès was sent the most daunting descriptions of life in the Boiron tile-factory headquarters in the rue du Faubourg-Saint-Honoré near the place de la Concorde. Despite the pleasant setting, Saint-Exupéry wrote as if he were trap-ped in a cage where he literally counted off the minutes until allowed to escape.

'The clock's second-hand is my only joy,' he wrote. 'Yawning, what a wonderful consolation.' The letter was so long that he obvi-ously had nothing to do, although he should have been estimating the profit margins on new tile production. The lunch-time break was greeted with a 'hurrah!' and then followed by the sentence: 'It's horrible – it's five past two and I'm back in my office.'

Routine did nothing to dampen his determination to become an author. Saint-Exupéry wrote to Sallès in July 1924 saying that he noted passages for his proposed novel on bits of paper and then wondered how to assemble what amounted to a jigsaw puzzle. Sallès was warned that he would not escape '*la corvée du roman*', novel duty, when he visited Paris. In other words, he would be obliged to listen to what had been written, a task which Saint-Exupéry imposed incessantly on friends throughout his life, just as he had made his brothers and sisters listen to stories and poems at Saint-Maurice at all hours of the day or night.

Renée de Saussine, whom he called his literary manager, also fulfilled his need for instant appreciation. In a long, platonic friendship, Antoine sent her many letters from foreign countries as a follow-up to literary discussions at her parents' home in Paris or in cafés on the Left Bank. She remembered his most familiar habit when carried away by a literary argument: holding an unlit cigarette while he burnt match after match and piled them up in an ashtray.

The need to write letters to sympathetic friends, usually cajoling them into a meeting, became even more urgent when he left his clerk's job to become a travelling salesman for a lorry-manufacturer, Saurer. The best part of this work, which he pursued for about two years, was a two-month apprenticeship in the Saurer factory in Suresnes in the Paris suburbs. Even though he was a heavy sleeper, Saint-Exupéry used to get up at 6 a.m. for the joy of working with engines.

Later, driving a sporty Zédal Sigma company car as Saurer's rural salesman, he was able to get away from the dreary bed-sitting-room at the Hôtel Titania at 70*bis* boulevard d'Ornano in the 18th *arrondissement*, where he boarded for two years. He often referred to his small room's depressing atmosphere, but his sales area provided only limited consolation. He had to drive hundreds of miles to cover three under-inhabited rural *départements*, the Allier, the Cher and the Creuse, where the monotonous life of small market towns both amused and repulsed him. Evenings spent in run-down hotels left him plenty of time to write to Renée de Saussine, sharpening his powers of observation and developing a writing style that became more and more sparse.

He summed up his existence in two sentences: 'My life is made up of bends I take as fast as possible and of hotels that look the same. I feel low.'

Whenever he could, Antoine abandoned the country to return to Paris and plunge into a contrasting social life. Some of the time was spent with Yvonne de Lestrange, his mother's cousin, whose apartment on the quai Malaquais was a meeting-place for Paris's cultural élite. An immensely rich woman, whose marriage to the

Duc de Trévise was later annulled, she was a liberated hostess of exceptional intelligence and wide interests. She acted like an elder sister towards Antoine, putting up with his eccentric behaviour which included falling asleep in the bath and flooding much of the flat.

Life at the quai Malaquais, next to the Institut de France, was impressively aristocratic with liveried servants and an endless stream of influential visitors to regular formal dinners. Saint-Exupéry was there so often that his unofficial headquarters in Paris became the Café Jarras just below.

He was deprived of Yvonne de Lestrange's guidance for much of 1925 because she left for the French Congo on a scientific mission for the Institut Pasteur to test a vaccine on a jungle tribe. On the first part of the trip she was accompanied by André Gide and Marc Allégret, a young film-maker.

At dinner-parties at the quai Malaquais, Yvonne de Lestrange made much of Antoine's determination to be a writer and spoke of his first short story, 'L'Évasion de Jacques Bernis' – Jacques Bernis's Escape – to several writers. In the tight literary world around the Left Bank, the news was carried to Jean Prévost, the twenty-three-year-old editor of a new literary review called Le Navire d'argent, the silver ship.

A powerfully built young man who broke Ernest Hemingway's thumb in a boxing match, Prévost had already had stories published by the Nouvelle Revue Française, whose most distinguished sponsors were André Gide and Gaston Gallimard, both regular visitors to the Lestrange apartment. Because of his seniority in the literary world, and despite being two years younger, Prévost was always treated like an elder brother by Saint-Exupéry.

Prévost introduced Antoine into the unique climate of the rue de l'Odéon with its two internationally known bookshops run by an American woman and a Frenchwoman. On one side was Sylvia Beach's Shakespeare and Company, with visitors such as Scott Fitzgerald, Ernest Hemingway and James Joyce. On the other side was La Maison des Amis du Livre run by Adrienne Monnier whose friends included Gide, André Breton, Guillaume Apollinaire, Louis Aragon and Paul Valéry.

In 1926, Adrienne Monnier was a solid forty-three-year-old spinster whose passion for literature was as strong as it had been when her father, a postman, gave her all his savings to found the bookshop in 1915. Over the years, it became a meeting-place for the Gallimard stable of writers and, in 1925, she decided to put all her meagre profits into the monthly *Navire d'argent*. Despite an astonishing gallery of contributors, the silver ship was doomed from the start and sank within a year, forcing Adrienne Monnier to sell all her stock to pay the debts. In the meantime, the magazine had introduced Hemingway to the French public (Gallimard immediately gave him a contract) and encouraged a number of young writers including, in Adrienne Monnier's words, 'our most glorious beginner, Antoine de Saint-Exupéry'.

'Jacques Bernis's Escape' was published in an abridged version as '*L'Aviateur*', a title which removed some of the essential mood of the story. Bernis's escape has a double meaning: he breaks free from the constraints of a tiresome existence by reaching for a magic sky and then shakes off life's heavy bonds in a plane crash.

Even though the love element is absent, the story foreshadows *Southern Mail* in its fatalistic tone. Bernis's exhilarating sensation of flying above a French airfield becomes the inevitable overture to a violent death in a fable as old as Icarus. In an ironical twist, Jacques Bernis is resurrected in *Southern Mail* only to die in the desert while flying the mail to West Africa. The short story and book give the fictional hero a unique place in literature for being killed off twice in different places by his creator.

Bernis's melancholy and indifference to survival echoed Saint-Exupéry's actual feelings and experience. When he wrote the story in 1926, he was suffering from the contrast between his boring job as a salesman and the freedom of the skies. He still made occasional flights from Orly to fulfil his obligations as an air force reserve officer, but each outing felt like a reproach for his failure to become a full-time pilot.

From his pedestal as a published author, Prévost introduced Saint-Exupéry to his magazine readers as an aviation and mechanical specialist whom he had met at a friend's home and whom 'I much admired for the strength and finesse with which he described his impressions'. Although Prévost said that Saint-Exupéry, 'whose gift of truth and directness is surprising for a beginner', was preparing other stories, nothing was heard of the novice author in the publishing world until 1929, when he returned from piloting in West Africa and emerged from years of personal trials like a man reborn.

Southern Mail

SAINT-EXUPÉRY'S months as a lorry salesman made him feel so low that he wrote to his sister Marie-Madeleine complaining of his 'terribly lonely life, always on the highway . . . Nothing happens in my life. I get up, I drive my car, I have lunch, I have dinner. I don't think about anything. It's sad.'

In all probability, Marie de Saint-Exupéry intervened personally to save him from this frustrating existence by asking Abbé Maurice Sudour to help her son start a professional flying career. The priest, who had kept in touch with many former pupils after being appointed head of Bossuet school, was a close friend of Beppo de Massimi, general manager of the Latécoère airline company. Massimi had served as an Italian volunteer officer in the French air force and later sent his son to Bossuet. At Maurice Sudour's request, the airline official interviewed Saint-Exupéry in his office on the Champs-Élysées in Paris on 12 October 1926, first offering him an administrative job and then giving in to his plea: 'Monsieur, I want to fly . . . only fly.'

During the Great War Massimi had served as an observer with Didier Daurat, who in 1919, at the age of twenty-eight, joined the newly formed Latécoère airline company, later known as Aéropostale. In his position as operations manager of the African route flying mail out of Toulouse, Daurat chose his own pilots and Massimi telephoned to ask him to give Saint-Exupéry a trial.

That telephone call led to five joyful years in Saint-Exupéry's life, the longest period of self-fulfilment and interior calm in an existence which was already half over. The mean and mundane preoccupations of a travelling salesman, melancholic Parisian, frustrated writer and

[83]

rejected suitor dissolved literally overnight. Saint-Exupéry entered the real world of aviation like a Knight Templar and emerged purified in thought and spirit.

The years of flying in Africa and South America were the most important in his development as a writer. Between 1926 and 1931 he gathered the material for most of his books. Long spells of solitude in the sky or in exotic climates opened up creative horizons. The trust placed in him restored his self-respect while camaraderie and self-sacrifice provided the fundamental tissue of his views on life.

Only two days after seeing Massimi, Saint-Exupéry walked across the bare and muddy airfield at Montaudran in Toulouse, headquarters of the Lignes Aériennes Latécoère, and made contact with the heart of pioneering aviation. From there he would draw the inspiration for portraits of courageous men and their exploits that have no equal in the literature of flying. Sometimes a few brief lines transformed a surname, like Bury or Lécrivain, into a figure worthy to sit at the Round Table. In *Night Flight*, which covered the Latin-American period, Didier Daurat's uncompromising leadership was sanctified under the character of Rivière and held out as an example to all men. Pilots like Henri Guillaumet, who might now be remembered only by students of aviation history, were raised to the status of moral leaders in the quest for courage and compassion.

From another viewpoint, Saint-Exupéry implicitly ignored those who did not conform to his ideals of self-sacrificing devotion or bravery. Among those forgotten men was Pierre-Georges Latécoère, an audacious businessman who formed an airline which became an integral part of French expansionist foreign policy between the wars. His ambitions resembled those of merchants and shipbuilders of the fifteenth and sixteenth centuries, but it was a comparison that left Saint-Exupéry indifferent. In *The Little Prince*, he did not hide his contempt for industrialists with no time to enjoy the money they make as they moved from enterprise to enterprise. The little prince's businessman was a composite image, but Pierre-Georges Latécoère would have been an acceptable model.

Born into a rich provincial family which had made much of its money from timber, Latécoère graduated from the Centrale, the civil engineering school. Photographs taken when Saint-Exupéry met him show a forbidding man with rimless spectacles and a neat moustache. He was remembered by his pilots as a cold, authoritarian employer, who had made a fortune out of supplying ammunition to the army during the Great War before turning to aeroplanes in 1917. What marked him out from many other industrialists enriched by battlefield carnage was his post-war vision. Within a year of the Armistice, he had turned his planes to peacetime use by inaugurating the first airmail service to North Africa. Letters which had previously taken a week to reach the Moroccan protectorate were now delivered regularly in a thirty-hour flight.

Latécoère's ambition was seen as a dangerous gamble by his competitors. Few planes in 1919 had a safe range above 500 kilometres or a top speed of much over 100 kilometres an hour. The pilot flew with his head in the open air, frequently looking below for landmarks or for emergency landing-fields. The Bréguet 14 biplanes which inaugurated the run in 1919 were built for a short life in war conditions. Mechanical weaknesses had to be compensated by the reckless dedication of pilots.

Most of the men who pioneered the mail service were Great War veterans undaunted by terrifying casualty figures. In all, more than 120 aircrew were killed opening up Latécoère's routes to North and West Africa and later to South America. This was a casualty rate that was unlikely to move the heart of a munitions manufacturer, but Latécoère also needed someone to inspire the hardened flyers and force them to stretch the limits of their primitive machines. The man he chose was Didier Daurat.

In *Night Flight* Daurat, portrayed as Rivière, is a born leader, a Nietzschean superman, capable of turning ordinary men into heroes by the force of his personality. For Saint-Exupéry, Daurat himself became a father-hero figure, an exemplary man who could do no wrong, even when he appeared unjust. Saint-Exupéry's perception of Daurat's principles and temperament is also at the centre of the personal philosophy expressed in *Wisdom of the Sands*, where the autocratic Berber chieftain rules by the strength of his character and accumulated wisdom.

Daurat was able to repay Saint-Exupéry's tribute in part in 1954 when he wrote a short book called *Saint-Exupéry, as I Knew Him*.

Daurat said that the author of *The Little Prince* understood that the value of life was 'everything that contributed to the glory and dignity of man; that is devotion and sacrifice, the giving of oneself'.

If Saint-Exupéry had lived to write Daurat's epitaph when his chief died in 1969 at the age of seventy-nine, the tribute would have been expressed in much the same words. Admiration and reverence were inevitable from a young man brought up on the heroism of the Great War. The stature of veterans had increased rather than diminished by 1926 and Daurat, a small neat man with a stern military bearing, had several claims to being among the bravest of the brave.

After graduating from the Paris horology and mechanical school he joined the army and was wounded at Verdun. When he recovered, he volunteered for the air force and teamed up with Beppo de Massimi. Daurat's most important exploit as a reconnaissance pilot was the discovery of the German long-range gun 'Big Bertha', whose shells had forced the evacuation of Saint-Exupéry's Lycée Saint-Louis to the Paris suburbs in 1918. On 1 September 1919 Daurat enhanced his wartime reputation by opening up the Toulouse-Rabat mail route for Latécoère. The pilots who followed him across the Pyrenees through the treacherous skies of Spain and North Africa reflected Daurat's devotion to an ideal of getting the mail through, no matter what the cost in human lives.

Saint-Exupéry's noble image of Daurat was not shared by all the pilots, some of whom felt that the portrait in *Night Flight* was lopsided and that the airline chief's faults had been overlooked. They were more aware of Daurat's coldness and lack of feeling which owed much to his experiences in the Great War where life had been so cheap. He transferred the theory of the expendability of man from the battleground to the delivery of mail.

Daurat's critics detected only resolute professionalism where Saint-Exupéry saw idealism. Rivière's inner motives and principles were the writer's own romanticized invention because no one came close to the austere and authoritarian operations manager who had built unbreachable barriers around himself. Not even his most senior pilots addressed him by his first name. Saint-Exupéry was no exception. In the dedication to *Night Flight*, he respectfully called him Monsieur Didier Daurat.

Saint-Exupéry's admiration for his new boss on his arrival at Toulouse was not immediately reciprocated. Recalling their first meeting, Daurat said that doubt over his new recruit's ability was considerable. Saint-Exupéry's log-book was thin, the main recommendation being 350 hours of training-flights in the air force. Nor was Daurat impressed by Saint-Exupéry's stiff attitude and his clumsy gestures, feeling that Antoine was afraid of not being up to the task after a life 'in which he had succeeded at nothing'.

Daurat was probably prejudiced by Massimi's unflattering assessment during the interview in Paris when the Italian remembered Saint-Exupéry as 'a big shy boy who appeared bothered by his height and the fact that he took up too much space in the armchair'.

Saint-Exupéry's own recollections of his arrival at Toulouse's Montaudran airfield in *Wind, Sand and Stars* have a trance-like quality and a trace of humility, as if he still could not believe his luck when he wrote about the event twelve years later. Well before his first take-off, he had moved out of the zone of ordinary mortal experience into the heady atmosphere of adventure. He mixed with men who had become national legends of courage and daring, flying fragile aircraft in which, in Saint-Exupéry's words, engines could fall from their mountings without warning.

No pilot at Montaudran could have been transported so suddenly from a humdrum job. Saint-Exupéry's memories of serving among this race of heroic craftsmen, his first task being to dismantle aeroplane engines, resurrected the legendary days of Ambérieu. The atmosphere at the Hôtel du Grand Balcon in Toulouse, where the airmen stayed, was similar to that of the Hôtel du Lion d'Or in Ambérieu in 1912. There was no common background among flyers; no noticeable rank and no social classes. They were joined together by a crusade: the mail had to get through. A postcard to a lover in Rabat was more important than either plane or pilot. The only reward worth having was the recognition of other flyers.

Saint-Exupéry's writing also exuded relief at just being himself and doing a useful job. There was no hint that recent months had brought their share of unhappiness with the death of his eldest sister Marie-Madeleine who had suffered much of her life from epilepsy. She was buried alongside her father and her brother François in the family vault.

In his letters from Toulouse, Saint-Exupéry made plans for his mother to join him for holidays, aware that she was now virtually alone. Gabrielle had married three years before and moved to Agay on the Mediterranean while Simone was preparing to leave for Indo-China as a librarian. His mother, though, was preoccupied with her own charitable work, assisting the resettlement of war-devastated villages in northern France. The fact that she did not rush to his side was part of a long-overdue process of storing away the sentimental props of childhood.

Over the coming years, there would be many brief reunions between the surviving children and their mother, but the conspiratorial spirit of Saint-Maurice-de-Rémens was disappearing. Soon after joining Latécoère, Saint-Exupéry wrote to Simone regretting that 'we are dispersed like the children of Babel' and wondering if he had ever lived the childhood memories his sister had evoked in a recent letter. 'People think I'm heartless because I say nothing but I could die from melancholy for the past in ruins, for all these pasts in ruins,' he added.

The mysteries of Saint-Maurice were to be replaced by clouds which resembled castles and dragons, and desert wastes which he coloured with dreams and fables. Nearly two decades passed before Saint-Exupéry's romantic childhood memories and his troubled adult life merged to produce the sad bewilderment of the little prince.

The Lamp of Confidence

Southern Mail, published in 1929, and the collection of essays *Wind, Sand and Stars*, released ten years later, contain descriptions of similar events which could have been written by different authors. The first book is marked by effort and self-consciousness, while the second flows with spontaneity and confidence.

Saint-Exupéry wrote far fewer works than many of his contemporaries, such as his rival pilot, Joseph Kessel, who published ten times more books and won the Académie française novel prize for *Les Rois aveugles* – The Sightless Kings – two years before *Southern*

Mail was released. Saint-Exupéry's output was restricted primarily by his search for perfection and a dogged pursuit of his own ideas of what constituted good writing, seeking encouragement rather than advice. His claim that he reworked manuscripts as many as thirty times before being satisfied was not far-fetched. He chipped away to the heart of his experiences and the literary result was evident.

Southern Mail is an average novel; *Wind, Sand and Stars* is a masterpiece. The first book is about 150 pages long in the original French, but its construction is uneven, with a clumsy imbalance between the flying scenes and the love-affair between Jacques Bernis and Geneviève. The essentially melodramatic situation is handled with much less assurance than the equally melodramatic plot in Kessel's *L'Équipage* – The Crew – which Saint-Exupéry read on its release in 1923.

Wind, Sand and Stars, which won the Académie française prize in 1939 and caused a sensation in the United States, is written with a deceptive simplicity which leaves the work suspended in a literary altitude of its own, somewhere between a compulsive travel book and a romantic reflection on the nobility of mankind. While *Southern Mail* falls into the general category of an autobiographical novel, *Wind, Sand and Stars* circles in a solitary and original orbit.

Like Saint-Exupéry's childhood memories, the events in *Wind, Sand and Stars* became fresher as the effect was distilled by nostalgia. The ten years between the two books was a period of intense personal trial, but this was brushed aside and only the brightest and most moving lessons appeared in their brilliant polish.

The outstanding example is in the opening pages of the book where he reworks a passage from *Southern Mail* regarding Henri Guillaumet. In the novel, Bernis is initiated into the perils of flying over Spain by the anonymous narrator, who reveals an intimate landscape, not of great cities, but of fields with real flowers and of Mediterranean beaches where a pilot in trouble has to avoid fishing-boats in the evening dusk.

In the later book, the same laconically recounted scene has evolved into a lyrical and gentle reminiscence of his brotherly relationship with Guillaumet and the few moments that changed Saint-Exupéry's perception of his first mail delivery to North Africa, 'transforming

Spain into a friend'. His admiration for Guillaumet illuminates the text. Guillaumet 'spreads confidence in the way a lamp gives out light'. Shoulder to shoulder 'with this veteran' Saint-Exupéry feels a sort of schoolboy peace as his mentor repeats his litany of the airmen's friends and foes: an orange grove, a flock of sheep and a hidden brook. The tense enumeration of dangers in the first book becomes more poetic and more personal, a pilot's-eye view that illustrates Saint-Exupéry's reflection that the plane has helped us discover 'the real face of the earth'.

The images in *Wind, Sand and Stars* make Guillaumet appear to be a much older man than Saint-Exupéry, a more humane version of Didier Daurat, possibly with an heroic Great War record. The impression might have remained if Guillaumet had not become one of the most daring and most photographed airmen of the inter-war years. By the time the book was published in 1939, he was a national hero and his young, innocent, round face had become familiar to millions of newspaper readers. Like Saint-Exupéry, who dedicated the book to his friend, Guillaumet had survived incredible dangers and incarnated the manly values and unflinching loyalty that Antoine had detected at their first meeting.

A pleasant-looking, good-humoured boy from a village called Bouy in the Champagne area where his father was a milkman, Guillaumet, who was actually two years younger than Saint-Exupéry, had been fascinated by planes since watching Henri Farman set off from an airfield near his home to fly to Reims in 1908. Eight years later, at the age of fourteen, he was taken for his first joy-ride in a military plane. He went to Roland Nungessor's flying-school at Orly in 1920 before joining the air force.

Life in a peacetime armed forces unit had lost its charm by 1925 and, with the help of another aviation hero, Jean Mermoz, whom he met during his military career, Guillaumet joined Latécoère after winning a 3000-kilometre air race. He already flew regularly on the Senegal run when Saint-Exupéry arrived at Toulouse, and those few months' experience had given him the veteran's gloss seen in the opening pages of *Wind, Sand and Stars*. Didier Daurat, who witnessed their first meeting, noted that it was the moment when 'a friendship of rare quality was born'.

Saint-Exupéry's esteem for Guillaumet as a man and a pilot during their years together in North Africa and South America inspires the finest pages of *Wind, Sand and Stars*. Nowhere is the author's generous recognition of the special stature of fellow human beings more patent. Guillaumet is not just a companion. He embodies all the human qualities that Saint-Exupéry aspires to and yet there is a faint feeling that this esteem is not fully returned by his surrogate younger brother.

Guillaumet has two assets that inevitably distance him from the self-questioning and often solitary Saint-Exupéry. He is totally self-confident and happily married. He has no intellectual pretensions, no time for self-analysis. He returns to his home among the vineyards and dairy farms of the Marne and feels content. Saint-Exupéry, conscious of his own shortcomings and struggling with an unsatisfactory marriage, goes back to Saint-Maurice and feels alienated.

Saint-Exupéry seemed always half a step behind Guillaumet, whose exploits and record attempts were more spectacular and more successful. And this reached a final cruel irony when Guillaumet was shot down in the Mediterranean four years before Saint-Exupéry's Lightning crashed in the same sea in 1944.

CHAPTER SIX

A Precise Idea of Nothingness

WIND, *Sand and Stars* is a confusing guide to Saint-Exupéry's flying career because it switches from France to North Africa to South America and back to North Africa without respect for chronology. Saint-Exupéry is more interested in sensations and moods than details of his planes or his journeys. A lack of facts intensifies the lyrical quality of his prose. Landings are described like the return from a purifying journey, invoking floods of revived hope in a colourful planet of flowers and smiling people. Airfields are seen as the centre of optimistic universes bounded by relief, friendship and the satisfaction of a job well done.

A few hours in the air intoxicated Saint-Exupéry and protected him from boredom on the ground. Montaudran gave him a sense of pride he had never felt before and it would have been churlish and disloyal to paint the scene in its true, slightly drab colours. Fortunately, Saint-Exupéry's love of letter-writing filled in much of the detail left out in the published work. Daurat and Massimi and several other Latécoère pioneers wrote memoirs that provided more accurate glimpses of a hard and wearing life with its share of tiresome problems.

Latécoère airport at Toulouse was far less romantic than Saint-Exupéry pictured. A cement apron was surrounded by concrete hangars and a nondescript collection of buildings. The base was not much better equipped than during the wartime years when Latécoère built railway carriages on the site. Aircrew were driven from their rooms at the Hôtel du Grand Balcon in an old Ford bus which picked up the duty flyers at 4 a.m. Following Daurat's inflexible rules, neither weather, nor human weakness nor mechanical failure was an obstacle to mail deliveries on the journey of nearly 5000 kilometres from the southern French city to the colonial West African port of Dakar in Senegal.

Saint-Exupéry compared the atmosphere created by Daurat at Montaudran to 'a sort of war', an image evoked in *Wind, Sand and Stars* in the passage where Antoine is driven to the dispersal point in the old bus and hears of the death of Émile Lécrivain, one of the company's bravest airmen. The sacrifice of lives was officially justified by the need to open up air links to expand France's African empire. Latécoère's first influential ally was Marshal Louis Lyautey, who 'pacified' the Moroccan protectorate before and after the First World War and understood the significance of rapid communications with the new African colonies.

In the race to conquer more territory in the West African desert, France was in direct competition with Spain. The Foreign Legion and other regular troops were involved in an endless combat with desert tribes or renegade bands refusing to accept French domination. Similar battles were going on in North Africa where Louis de Bonnevie, Antoine's school-friend from Fribourg, had been sent as a regular artillery officer. His death from typhus in Morocco in 1927 was another tragic event which Saint-Exupéry did not mention in his public writing.

Only good luck had saved Saint-Exupéry from death long before his friend Bonnevie. His first flight to Africa was a routine trip as a passenger in an open cockpit filled with mail-bags, but on his inaugural run as a professional flyer he was a victim of treacherous weather. Deliveries to Casablanca were made in two relays. The first pilot made landings in Barcelona and Alicante before being replaced by a colleague who, again in two hops, reached Morocco. Saint-Exupéry's outward flight to Alicante went without a hitch but on the way back he flew into the confusion of an early dusk and ground mist near Carcassonne. He was forced to crash-land in a field and had to wait throughout the night until a car came to rescue him.

Sometimes he had to fly all four hops to Casablanca. On one journey he thought his controls had snapped when the plane plunged towards the ground after encountering an air-pocket. On another occasion, he walked away from a wrecked plane in Rabat and then had to travel the 2000 kilometres to Toulouse through a nine-hour storm which bounced him about like a tennis-ball. Following that episode, he wrote to a friend, Lucie-Marie Decour, saying he could not believe that a plane could take so much punishment. After braving more bad weather, Saint-Exupéry flew into Alicante to be told that a passenger on an earlier flight had been flung to his death after his seat-harness snapped.

If Saint-Exupéry made little reference to these hair-raising trips in his published works, there were two reasons. One was modesty. His adventures rated little against the exploits of fellow Latécoère pilots like Jean Mermoz, the most famous of all French prewar flyers, who was killed three years before *Wind, Sand and Stars* was published. The other reason was that risk alone lacked the spiritually elevating element of other memories which he later revived and transformed.

Central to these recollections was his period in 1928 as airfield manager of the Latécoère base at Cape Juby, now known as Tarfaya, a West African Atlantic stopover on the route to Dakar. This desolate desert retreat on the shores of the ocean left profound traces in *Wind, Sand and Stars*, *The Little Prince* and *Wisdom of the Sands*. Solitude, cut by brief bursts of companionship, touched Saint-Exupéry like an act of grace. Years later, his sense of loss at abandoning this patch of the Sahara inspired him to fill the vacuum with simplistic idealism. In the claustrophobic and amoral atmosphere of a demanding social life in Paris, where he lived for most of the thirties, nostalgia for the purity of Cape Juby made him believe that European civilization had lost its way and had to be rebuilt from scratch.

He was fully aware that time totally transformed his perception of this wasteland paradise. A frank admission that a monotonous existence could gradually change into the sublime with the passing of the years was made in an undated letter he wrote to Charles Sallès, recounting a long and boring flight over the deserts of southern Morocco. Saint-Exupéry described the experience as giving a 'precise idea of nothingness', but he also wrote: 'I have gone through days of sinister gloom in a rotten hut and yet all I can remember now is a life full of poetry.'

An even more specific description of the 'sinister gloom' was contained in a letter to Simone de Saint-Exupéry in which he depicted the desert tribes as 'thieves, liars, bandits; treacherous and cruel'. Although he had arrived in Cape Juby full of humanitarian illusions, he had begun to judge the Moors in harsher terms.

'They kill a man as if he were a chicken, but lay their lice carefully on the ground', he recalled in 1928. And yet he wrote ten years later in *Wind, Sand and Stars* that he had succumbed to the desert as soon as he saw it, and been struck by the nobility of man playing out a secret drama in the seemingly empty Sahara.

CAPE Juby was neither a noble idea nor a noble setting. Geographically it was part of the Spanish possession of Rio de Oro, south of Morocco, which Spain abandoned in 1975. The enclave was annexed forcibly by Morocco in the wake of the Spanish pull-out, but the same nomadic tribes who disputed Spanish and French colonial domination in the thirties claimed the territory for the Polisario Front. In 1928, when Saint-Exupéry was sent to run the landing-strip after more than a year's flying to North and West Africa, Spain was suspicious of French motives. Centuries of rivalry between Paris and Madrid had created difficulties in establishing Latécoère's precarious rights to fly over Spain where sympathies were pro-German.

The Spanish had been defeated in the Rif area of northern Morocco in 1924 when 20,000 Spanish troops died in a battle with rebels led by Abd el-Krim. The French seized on the defeat to establish their hold on the territory, sending Marshal Philippe Pétain to Morocco in 1926 with an expeditionary force of more than 100,000 men to destroy the Moroccan rebel army.

The nomadic tribes in the southern Sahara, usually known as Moors, also resisted French attempts to dominate all of West Africa, fighting a colourful guerrilla war with the French Foreign Legion and specialist camel corps. The struggle had reached its peak when Saint-Exupéry was sent to Cape Juby. Planes on the mail-delivery run were regularly shot at like wild birds as they flew over Arab encampments along the Atlantic coastline.

In the enclave of Rio de Oro, small Spanish garrisons occupied isolated posts where the soldiers depended on food supplies and water delivered by a twice-monthly schooner service from the Canary Islands, another Spanish possession. The Spanish forces avoided clashes with the desert tribes by making temporary pacts or by providing a refuge for raiding-parties escaping from French reprisals. Behind this attitude was a web of European imperialistic intrigue in which the desolate territory of Rio de Oro was no more than a pawn, but without permission to fly over this vast uninhabited stretch of desert, Latécoère's ambition of opening up a South Atlantic mail route from Dakar to South America would have foundered.

While a diplomatic battle raged over rights to overfly Spanish territory, Daurat decided to send Saint-Exupéry to Cape Juby in the hope of establishing better relations with the local Spanish governor. 'Saint-Exupéry was a natural ambassador, capable of soothing other people's touchiness,' Daurat said.

Antoine could not speak Spanish but his aristocratic background was considered an advantage in dealing with Spain, which was under a military dictatorship led by a marquis, Miguel Primo de Rivera. The transfer to this desert outpost, where he had previously landed during mail runs the year before, was not a very tempting prospect. It meant exchanging the excitement and camaraderie of the postal flights for a stationary base. As a compensation, the station chief could act on his own initiative. Because one of his principle roles was to rescue pilots brought down in the desert, Saint-Exupéry was given the chance to show qualities of leadership for the first time in his life.

Whatever the consolations, he must have felt a sense of apprehension when his plane circled Cape Juby. He knew that months of loneliness lay ahead, broken only by radio contact with Aéropostale landing-fields in Morocco and Mauritania. The settlement centred around a run-down, high-walled white fortress backing on to the Atlantic only a few yards away. In front there was only flat desolation, except for a group of outbuildings, surrounded by barbed wire, which served as an air terminal. From the ground, the scene was even more inhospitable. The fort was next to a penal colony. The Spanish Foreign Legion garrison, commanded by a colonel, had little to do except wait for an unlikely attack by an invisible Arab enemy whose spies lived in tents under the mud-stained fort walls.

As Saint-Exupéry discovered, the only indication of the passing of time was the regular quarter-hour calls of sentries as they paced the walls looking for a foe who never came.

Joseph Kessel visited Cape Juby and wrote that the soldiers were hardly distinguishable from the dangerous prisoners they were guarding. They went weeks without washing and their uniforms were in rags. The isolation oppressed the officers as much as the private soldiers. Kessel spent an hour in the fort's mess where the only sound was the roll of dice. In his mind, Cape Juby housed an assembly of ghosts.

Not even the years of living in cheap lodgings and poor hotels had prepared Saint-Exupéry for the restricted accommodation provided for Latécoère's representative. The suspicious Spanish did not want the new airfield manager or his three mechanics in the fort, and they had to live in a hut against the northern wall and facing the sea. At night they were a target for nomadic marauders and thieves, with only a primitive security system for protection. A wire leading to a propeller-operated generator was attached to the door-handle, giving an electric shock to unwelcome visitors.

In the long silence of the evening, disturbed only by the waves breaking on the shore and distant shouts from the sentries, Saint-Exupéry wrote and rewrote *Southern Mail* by the light of a paraffin lamp, perfected his skill at card-tricks and drew up long reports to Latécoère, some of which filtered back to the colonial planners at the French Foreign Ministry. He had to await the arrival of mail-planes which landed twice a week, coming from north and south, while trying to remain on good terms with the Spanish governor and the local tribes. Although he later wrote about exciting rescues of downed pilots, sometimes under fire, his impressions written during the first months were acutely depressing. In a letter to his mother in 1928, he described the setting as 'more and more absurd'. His corner of the desert, he said, was inhabited by 200 Spanish soldiers who had clung on to the fort for thirty years and whose only callers were the filthiest of Moors.

'These corridors of the Sahara, decorated by a few extras, bore me like a dirty suburb,' he wrote, denigrating a forbidding scene which would one day be glorified in *Wind, Sand and Stars*.

[97]

Le Grand Marabout Blanc

DIDIER Daurat wrote about his 'magnificent ambassador' at Cape Juby in such resounding terms that Saint-Exupéry was credited with 'enlightening the confines of the desert with the shining prestige of France and spreading the nobility of sentiments and the generous vitality of our country'. Eulogies like these earned Saint-Exupéry a Légion d'honneur for his work in the Sahara where the local nomads called him *'le grand marabout blanc'*, the great white prophet.

Daurat also touched on a less dignified image, remembering that Saint-Exupéry usually dressed shabbily in an old pair of pyjamas while his 'embassy' was furnished with a few wooden boxes and a makeshift table set on oil-drums. The eccentric side of Saint-Exupéry's character was rarely revealed in his own writings but perhaps the best contemporary portrait was recorded by one of his mechanics, Jean-René Lefebvre, who later became principal inspector for Air France, the state network which developed from Aéropostale.

'No one could believe that Daurat would appoint such a disorganized person to run the base at Cape Juby,' he said. 'Going into his office terrified me. Everything was mixed up – official documents, working notes, personal letters and drawings. How could he know what he was doing in such a mess?'

Even though Saint-Exupéry used to chat for hours with his mechanics while they worked, Lefebvre admitted that he felt more at ease with other pilots like Guillaumet. 'Saint-Ex wasn't a snob,' he said, 'but there was something of the *grand seigneur* in him.

'What really charmed me was his odd, dreamy side, but from a mechanic's point of view he made mistakes and he liked his little fantasies which could be quite dangerous. I was a rather scared witness of this characteristic on numerous flights.'

Saint-Exupéry's unnerving nonchalance was apparent on a trip to Villa Cisneros in the south of the Spanish enclave when he went to deliver the garrison's mail with Lefebvre as passenger. On the onward flight the plane had trouble taking off and, in the mechanic's words, began coughing, shaking and spewing out steam as it circled over the Rio de Oro bay.

'The engine was overheating and Saint-Ex went down to sea-level,' Lefebvre said. 'I began peeling off my socks and shoes, ready to jump in and swim for it. Saint-Ex simply started doodling cartoons which he handed back to me with a big grin.'

The cartoon figures were swimming in high seas, or were stranded like Robinson Crusoe or held as prisoners in the desert. Saint-Exupéry ignored the warnings from his engine and flew the 400 kilometres to Port-Étienne in French territory where he wrote in his log-book: 'Good motor. Nothing to report.'

At dinner, when Lefebvre expressed astonishment at such a dismissive note, Saint-Exupéry retorted that the engine had got them to their destination, hadn't it? He knew very well that Lefebvre would carry out the repairs because the mechanic was returning to Villa Cisneros in the same plane.

On another mission when an engine started missing a beat, Saint-Exupéry reassured the mechanic that piloting a plane was not like driving a car. 'You don't have to watch where you're going,' he added. 'A plane is built to fly straight ahead without anyone worrying about it.'

At the time, planes did not have automatic pilots. Like other airmen, Saint-Exupéry fixed the joystick in place with a big strip of rubber. It was on those long monotonous flights, when the controls could be forgotten, that he allowed his imagination to wander off into creative fields. He was not only taken up by writing and philosophy. During the thirties he patented fourteen inventions for the air-craft industry, including navigation and landing aids.

Lefebvre was frank about his reluctance to fly with Saint-Exupéry because of Antoine's reputation for absent-mindedness. Another unfavourable impression was given by Paul Nubalde, a mechanic at Villa Cisneros in 1928, who later became head mechanic for Air France. Nubalde's assessment of Saint-Exupéry's ability was listened to because he was Didier Daurat's godson. Many years after travelling as a passenger with Antoine in the desert, Nubalde said he preferred flying with what he called 'the real pilots'.

'He was not a great flyer,' he said. 'He was always thinking of something else and didn't always look at what he was doing.'

Over the years there were many strange incidents which could be attributed to human error, but judging whether Saint-Exupéry was a less-than-average flyer would be an impossible task. His record would have to be compared with that of other aviators of his generation, and account taken of the number of hours flown and the types and reliability of planes. Even this would be meaningless in desert conditions where Aéropostale's Bréguets had trouble at least once on every six trips.

Sand caused havoc in the engines as well as making life at Cape Juby a misery. The sea wind never dropped, building up huge dunes along the walls of the fort every night. Saint-Exupéry's habit of wearing pyjamas was less strange than it seemed. Most of the Spanish garrison also wore them because sand made their uniforms uncomfortable, but the most disagreeable problem was the amount of grit which got into the food.

While Joseph Kessel remembered the cheerless atmosphere of Cape Juby and Saint-Exupéry wrote dismal letters home, a more amusing picture of the Latécoère desert base was recorded by Henri Delaunay, a pioneer airmail pilot, who later flew with RAF Bomber Command during the war. Delaunay wrote a book called *Araignée du Soir* – Evening Spider – which included a remarkable passage in which three of the most famous aviators of the pre-war years, Guillaumet, Mermoz and Saint-Exupéry, spent the day together at Cape Juby.

'Our little hut echoed with laughter,' Delaunay wrote, remembering a juvenile atmosphere of practical jokes, disorder, warmth and comradeship. The most bizarre element was the hut's small menagerie of repulsive-sounding pets. A hyena had to be kept tied up outside because it smelled too much, but the constricted space of what served as the crew's mess was partly taken up by a half-mad monkey called Kiki, which ate razor-blades, a greedy and noisy mongrel bitch called Mirra and a fat cat named Paf who fought with the monkey.

Delaunay recorded one of the rare distractions in Saint-Exupéry's austere existence when four planes, two from the north and two from the south, touched down for refuelling and servicing. Aircrew were given a meal in a primitive kitchen where food had to be heated with a blowlamp. While lunch was prepared by two Arab servants,

Guillaumet and Saint-Exupéry played idiotic word-games and Mermoz concentrated on a crossword, tilting his chair on to its back legs.

'We had fun like kids,' Delaunay added, relating how they tied a string to Mermoz's chair and attached it to the sleeping dog knowing that it would leap up when its dinner was served.

Hidalgo de Cisneros, future commander-in-chief of the Spanish Republican air force, described Saint-Exupéry's role as an entertainer at Cape Juby in an interview in *Icare,* the French airline pilots' magazine. De Cisneros was attached to the Cape Juby garrison as a young airman and felt that Antoine's good humour and easygoing character lessened Spanish hostility towards the French aircrews.

He was a regular visitor to the fort and used to amuse the bored Spanish soldiers with card-tricks and hypnosis, a technique he had learned from a fellow conscript at Strasbourg seven years earlier. The most memorable night was when the whole garrison took part in an improvised banquet in honour of Saint-Exupéry to make amends for a near tragedy. To reduce the number of guards needed on the airfield, de Cisneros had imported an enormous watchdog from Spain. Soon afterwards, the Spaniard heard calls for help and found Saint-Exupéry on the ground being furiously mauled.

'The hound had bitten his shoulder and was ready to tear him apart,' de Cisneros said. 'I tried to pull him away but the brute would not let go. There was an iron bar on the ground and I used it to knock the beast half unconscious.' Saint-Exupéry needed a week of treatment before the garrison could apologize with the surprise dinner.

The dog's attack was one of the rare occasions when Antoine's gift of taming animals let him down. His fascination for pets dated back to his days at Saint-Maurice when he used to take a tortoise for walks on a leash. In Cape Juby his contacts with wildlife were one of the inspirations for *The Little Prince* fifteen years later.

'My role here is to tame,' he wrote to his mother from the air base about a pet chameleon who resembled a diplodocus and whom he watched for hours. He also kept desert gazelles which ate from his hand, but the most lasting experience was an encounter with a desert fox, an animal smaller than a cat. He wrote about the experience in a letter to his sister Gabrielle and included a sketch of the fox with its 'huge ears'. He became very fond of the little creature, spending hours befriending it. The fox was 'particularly wild and roared like a lion', he wrote. In *The Little Prince*, the desert fox with its long sharp ears reappears in a passage where Saint-Exupéry talks of the mutual love created between two beings each searching to be 'tamed' by the other.

'If you tame me, we will only need each other,' the fox tells the little prince. 'You will be the only one in the world for me. I will be the only one in the world for you.' During the aftermath of Saint-Exupéry's crash in the Libyan desert in 1935, which provided the longest reminiscence in *Wind, Sand and Stars*, a desert fox, or fennec, gave him the will to survive when he was faced by slow death from thirst.

Le Commandant Des Oiseaux

SAINT-EXUPÉRY spent much of his spare time at Cape Juby reading technical and philosophical books brought by his colleagues whom he used to entertain with lectures on everything from geometry to metaphysics. If they were bored, he produced card-tricks which he had perfected to professional level while trying to maintain his sense of humour in an atmosphere of carefree banter of which he was often the target. Henri Delaunay wrote that Saint-Exupéry had such a self-deprecating sense of fun that the mechanics were often in fits of laughter when he deliberately made a fool of himself. Other eye-witnesses contradicted this account, saying that Antoine was often quick to take offence when he was ribbed although he was just as fast to forget a grudge.

Saint-Exupéry was not only a diplomat, an air-base manager and camp entertainer. He was there to save crashed pilots from the savagery of nomadic tribesmen or from dying of thirst. In carrying out this mission he formed the basis of his philosophy that all men were interdependent, that there were no areas of exclusion and no conflict of race.

His success as the central link in a permanent desert rescue operation was founded mainly on instinct and temperament with a dash of idiosyncrasy. The need for allies was paramount and after 'taming' the Spanish by regular visits to the fort to play chess or *belote*, he broke through the hostility of the Arab tribes by treating them with a level of respect they rarely received from a European. His first friends were the half-naked, underfed children living in the tented encampment around the fort, whom he fed with chocolate and biscuits. To them, he was *'le commandant des oiseaux'* – chief of the birds. Saint-Exupéry's openness and generosity also attracted friends among tribesmen resolutely hostile to the beleaguered Spanish and he made further progress by taking lessons in Arabic in the chieftains' tents. His influence was increased by his access to company money to pay for interpreters, who flew on the airmail planes, and his successful bid to raise cash to free a slave called Bark, as related in *Wind, Sand and Stars*.

By the summer of 1928, Saint-Exupéry had joined forces with the least aggressive tribe, the Irzaguin, who provided armed escorts on several missions into the desert. Later he achieved an uneasy peace with the leaders of rival warrior bands despite their regular raids on French troops outside the Spanish enclave, but he never reached agreement with the R'Guibat, the most belligerent nomads. They were suspected of receiving arms from the Spanish to disrupt French interests although many of their weapons were bought with ransom money raised from the capture of French pilots.

Saint-Exupéry's first task each morning was to take planes at the air base for a spin to reduce the effect of condensation. Often he was out for an hour or more, gradually widening his area of reconnaissance until he knew more about the surroundings of Cape Juby than the Spanish garrison did. Occasionally he would take one of the local chieftains for a ride in the hope of overawing him.

At the same time, he was able to survey potential emergency landing-grounds and keep a check on marauders. Accidents in the desert were frequent and airmen were often tortured before being ransomed. Saint-Exupéry arrived at Cape Juby fully aware of gruesome murders carried out by the rebellious Moors, some of whom took revenge for attacks by the French air force which operated similar aircraft to those of Aéropostale. Few planes overflew the desolate Spanish enclave without attracting a volley of bullets from Arab raiding-parties.

Some months before being posted to Cape Juby, Saint-Exupéry had been given a foretaste of the dangers while a passenger with a pilot called René Riguelle. Henri Guillaumet flew as escort in another plane, in accordance with strict company orders that no aircraft was to fly alone. The trip was made soon after the murder of a French flyer and a Spanish mechanic. Another Frenchman, seized at the same time, tried to commit suicide rather than endure torture and died soon after being released. The two burnt-out Bréguets involved in the tragedy could still be clearly seen by overflying mail-planes.

At the southernmost point of the Spanish enclave, Riguelle's engine exploded and he was forced to crash-land. Guillaumet flew back to help him, transferring the postal bags to his plane. While Saint-Exupéry stayed with the remaining sacks of letters and the downed aircraft, Riguelle and Guillaumet flew off to seek aid.

His two friends had given him their loaded pistols, leaving a solitary Saint-Exupéry to dig a defensive position in the dunes, proudly guarding the letters with his life. He sweated it out for the rest of the day, waiting for an attack by desert warriors who had recently captured and ransomed his friend, Jean Mermoz.

After laying his pistols and five cartridge-clips beside him on the sand he felt for the first time that he was responsible for his own life and, as the day wore on, the mystery and danger of the Sahara bowled him over. Writing in *Wind, Sand and Stars*, he said he was bewitched by something half revealed and yet unknown. It was the love of the Sahara, which, like love itself, was born of a face which was perceived and never really seen. 'For ever after this first sight of your new love, an indefinable bond is established between you and the veneer of gold on the sand in the late sun.'

When the others returned at dusk, Saint-Exupéry was told there had been no need to worry. They had deliberately omitted to inform him that this was pacified French territory where he could have sat for half a year without running the least risk.

This episode also inspired another memorable passage in *Wind, Sand and Stars*. After being reunited with his friends, Antoine stayed overnight at a colonial fort near the present-day city of Nouakchott, capital of Mauritania, an incident also romanticized in *Southern Mail*. The military outpost was guarded by fifteen tribesmen and a lonely French sergeant, stricken by homesickness and ashamed of the fact that he once had no wine in the cellar to fête a visiting captain. That night, Saint-Exupéry slept in the open. As he watched a magic desert sky full of stars and shining asteroids his love for the Sahara intensified and he wished the night could last a thousand years.

By July 1928, Saint-Exupéry was no longer the awkward, self-doubting young man that Didier Daurat had met nearly two years before. He had become a leader of authority with enough self-confidence to ignore company rules and act on his own initiative. His most conspicuous disregard for Aéropostale's regulations was shown during his successful attempt to recover a wrecked plane in enemy territory. On 18 July Riguelle was forced down about 30 kilometres south of Cape Juby in an area where rebels had captured and ransomed a Spanish pilot a few months before. While Riguelle was flown to safety, Saint-Exupéry set out to bring back the plane in what his official report described as an unprecedented operation. After two days of discussions with reluctant Moors, he had hired an armed guard of fifteen men to take him to the crashed aircraft.

Along with a mechanic, Saint-Exupéry set off on horseback with a weird caravan of six horses, two donkeys, a pack-camel and two other camels pulling a makeshift wheeled cart of his own design carrying a spare engine. 'This is the first time that camels have been used as draught animals, at least here,' he wrote in the official report, one of several accounts of this trip.

Despite the threat from an Arab raiding-party, Saint-Exupéry oversaw the preparation of a 90-metre long take-off strip completed by a ramp. While his mechanic was still working on the engine, the Moors, Irzaguin, panicked after hearing rifle-fire from a rival group of Aït Toussa. Twelve Irzaguin had recently been killed in an ambush by the enemy tribe and they made up an excuse to abandon the rescue work. An Arab messenger pretended that the commander of the Cape Juby garrison had ordered a retreat and the little caravan was forced to start its return march without completing repairs.

In his official report, Saint-Exupéry said that his nomads only turned back to the damaged plane after being 'wounded in their pride', a sentence explained in a letter to Yvonne de Lestrange. He rallied his shaky Moors by saying he would have been better off with a party of women.

The tone of his report and two subsequent letters on the incident made it sound as if he had set up the expedition as a test of his own courage. Two Spanish planes flew overhead to warn him that Arab raiders were approaching, but he ignored the message and spent the entire day under enemy fire defending the plane. While his warriors lay flat or crawled around on all fours, Saint-Exupéry strode boldly along the dunes defying the Arab riflemen. In a letter to Raymond Vanier, Aéropostale's Dakar representative, he described his baptism of fire as 'magnificent'. His apparent lack of concern for his own safety encouraged the men to complete work on the take-off strip. By five in the afternoon Saint-Exupéry was able to fly the plane back to Cape Juby with his mechanic as passenger.

In an account sent to Didier Daurat, Saint-Exupéry pointed out that the Spaniards had used a warship to protect a working-party salvaging one of their planes which had crashed on the beach near Cape Juby while he and his mechanic had spent two days and two nights in hostile territory to save Latécoère's aircraft. This little show of literary bravado was followed by a request not to count the cost of the rescue because it was impossible to produce receipts.

Later, Saint-Exupéry seemed embarrassed by his delight at playing the desert warrior. André Gide's preface to the French edition of *Night Flight* quoted a letter from Saint-Exupéry referring to this incident. The cited passage was part of the account contained in his correspondence with Yvonne de Lestrange, in which Saint-Exupéry wrote that he heard bullets whizz past his head for the first time in his life and was proud of the fact that he was much calmer than his Arab soldiers. But the adventure made him realize why Plato placed raw courage at the bottom of the list of human virtues.

'It is not made up of fine sentiments but a dash of anger, a little vanity, plenty of stubbornness and vulgar sporting pleasure,' he said. 'Never again will I be able to admire a man who is only brave.'

The truth may have been that the achievement hardly raised much interest among fellow pilots who had undergone far worse hazards. Pressed for the truth, Saint-Exupéry admitted that his battle of the dunes had been limited to three rifle-shots fired from a long way off.

His colleagues showed greater appreciation for an exploit of Saint-Exupéry's, the three-month search for two marooned airmen, Marcel Reine and Édouard Serre, which brought out unexpected reserves of skill, persistence and diplomacy. Several of the most memorable passages in *Wind, Sand and Stars* are scenes from the rescue mission involving Reine, a veteran pilot, and Serre, head of Latécoère's radio department, who was on his first inspection mission of West African bases.

The background to three months of perilous and exhausting attempts to persuade the R'Guibat to release the two men was only hinted at in the book, although Saint-Exupéry received a congratulatory telegram from Toulouse for his 'brilliant handling' of one of the worst crises suffered by Aéropostale. Those months were also significant from a literary viewpoint because it was during this operation that the setting for *The Little Prince* grew out of two separate desert landings, one on the top of a plateau and the other among desolate sand-dunes under a star-splashed sky.

The ordeal which Reine and Serre underwent began with an experimental night flight southwards from Agadir in a new plane, the Latécoère 25. Equipped with a proper cabin capable of carrying two crew and two passengers, the plane had a range only slighter greater than the Bréguet 14, but could carry nearly four times the load. A few successful night flights had encouraged exaggerated confidence in the new craft. The plane carrying Reine and Serre left Agadir without proper preparation and no advance wireless contact, turning up in darkness without warning at Cape Juby late on a June night in 1928. The landing took Saint-Exupéry by surprise and he had to rush out from his hut to organize the lighting of flares.

A senior inspector, who was one of the passengers, ordered Reine and Serre to continue flying southwards in the dark without him because this was the first clear night for weeks. Even so it was a reckless decision as Villa Cisneros had already gone off the air. As there was no news of the plane the following morning, it was presumed to have crashed. A furious Saint-Exupéry sent the irresponsible inspector packing and took charge of tracing the lost aircrew while a replacement took over his post at Cape Juby.

Because the missing Latécoère had not been signalled by any base on its planned route to Mauritania, Saint-Exupéry joined two other pilots at Port-Étienne in a formation flight over 1000 kilometres of desert coastline. The planes flew a mile apart, but the reconnaissance was cut short when the machine flown by Riguelle crash-landed and a second aircraft which went to his aid developed an oil leak. At dusk, Saint-Exupéry touched down alongside and while his mechanic, Jean-René Lefebvre, carried out repairs, the stranded pilots built themselves a little settlement, 'a village of men', using empty crates to protect them from the desert wind. This time, Saint-Exupéry was in extreme danger. The planes had landed 'on the naked crust of the planet' in a region controlled by the R'Guibat. It was almost the exact spot where a French pilot and a Spanish mechanic had been murdered the previous year.

Saint-Exupéry knew that 300 rebel tribesmen were camped near by and that they might have spotted the three planes. Comforted only by the light of candles, the marooned pilots and their Moorish interpreters began what they believed could be their last vigil. Despite the threat, the night had a taste of Christmas for Saint-Exupéry. The airmen told each other stories, exchanged jokes and sang. There was the light-hearted feeling of a well-prepared feast, he wrote, yet they were infinitely poor.

'Wind, sand and stars; an austere life for Trappists. But on this badly lit cloth, six or seven men, who owned nothing in the world except their memories, shared invisible wealth.'

Saint-Exupéry was so struck by these words when he wrote them nearly ten years later that '*Étoiles par grand vent*' – Stars in a High Wind – was his first choice for the title of *Terre des hommes*, as the book is known in French. He changed his mind only when he was given the uncorrected proofs. When the fuller American edition was commissioned, he preferred *Wind, Sand and Stars*. This became the inspiration for most translations.

*

THE Christmas-night images in *Wind, Sand and Stars* and its interdependent community of men are seminal to the philosophy expressed in Saint-Exupéry's wartime writings and *Wisdom of the Sands*. In two other passages, more magical and nostalgic, lie the seeds of *The Little Prince*. In the first, he speaks of a landing on a 300-metre-high plateau when trying to make contact with the R'Guibat kidnappers. He intended sending a Moorish guide to meet the nomads, but there was no way down from what he called a desert iceberg made up of shells from the time when the Sahara was an ocean-bed. These untrodden few acres of the world, which he saw as a table-cloth spread under the apple-tree of the night sky, contain the elements of the innocent poetry of the *The Little Prince*. The discovery of fist-sized black pebbles which have been thrown down to earth over thousands of years is the embryo of the interplanetary images in the fable he wrote during the war.

The imagery comes through even more strongly in another adventure immediately following this landing on his timeless and tiny world. Forced down at night among dunes, Saint-Exupéry is transfixed by a fascination with the night sky and pinned to the earth by an unknown force. Giving himself up to the 'enchantments of my memory', he returns almost physically to the scenes of his childhood.

In his reference to the 'provisions of gentleness' once gathered at Saint-Maurice-de-Rémens and the warmth he felt for his house-keeper and confidante, Moisy, there are glimpses of a creative process that seizes Saint-Exupéry like a vice while his mind fights to force meaning out of obsessive and elusive emotions. Few writers confess to their total helplessness when falling under a spiritual spell which they cannot understand. There is something terrifying about this passage containing the admissions of a man trapped by his own genius. 'What is going on inside me, I cannot tell,' he wrote.

In the coming years he would submit to this invisible strength or fight against it with limited success. In the end, the result was the same. The invasion of his imagination by reminiscence, tortured self-analysis, bewilderment over the destiny of adult man, and the belief that there was a hidden controlling force far beyond humankind's comprehension both transfigured him and crushed him. In his letters, there is the implicit recognition that this exquisite torment of

[109]

the mind spilled over into his personal life, notably complicating his relationship with his wife and causing swift transformations from sublime happiness and trust to remorse, suicidal depression and doubt.

Memories of the lost desert wastes, like the distant country of his childhood, became refuges in periods of corrupting melancholy. He forecast his coming sadness at separation from the Saharan wilderness in a letter to Charles Sallès just before leaving Cape Juby in November 1928. Saint-Exupéry had tasted an austere and challenging life and believed he would never be capable of making the effort to be happy again. He compared the after-taste of his stay in the desolate Spanish Sahara to eating the forbidden fruit. Soon he was to be shut out of this paradise, just as he was shut out of that other Eden, the walled garden of Saint-Maurice, and would yearn for ever to return to this land of simple values.

CHAPTER SEVEN

The Lost Navigator

REINE and Serre were not freed until September, a month after
Saint-Exupéry should have returned to France. His departure was
delayed further by other missions, including the rescue of a wounded
Spanish air force lieutenant whose plane had been brought down by
gunfire. A Spanish sergeant also went to help but his plane stalled
on landing. Saint-Exupéry had to return to save him after taking the
injured lieutenant to the fort at Cape Juby.

The undertaking was constantly threatened by a group of R'Guibat warriors whose efforts to capture the Spaniards were frustrated
by a battle with other tribesmen. The failure of this latest kidnapping
was a sign of the waning power of the R'Guibat whose fighting
history could be traced back hundreds of years. Their main raiding-
units had been destroyed in a pitched battle with the French just
before Saint-Exupéry arrived in the Spanish Sahara and the belligerent remnants were finally forced to accept an uneasy truce when
France established its administrative grip on the West African empire.

Saint-Exupéry had chronicled the dying months of an era. Relatively routine flights over friendly territory soon replaced the heroic
period of desert mail deliveries which had lasted ten years. 'Pacifi-
cation' on the ground was matched by a revolution in the air. The
longer-range Latécoère 25 was soon to begin regular service, ending
the reign of open-cockpit planes and making night flights safer.
Postal delivery times were cut by more than half and forced landings
were a rarity. New pilots recruited by Daurat expected their machines
to have comfortable cabins, dependable navigation aids, reliable wireless communications and long-range engines.

Saint-Exupéry returned to France with the veteran's gloss he had admired in Guillaumet, making him a candidate to join an even more risky Aéropostale venture in South America. Nearly a year was to pass before he arrived in Buenos Aires, but 1929 established him in a double career as aviator and writer. In the spring, he was sent to the navy's aerial navigation school at Brest for an advanced course run by Lionel-Max Chassin, a future air force general. Nine of the eleven students were military officers whose strict respect for discipline contrasted with Saint-Exupéry's nonchalance. Chassin said that Saint-Exupéry turned up late for the first meeting with his fellow students at a café in Brest, making a poor impression at the beginning of the specialist navigation course. He had got lost among the narrow streets in the Brittany port.

Chassin, who became a military historian, was younger than most of his students and the relaxed atmosphere of his course perhaps contributed to Saint-Exupéry's odd results. The introductory meeting ended in a drinking-session in which all eleven students, their teacher and another instructor bought rounds of vermouth-blackcurrant cocktails before setting off for a dinner remembered mainly for Saint-Exupéry's exuberant drinking-songs.

Much of the specialist course involved higher mathematics and astral observation from viewpoints on Brest's fortifications. While most of the theoretical lessons passed off well, Chassin said that Saint-Exupéry made some enormous blunders during practical courses. 'On the theoretical level he was sometimes brilliant but on practical exercises he was often clumsy, awkward and downright bad,' Chassin added.

In an ominous precedent for a later accident in which he nearly drowned, Saint-Exupéry forgot Chassin's instructions for landing a seaplane and would have sunk with his aircraft without rapid rescue work with a crane. On another occasion, when Chassin was co-pilot, Saint-Exupéry ignored his instructor's lessons on specific manoeuvres for flying-boats on take-off and pulled the joystick the wrong way, nearly driving the aircraft under the waves. However, Chassin judged Saint-Exupéry 'very strong' in mathematics, while with regard to navigation aids he continually outlined new ideas and inventions, some of which were later patented.

Saint-Exupéry was given a pass-mark and would have received

a certificate of advanced navigation if a Defence Ministry inspector had not intervened. He told Chassin that the course would not be considered credible if everyone succeeded and insisted that two names were removed. Saint-Exupéry was one of the unlucky pair.

Chassin attributed much of Saint-Exupéry's loss of concentration to his preoccupation with the imminent publication of *Southern Mail*. The first proofs were sent to him during the training-course and at every opportunity Antoine recited passages to fellow students. Later he read chapters to his cousins in Carnac, among them Honoré d'Estienne d'Orves, who had joined the navy after graduating from the Lycée Saint-Louis and the École Polytechnique.

Few outsiders admitted having made adverse comments because Saint-Exupéry's sulky reaction to literary suggestions had been characteristic since early childhood. He preferred to make corrections in secrecy at night when he should have been studying for his navigation course. Usually, he went to bed in the early hours after long sessions of editing and some of his inattention during Chassin's early-morning lessons was caused by pure physical and intellectual fatigue.

BECAUSE of André Gide's influence, *Southern Mail* was always destined for Gallimard's *Nouvelle Revue Française*. André Beucler, who had written three novels for Gallimard, was asked to write a preface while Jean Prévost, the editor of the now defunct *Navire d'argent*, was chosen to write a review which appeared two months before the book was released in April 1929.

During a radio broadcast in 1954, Beucler spoke of his first meeting with Saint-Exupéry, when he was struck by his 'mischievous look and a nose that quivered like an insect's antennae'. The two men discussed the new book in a café of the avenue Wagram where Saint-Exupéry had contrived to make a good first impression, arriving with a bundle of newspapers, books by Gide, Colette and Georges Duhamel and a clockwork toy he had bought for a friend's child. As soon as the conversation started, Saint-Exupéry described himself both as a Nietzschean and a Marxist who believed that ordinary people had to be led and organized. He had taken up flying, Saint-

Exupéry said, because it combined personal fulfilment with comradeship, danger, sacrifice and emulation.

Beucler received the message with enthusiasm and wrote a preface full of admiration for a novelist he described as a hero, soldier and man of action. Nor did Saint-Exupéry's other young literary sponsor, Jean Prévost, let him down in his review in the *Nouvelle Revue française*.

Southern Mail was the subject of several other reviews that were kind without being eulogistic. Most reviewers tended to echo Beucler's praise for an author who could turn out a novel despite an intense, adventurous life, but often agreed with the prefacer's reckless comment in support of his enthusiasm for the man of action that 'Saint-Exupéry is not a writer'.

Disregarding this remark, Antoine had already started on another book about aviation, even showing the first passages to Gaston Gallimard. The finished work would have little relation to the original draft because, in September 1929, Saint-Exupéry was given only a few days' notice of an imminent transfer to Buenos Aires as Latécoère's traffic manager in Argentina. More than a year of intensive flying in South America would give a different shape to what eventually became *Night Flight*, a literary classic which would make nonsense of Beucler's judgement.

At the heart of Saint-Exupéry's experiences in Africa was the struggle of man against man, with the desert and sky providing the backdrop for the clash between two civilizations. Disillusion and idealism relentlessly contradicted each other. The despair he felt regarding the life of decadent French colonizers in Dakar was compensated by the uplifting episode when he and his colleagues bought a slave called Bark for 50 Spanish pesetas so that he could return home with dignity as a free man. Nobility and disgrace changed camps frequently until neither European nor Arab had a monopoly of good or evil.

When Saint-Exupéry wrote of his life in South America, the adversaries became the elements and the Andes. The only worthwhile challenge was for man to surpass his own self, achieving unexpected levels of physical and intellectual courage exemplified by Guillaumet and Daurat. Saint-Exupéry's own experiences also went far beyond anything he hinted at in his books. The air-currents over the mountains lifted man and machine thousands of metres above the normal ceiling of most modern aircraft, and much the same effect was induced in Saint-Exupéry's soaring perception of mankind.

A Land of Moonlight and Stones

ALTHOUGH Saint-Exupéry's posting to Buenos Aires was essentially an office job, he was also responsible for pioneering the world's southernmost air service to Patagonia and did more long-distance flying than in Africa, often in appalling conditions. His intuitive skills were sharpened by risk and he surpassed his own limits in the same way as his heroes, Mermoz and Guillaumet.

While Saint-Exupéry showed a familiar humorous disregard in the face of acute danger, the South American period furnished no anecdotes indicating a lack of concentration to match those recounted by Lionel-Max Chassin. Antoine had less time for a literary career, the source of much of his distraction, although the urge to create was hardly diminished. His imaginative situation reports and continuous flow of inventive suggestions for improving the service seem to have irritated Daurat/Rivière.

In *Night Flight*, Rivière's aide, the self-doubting Inspector Robineau, owes much to Saint-Exupéry himself. Ill at ease in his role as a cadre denied the right even to drink with the pilots, Robineau sombrely digests a rebuke from Rivière. '[Robineau] had given up suggesting new methods and technical solutions after Rivière had written: "Inspector Robineau is requested to submit reports, not poems".'

Robineau was told to use his skills to stimulate the airline staff's enthusiasm, and from then on he 'threw himself into the question of human weaknesses as if they were his daily bread'. Just in case anyone reading between the lines assumed that Saint-Exupéry was inflating his self-importance by describing the inspector's hunt for the mechanic who drank, the air-base official who spent the night on the tiles or the pilot who made bad landings, he added Rivière's ambiguous judgement on Robineau: 'Even if he's not very intelligent, he's quite useful.'

At best, in the author's own analysis, Robineau/Saint-Exupéry is a loyal NCO ready to follow his defeated general into exile when the night flight from Patagonia crashes – the book's central theme – and the disaster threatens to ruin Rivière's career. Saint-Exupéry must have felt that his portrait of Robineau was particularly unsympathetic, as he later told his friend Georges Pélissier that it was an act of revenge against a pompous airline inspector he disliked. The man had borrowed geological samples Saint-Exupéry had collected in the desert and had never returned them.

GUILLAUMET, Mermoz and Reine had been at the quayside on Saint-Exupéry's arrival in Buenos Aires and they recreated the atmosphere of Toulouse's Hôtel du Grand Balcon in the Hotel Majestic. Aéropostale's officers were nearby in the Calle de la Reconquista where the most influential executive was the Argentinian technical director, Vicente Almandos Almonacid, a Great War volunteer officer in the French air force.

Almonacid was a national hero and without his political contacts Aéropostale would never have been allowed to establish a network in South America where local political sentiment was mostly pro-German. It had taken four years of negotiations to develop an airmail service from Europe which included an Atlantic link by fast motor boats between Senegal and Natal on the Brazilian coastline.

The French government's lack of support had so disgusted Pierre-Georges Latécoère that he sold his control of the airline in 1927 to a French financier, Marcel Bouilloux-Lafont, who became chairman of a joint French-Argentine enterprise called Aeroposta Argentina. By the time Saint-Exupéry reported for duty in October 1929, Aeroposta Argentina was running a twice-weekly service from Buenos Aires to Asuncion del Paraguay, connecting with mail-flights from Santiago de Chile and the Brazilian port of Rio de Janeiro. On the strength of his successful handling of the Cape Juby sector, he was appointed traffic manager with the task of pioneering a regular service to Patagonia and Tierra del Fuego, about 2500 kilometres south of Buenos Aires.

Above: Saint-Exupéry's father, Jean.
(*Frédéric d'Agay*)

Left: Saint-Exupéry's mother, Marie.
(*Frédéric d'Agay*)

Below: Marie and Jean's wedding. Tante
Gabrielle is in the foreground.
(*Frédéric d'Agay*)

Saint-Maurice-de-Rémens from the garden. (*Frédéric d'Agay*)

Marie with Saint-Exupéry and François, in the cart. (*Frédéric d'Agay*)

Saint-Exupéry with Tante Madeleine, Marie's sister. (*Frédéric d'Agay*)

The plane in which Saint-Exupéry took his first joy ride at Ambérieu in 1912. The pilot, Gabriel Salvez-Wroblewski, is in the pilot's seat with his brother Pierre seated behind. (*René Wroblewski*)

Father Auguste Launay's class at Le Mans in 1913. Saint-Exupéry is second from the right in the back row. (*Saint-Croix-du-Mans college*)

Left: Studio portrait of Saint-Exupéry aged twenty-two. (*Frédéric d'Agay*)

Below: Saint-Exupéry's sister Gabrielle's wedding to Pierre d'Agay in October 1923. Saint-Exupéry is seated second from right in the front row. (*Frédéric d'Agay*)

Saint-Exupéry and his best friend, Henri Guillaumet, standing in front of their plane. (*Musée d'Air France*)

OPPOSITE PAGE

Top Left: Louise de Vilmorin, Saint-Exupéry's first fiancée. (*Andrée de Vilmorin*)

Top Right: Didier Daurat, Aeropostale's operations manager. (*Musée d'Air France*)

Bottom: An aerial view of Cape Juby. (*Musée de Air France*)

Right: Consuelo Suncin, Saint-Exupéry's wife. (*Claude Werth*)

Below: Saint-Exupéry and Consuelo on their wedding day at Agay, April 1931. The bridesmaids, Marie Madeleine and Mireille, and the page boy, François, are Gabrielle's children. (*Frédéric d'Agay*)

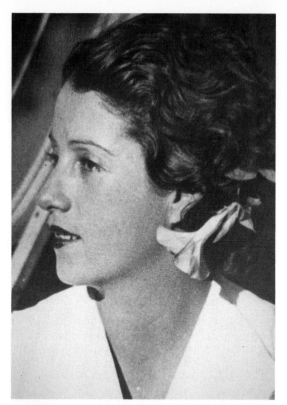

Jean Mermoz was later sent back to France to perfect a seaplane service between Africa and Latin America that would soon turn Aéropostale into an international airline in which punctuality and reliability became more important than bravery and ingenuity. But the airfields in Argentina were as primitive as in the early days at Toulouse or Cape Juby. From the air, the great flat and empty expanses of the Argentinian pampas were reminiscent of the Sahara, as Saint-Exupéry discovered on his first flight southwards to Bahía Blanca only two days after arriving in Buenos Aires. On arrival he was met by an Argentinian pilot, Luro Carambaceres, whose own book on these pioneer days, *Rumbo 180°, Huellas en el Cielo Austral*, Traces in the Southern Sky, fills in essential detail on the Patagonia line.

The two men became close friends, and some months after Antoine had returned to France he told Carambaceres in a letter that no period in his life was preferable to the time he spent in South America. He saw the immense open spaces with such clarity that the memories hurt him. This was not the poetic licence of his re-creation of the Sahara period, but a genuine regret for the most intensely satisfying months of his professional flying career.

Saint-Exupéry wrote surprisingly little in *Wind, Sand and Stars* about his personal experiences during this period. He explained his reluctance to reawaken these memories in the letter to Carambaceres, saying that if a man had loved a woman desperately and wanted to live in peace he had to destroy her portraits. This was what he had done in relation to his months in Argentina.

Carambaceres was more generous with detail in his book, even recounting the inaugural commercial flight to Patagonia out of Buenos Aires which he shared with Saint-Exupéry on 30 October 1929. The countryside before the first refuelling stop in San Antonio Oeste was bleak, the barrenness being broken only by flights of flamingos rising from salt lakes. San Antonio was little more than a lost village of mud huts scattered among sand-dunes but the next leg along the Gulf of San Matías was over a relatively populated area of extensive fruit and vegetable farms. Trelew was a new boom-town, sheltered from the violent winds off the Patagonian plateau which would nearly destroy Saint-Exupéry's plane on a later trip.

The next stopover, Comodoro Rivadavia, turned out to be an

ugly, sprawling oil settlement surrounded by derricks, where 10,000 oil-workers created an atmosphere resembling the gold rush, with the main street overlooked by saloons and brothels. The town's Atlantic beaches teemed with seals and walruses. Saint-Exupéry caught a baby seal which accompanied him back to Buenos Aires, sitting on top of the mail-bags.

When Carambaceres had completed the survey of other landing-strips as far as Cape Horn, Saint-Exupéry flew the whole length of the route to Tierra del Fuego. Borne along by strong winds on the return flight, he covered the 2500 kilometres from Patagonia to Buenos Aires in the same day, one of several marathon trips of eighteen hours or more. Much of the journey was in darkness, with the empty earth eerily lit by a pale moon. This voyage through hours of solitude over the silent pampas left its indelible impression on *Night Flight*, where Saint-Exupéry portrayed the Argentinian plateau as a 'landscape of moonlight and stones.'

Three months later, after the crude airfields had been equipped with wooden hangars and wireless shacks, a weekly service was started to the southernmost inhabited area of the world. Most of the time, pilots flew in atrocious weather conditions: raging tempests were a daily hazard which flyers had to put up with or risk being fined for delays, although at Comodoro Rivadavia there was a notice forbidding pilots from landing when gusts exceeded 150 kilometres an hour. After Saint-Exupéry had to battle with a cyclone off Trelew, where winds reached nearly 200 kilometres an hour and nearly tore off the Latécoère's wings, it took 120 soldiers an hour to drag the plane into a hangar.

There were at least two occasions when Saint-Exupéry's eccentricity earned rebukes. While flying a new Latécoère 28 with nine passengers aboard, he was forced to land during a terrifying rainstorm. His passengers, members of a French theatre group, were soaked to the skin while running for shelter in a nearby village. When the plane landed at Buenos Aires after going missing for more than a day, the portholes were bedecked with women's underclothes hung up to dry and the passengers were attired in ill-assorted cowboy clothes bought at a local store. Saint-Exupéry himself wore slippers and was covered in mud. His self-satisfied smile exasperated the local air-base chief, who threatened to send him back to France for 'playing the fool'.

A more dangerous act of bravado occurred during a flight from the Uruguay border. Saint-Exupéry had been sent to pick up mail driven overland from Brazil, where air traffic was stopped because of a revolution. Taking off from a primitive airstrip, the overloaded plane struck barbed wire and hit the ground. The bump popped the rivets holding the cabin to the corrugated-steel fuselage. An emergency soldering job was carried out by the local blacksmith, but the cockpit and fuselage began splitting in mid-flight. In dismay, the radio operator reported that he could clearly see the ground through the crack.

On touching down at Buenos Aires, Saint-Exupéry called over a mechanic, Raoul Roubes, and said with pride, 'Pretty good work, eh?' The trembling radio operator swore he would never fly with Saint-Exupéry again after Roubes confirmed his worst fears. 'You must be nuts,' Roubes told the pilot. 'The plane was about to break in two.'

The Diamond Lake

THERE is no story which tells more about Saint Exupéry's own feelings and personality than his account of Henri Guillaumet's extraordinary courage after a crash in the Andes in the depths of the South American winter. Saint-Exupéry was the first pilot to welcome him back to safety and record Guillaumet's remark, 'I swear that what I went through no animal would have gone through.'

That sentence in *Wind, Sand and Stars* has become one of the most quoted in French literature, a summing-up of the author's belief that man was born to surpass nature and himself. Saint-Exupéry described it as the noblest sentence ever spoken, defining man's place in the universe and re-establishing the true hierarchy. Whatever can be said about Guillaumet's professional skill, he was a modest and ordinary man at heart, and not predestined to be singled out in a crowd. After Saint-Exupéry's account of the crash in the mountains, he has rightly been held up as an exemplary moral and humane figure for generation after generation, a model of integrity and resolution.

Wind, Sand and Stars, with its essential lesson that man can overcome the most terrible adversity, illuminated France like a beacon after the defeat in June 1940. In prisoner-of-war camps where a million and a half Frenchmen had little to cling to except despair, Guillaumet's experience contained the fabulous message that salvation could come out of the depths of night.

Saint-Exupéry's own sparse retelling of Guillaumet's resurrection and the tears that flowed spontaneously when the two men hugged each other with relief is not only a moving piece of writing. It is an accurate report, written nearly ten years after the event. He had long ago got into the habit of taking extensive notes, which enabled him to write much of the story in Guillaumet's own words. Saint-Exupéry sat for hours by his friend's bedside after the rescue, listening to a recital given between bouts of sleep disturbed by appalling nightmares. He also read Guillaumet's own official report written within days of recovering from his week-long ordeal. In a letter, illustrated by a cartoon of Guillaumet standing on top of a mountain, Saint-Exupéry described the summary as 'stunning' and suggested that his friend should seek membership of the Académie française.

Guillaumet's report, while lacking the literary quality of *Wind, Sand and Stars*, contains much information that Saint-Exupéry overlooked for the sake of a narrative which concentrates on the resilience of man more than on the near-tragic event. But even though there was no intention on Guillaumet's part to play on emotions, the simplicity of his own words was often as moving as Saint-Exupéry's version.

Astonishingly, the flight of Friday 13 June, 1930 was Guillaumet's ninety-second crossing of the Andes. Despite the often alarming task of seeking air-currents to lift planes over mountains of up to 7000 metres high, he had been shaken by only two serious incidents during what had become a fairly reliable airmail service from Santiago de Chile to Buenos Aires.

This was a tribute as much to his extraordinary skill as a pilot as to the solidity of the Potez 25 open-cockpit biplane which was the workhorse of the route. Guillaumet, who flew alone, believed the plane's superior flying qualities saved his life during an earlier flight when conditions were so cold that the whole aircraft was covered with ice during a thirty-minute shaking in the middle of heavy snow-clouds. On another occasion, the plane had plunged several thousand metres in an air-pocket, sometimes being turned on its back, but Guillaumet treated these occurrences as all in a day's work and ignored the dangers. On Thursday 12 June, though, he admitted defeat in the face of a blizzard and turned back seventy minutes out of Santiago because impenetrable snow-clouds blocked the route over the Andes.

The following day he took off again at 8 a.m, pushing super-stition to the back of his mind. His only other crash as a pilot had been during service in the air force and had occurred on another Friday the 13th. This time, clouds rising to 9000 metres again cut off the normal passage over the mountains and, after more than three and a half hours of vain effort battling against a snowstorm, he was forced to land on the edges of the Laguna Diamante, the Diamond Lake.

Only the night before, a local hunter had told him that the lake's edges were usually frozen solid and clear of snow. The touchdown was successful until the wheels hit a drift and the aircraft turned upside-down, twisting the propeller. For the next thirty-eight hours, while the tempest raged, Guillaumet sheltered in the fuselage after wrapping himself in a parachute. During two nights he was tormented by images from a novel he had just read about Alaska called *Le Grand Silence Blanc*, The Great White Silence.

At 2 a.m. on Sunday the wind suddenly dropped, the sky cleared and he could see the moon over the chill lake. Seven hours later he heard a plane circling around but his effort at lighting smoke-flares was useless. The crashed silver aircraft and the grey smoke of the flares blended with the landscape and were invisible from the sky.

'I had only one chance of escaping and I knew that if I was going to try it I would have to walk without any equipment over a pass 4200 metres high,' Guillaumet wrote in his report. 'I didn't have the slightest idea about mountain-climbing but I nevertheless decided to set out. I don't know what I would have done if I had known the physical and moral suffering ahead of me.'

Into a suitcase he packed half a bottle of rum, some condensed milk, tins of sardines and corned beef and a little solid-fuel stove. His only navigation aids were a small pocket compass and a torch. Before leaving, he used a stone to scratch a message on the crashed plane which read: 'Because an aircraft would not be able to spot me, I have headed towards the east. Adieu, everybody. My last thought will be for my wife.'

At 10 a.m. on Sunday he began a five-day forced march that continued day and night without sleep until Thursday 19 June. From the beginning, when he had to climb through snow 3 metres deep, his spirit and resistance were tested to breaking-point. He lived on boiled snow and condensed milk because the other tinned food was frozen solid and barely edible. The tin-opener became more useful as a makeshift ice-pick.

On the first day, Guillaumet rolled 300 metres down a mountain-side and was saved only by falling into soft snow. On the second day, he painfully retraced most of his steps when he was confronted by an impassable slope. Later, his soaked flying-overalls became too heavy and he had to throw them away along with his wet socks. Sometimes blinded by whirling snow, Guillaumet struggled on despite nature's cruel tricks. While he was trying to eat, a blast of wind blew away one of his gloves. The wind also raised false hopes. Several times he thought he heard cocks crowing or trains whistling as if civilization were approaching.

Tuesday, the third day, tested his will to the limit. Guillaumet followed a small river and half fell as he stumbled over huge rocks. His suitcase filled with water, ruining his solid fuel and his boxes of matches. Even by walking at night, guided by torchlight, he covered only 3 kilometres. Blood from his damaged ankles stained the snow.

'This was the hardest day,' he wrote, although Wednesday turned out to be another nightmare. He fell 50 metres into a ravine, losing his suitcase containing his food and torch. At that point, Guillaumet thought he had reached the end of his endurance. Often, he could only advance by crawling on all fours. He had to cut his shoes open because his feet were swollen and then fell into the river and was nearly swept away.

Later he told his friends that what kept him going was three little photographs of his wife, Noëlle. 'I often drew new courage by looking at those photographs,' he said in his report, but at the same time he contemplated the fast-flowing river and thought it would be easy to 'let myself go peacefully'.

By Thursday he was so weak from physical effort and lack of food that he staggered under the weight of his overcoat and he had to discard it. Soon afterwards he was convinced that his last hope had vanished at the very point of rescue. A peasant women and her child took fright and fled on horseback on seeing what they thought was a haggard madman stumbling from the mountain pass. Guillaumet used all his remaining strength to call out, 'I am the lost pilot – muchos pesos,' and they turned to help him. After being nursed back to health in the family's one-room house, Guillaumet was being taken by car to his air base when a plane landed on the highway.

The pilot was Saint-Exupéry, who had flown relentlessly through the mountain passes in search of his friend. Guillaumet summed up the meeting in one sentence: 'Our reunion was excessively moving.'

Jean-René Lefebvre, who had overcome his reluctance to fly with Saint-Exupéry so that he could join in the rescue, was the mechanic. He later organized an overland expedition which recovered the mail from Guillaumet's aircraft and brought the machine back to base.

As for Guillaumet, he summarized the accident in his log-book with these few words: '13 June. Potez N25, No. 1522. Santiago/ Laguna Diamante. 3 hours 35. Landing in the middle of the Cordillera. Overturned. Violent blizzard. Returned on foot, 19 June.'

The Fashioning of Men

WHEN the missing pilot had recovered, a celebration was held in the Guillaumet flat in Buenos Aires. Saint-Exupéry's exuberance was remembered for years afterwards. He sang bawdy French folk-songs at the top of his voice, only breaking off to question Guillaumet on whether he had seen planes flying overhead. There had been at least two occasions when his friend heard or saw aircraft circling vainly over the mountains and Saint-Exupéry became even more euphoric when it was clear that he had been in command of one of the machines.

To get some peace, Henri and Noëlle Guillaumet, who had been married only the year before, eventually had to hustle Saint-Exupéry out of the flat in the early hours of the morning. There was rarely a night when he did not drop in or drag the couple off to the cinema, a night-club or an amusement park. Sometimes he would fall off to sleep on the couch and had to be helped downstairs to a taxi. One evening he left unaccompanied and fell asleep in the lift. He would have spent the night there if Noëlle had not found him curled up in the corner.

The Guillaumets also had to put up with a succession of girl-friends. The Saint-Exupéry of *Southern Mail*, who was so contemptuous of casual pick-ups, had discovered the joys of being a star pilot in a profession that attracted a flock of admirers. His aristocratic name and literary success added extra touches to his glamour, but all pilots were adulated in their own right like great sporting heroes. Although Saint-Exupéry resented a comparison with toreadors, flyers had the same compelling aura which he exploited to attract '*mignonnes*', his bachelor conquests.

THE strong sense of fellowship that he experienced during Guillaumet's rescue reinforced Saint-Exupéry's belief that he was not cut out for leadership. He wanted to remain one of the boys. His job as air-traffic chief, in which he had to hand out punishments for flight delays and accidents even when the pilot was not at fault, alienated him from his colleagues.

In *Night Flight* Saint-Exupéry implicitly criticizes his *alter ego*, Inspector Robineau, for enjoying power over men. Between the lines, he admits that his own decisions were only a parrot-like transcription of Rivière's carefully weighed severity. In fining pilots who break regulations, Robineau offers no other justification for his decisions than the application of standing company rules. Rivière, on the other hand, understands the necessity of a strict code of conduct.

'Regulations,' Rivière reflects, 'are like religious rites which seem ridiculous but which fashion men.' For Rivière, Saint-Exupéry writes, it is a matter of indifference whether he appears to be fair or unfair. He doesn't intend to enslave men by this severity, but rather to launch them beyond themselves.

As *Night Flight* is an argument in favour of Jesuit-like authority and a rigid doctrine of leadership, it is paradoxical that Saint-Exupéry avoided senior posts himself, preferring to be seen as a blindly obedient NCO rather than an officer. Even during the war, when he was much older than the average pilot, he shunned the possibility of command. His hyper-anxiety often induced excessive remorse and doubt. One of the few recorded incidents of a punitive decision taken by Saint-Exupéry was attributed in *Night Flight* to Rivière/Daurat as if Saint-Exupéry could not come to terms with having taken the action personally.

A veteran mechanic called Roblet is summarily sacked for incompetence by Rivière despite the fact that he has worked for twenty years on planes and built the first aircraft to fly in Argentina. Rivière wonders whether it was unjust to dismiss the man so brutally until he receives confirmation that the mechanic is unreliable. A plane lands with all its instruments out of action and an investigation shows that Roblet installed the faulty wiring.

Roblet was the name of a real person. He was chief mechanic at San Antonio Oeste and was more than sixty years old. According to Paul Decendit, a future chief test-flight mechanic with Latécoère, the engineer was summarily sacked by Saint-Exupéry after a crash caused by a mechanical failure.

On another occasion, Saint-Exupéry fined an airmail pilot 200 pesos on the spot for coming to his rescue after a forced landing. If the airman had followed Daurat's inflexible instructions, he would have taken his cargo to an air base before setting out to help his traffic chief.

These decisions based on harsh company rules drawn up by Daurat caused long-standing resentment, feeding Saint-Exupéry's fears of being ostracized by his men. If this apprehension was not enough to put him off seeking leadership, he was incapable of assuming the harsh responsibility, accepted by Daurat, of compelling pilots to take acute and often fatal risks.

The accident at the heart of *Night Flight* had its origins in a crash in Montevideo Bay in May 1930 which killed the Latécoère pilot Élysée Négrin. Three other people died, including Daurat's former deputy in Toulouse, Julien Pranville. In the previous fifteen months Daurat had lost six flyers and three radio operators, but this was a particularly inauspicious accident. Pranville was being flown to Natal in Brazil to welcome Mermoz's first flying-boat airmail link between Africa and South America which Daurat had organized.

The accident put the safety of the new service into question but Daurat's nerve did not crack. He went ahead with the inaugural flight from Senegal which left on 12 May 1930, with 150 kilos of mail flown in a record twenty-five hours from Toulouse. Undeterred by the Montevideo disaster, Jean Mermoz flew the Latécoère 28 seaplane *Comte de la Vaulx* on one of the most important long-distance flights in history, opening up a permanent mail and passenger service over the southern Atlantic. This same flight inspired a dramatic episode in *Wind, Sand and Stars* where Saint-Exupéry recounts Mermoz's description of huge waterspouts rising out of the Atlantic Ocean like the black pillars of a temple.

Despite bad weather, the mail was transported from France to Africa, across the Atlantic and over South America to arrive at its destination on the Pacific only four and a half days later. The event caused a sensation in South America where Aéropostale's flyers were commemorated in folk-songs and souvenirs. Six years later Saint-Exupéry was interviewed by a French newspaper, *La Flèche*, following Mermoz's death during another Atlantic crossing. One paragraph stood out. Referring to the South American period, Saint-Exupéry said that all pilots felt they had completed a '*tour de force*' and fulfilled a duty after succeeding in a particularly dangerous flight.

'Mermoz felt this more than any other man,' he added. 'He felt a sort of interior jubilation, a confused reaction, but he was sure that, as far as we were men, we had been ennobled.'

Saint-Exupéry participated in the record-breaking flight from southern France to the Pacific only vicariously, stuck in his office at Buenos Aires, worried by the long silences when radio communications broke down. For him, 'interior jubilation' was limited to praising the achievements of his fellow pilots. Any ambition to rise through the executive hierarchy went. He yearned to go back to the routine work of a mail pilot, unaware that his personal life, job and literary career were now set on conflicting courses which would not be reconciled until the publication of *The Little Prince* thirteen years later.

PART TWO

❦

1931–1939

CHAPTER EIGHT

Gomez Carrillo's Widow

IN 1931, Saint-Exupéry's professional, personal and literary life appeared set on an upward curve towards happiness and success. The challenges of Africa and South America had established his reputation as a fearless pilot. A few weeks before leaving Argentina he met his Salvadorean wife, Consuelo Suncin de Sandoval, whom he married in France in April 1931. By the end of the year his second novel, *Night Flight*, had been published to critical acclaim.

Instead of fulfilment, he stumbled clumsily through emotional upsets and career disappointments. As a flyer, he was often unemployed or had to take mundane jobs while attempts to break long-distance records ended in accidents. Although he wrote many newspaper and magazine articles, his higher literary ambitions petered out and it was not until the publication of *Wind, Sand and Stars* in 1939 that he made another lasting contribution to French literature. His greatest failure was his marriage, where he was torn between exaltation and bitterness.

His relationship with Consuelo began after they met in Buenos Aires during an Alliance française reception for French writers and entertainers on a lecture tour. The group's leader, Benjamin Crémieux, was a contributor to the *Nouvelle Revue Française* and had been introduced to Saint-Exupéry at a Gallimard cocktail-party in Paris. Among Crémieux's group was Consuelo, widow of the Guatamalan-born writer, Enrique Gomez Carrillo, an extravagant figure renowned for his feminine conquests, his tempestuous duels and a book on Mata Hari based on personal acquaintance.

Accounts of Consuelo's relationship with Gomez Carrillo usually record their first meeting as taking place in Paris in 1919 when she was supposedly only seventeen. However, a 1993 investigation into Consuelo's life by a Salvadorean filmmaker, Manuel Sorto, discovered considerable contradiction over dates. Confusion was added by the existence of several official declarations on her birth in the Central American state of El Salvador. At her wedding to Saint-Exupéry she said she was born in 1902, but claimed that the registration certificate had been destroyed during a Salvadorean revolution. Some friends believed the real date was 1898, making her two years older than Antoine, but her tombstone in Paris gives her birth-year as 1907.

Apart from members of Consuelo's family, Manuel Sorto's main source for his TV documentary was the Salvadorean journalist and historian Francisco Mena Guerrero, who interviewed Consuelo many times. He said that she and Gomez Carrillo first saw each other in Paris in 1925 when he was fifty-four and she claimed to be twenty-two.

Gomez Carrillo, who was still married to his second wife, had written more than fifty books and was the Paris correspondent for the Madrid paper *ABC* and two Argentinian journals. After taking Argentinian citizenship, he was appointed Buenos Aires' consul in Paris and, in Consuelo's own words, became 'immensely rich'. The Salvadorean TV inquiry revealed that the couple lived together for some months before they married in Nice in December 1926. Less than a year later Gomez Carrillo died, leaving Consuelo property in France and Argentina. It was partly to claim her inheritance and a diplomatic pension from the Argentinian government after three years of widowhood that Consuelo joined Crémieux's lecture-group.

By this time, Saint-Exupéry was sexually much less naïve and far less of a romantic than during his hopeless love affair with Louise de Vilmorin nearly ten years earlier. He had even become a little cynical about women, lavishing his money on night-club hostesses or frivolous admirers, but Consuelo's effect on him was as immediate as her success with the experienced Gomez Carrillo.

Contemporary photographs show a tiny, slim, beautiful woman, whose face radiates the vitality of a patently vivacious, artistic and playful character. Behind her large, dark eyes there is an element of provocation as if she knows from experience that few men can resist the appeal of her apparent vulnerability and need of protection. Her attraction went far beyond her looks. A soft voice and exotic South American accent added colour to a mysterious and fantastic personality that must have been spellbinding in the dull environment of Buenos Aires and amidst the formality of the Alliance française cocktail-party.

A spontaneous imagination made her a gifted and amusing story-teller, weaving an inextricable and often changing pattern of fact and fiction about her adventures since leaving El Salvador. One of her most dramatic anecdotes concerned her marriage to Gomez Carrillo when his former wife turned up at the ceremony. The woman, dressed in black, confronted the bride with a loaded revolver, cursed her and pulled the trigger. The gun misfired.

Consuelo claimed to have been born during an earthquake before being fostered by a peasant couple who fed her on goats' milk. Other apocryphal stories about her childhood in El Salvador included witchcraft and divine intervention. She continually invented conflicting accounts of her family background and hinted that her mother, whose maiden name was Sandoval, was related to the Spanish royal family. The aristocratic particle 'de' was added to impress the French.

Her real life-story needed no fairy-tale embellishment. She was born into a big family at Armeni, a village of about 500 inhabitants in the north-west of the tiny state of 3 million people. Her father, a cold, authoritarian figure, was a colonel and had bought a small coffee plantation. Two of his brothers who lived in the same village were also colonels.

The first known impression of Consuelo was recorded by a Salvadorean poet, Claudia Lars. The latter was also born in Armeni and the two girls occasionally stopped to chat in the main street. Once, when they were about twelve, they discussed their future plans. When Claudia Lars said she wanted to be a writer, Consuelo, who even at that age was considered exceptionally pretty, said she intended to be queen of a foreign land.

At fifteen, Consuelo qualified as a village schoolteacher under a system which allowed anyone with three years' secondary education to teach at primary level, but she was determined to go abroad to learn English. She went to see the President, Alfonso Quinonez

Molina, who gave her a grant to study in San Francisco with Ursuline nuns.

During a visit to Mexico when she was only seventeen, Consuelo fell in love with a handsome soldier, Captain Ricardo Cardenas, and they married soon afterwards in a civil ceremony. It was an ill-fated passion lived out against the background of a country in permanent revolution. A few months after the wedding, the Mexican captain was killed when a train in which he was travelling was blown up by guerrillas.

The young widow's distress was brought to the notice of the Mexican Education Minister, José Vasconcelos, who had first met her when her teaching-grant was transferred from the United States to Mexico. Consuelo told the historian Mena Guerrero that they became lovers. The minister was forced out of office in 1924 during Mexico's anticlerical period when 20,000 schools were forcibly shut down because of his reputation as one of Mexico's best-known contemporary philosophers he was sent to Paris as ambassador.

Consuelo left for the French capital two months later, booked into a small hotel near Les Halles and got in touch with him. She was quickly introduced into influential Latin American circles where her beauty won her many admirers. Consuelo's first meeting with her second husband, Enrique Gomez Carrillo, was at a reception given by the artist Van Dongen, one of her contacts in the world of painting and sculpture in which she became even more involved after Gomez Carrillo's death in 1927. By the time Saint-Exupéry met her, Consuelo was experimenting in sculpture after taking private lessons in Nice and Paris. One of her first works was her late husband's death-mask, which hung in her Paris flat and supposedly had mystical powers, emitting noises of disapproval when Consuelo invited friends whom Gomez Carrillo had not liked.

That anecdote was recounted by a Russian actress, Xenia Kouprine, a regular visitor to the apartment where Consuelo was the centre of a Bohemian crowd of writers, artists, actors and musicians. Consuelo was about twenty-five at the time but Kouprine said she appeared much younger.

'She was a typical South American; small and graceful with strikingly beautiful hands and arms,' she wrote in an article in a Soviet magazine to explain why Saint-Exupéry became infatuated from the first meeting. 'Her black eyes were captivating, rather like small stars, and her skin was wonderful.'

A Kiss While Flying

THERE are several versions of the first encounter between Consuelo and Antoine. Most have been contracted or inflated by family folk-lore, although the dominant story owes much to Saint-Exupéry's severe editing. He must have been questioned many times about the circumstances which led him to break family traditions and flout the imperatives of a rich and aristocratic marriage. His reply was usually limited to a statement that Consuelo, whom he described as his *'oiseau des îles'* or tropical bird, smuggled herself aboard his plane and hid behind the pilot's seat. In mid-flight she stood up triumphantly and said that she was a respectable widow. Because she had been compromised, he had to marry her.

Consuelo told a much fuller story which had the ring of truth. She not only repeated it many times at public lectures but included the account in unpublished reminiscences. She said that Benjamin Crémieux had enthusiastically recommended Saint-Exupéry long before he introduced him, showing her a letter to demonstrate his gift for writing. When she saw Antoine for the first time at the reception, soon after his return from the long haul from Tierra del Fuego, she felt an immediate attraction despite being overwhelmed by his height and bulk.

Instead of paying a compliment, Saint-Exupéry began the conver-sation with a clumsy remark which sounded like a complaint that Consuelo was too small and skinny. She took offence and he had to stop her leaving the reception by apologizing for being a 'big bear' and offering to take her for a joy-ride over Buenos Aires.

'Don't you want to tame me?' he pleaded, while explaining his initial awkwardness by the fact that he had not spoken to a woman since leaving on a week-long inspection tour of Aeroposta's distant installations.

Consuelo's handwritten description, full of first-person quotations, has a convincing tone. Frightened by the idea of an aerial baptism, she tried to get out of the invitation by saying she had to stay with her friends, but Saint-Exupéry suggested they came along as well. He used his authority as Aeroposta's traffic chief to commandeer a Latéoère 28 with space for nine passengers. While the rest of the party sat in the back in club-like armchairs, Consuelo was given the co-pilot's seat, hidden from the rest of the party by a veneered panel. From there she contemplated the landscape until suddenly confronted with an order from the pilot.

'Give me a kiss,' he demanded.

When she declined on the grounds that a Spanish woman would only kiss the man she loved, he assumed an air of extreme sadness and said she did not want to because he was too ugly. In the silence that followed, he cut the plane's motors and announced that he was going to crash into the Río de la Plata where they would both drown. Consuelo wrote that two tears trickled down his cheeks, breaking her resolution, and she pressed her lips against his face before reassuring him that he was not ugly.

This was probably not the first time that Saint-Exupéry had used a mixture of emotional and professional blackmail to impress a woman. A daredevil flight was standard courting routine for pilots, notably for the handsome Jean Mermoz, a rival in the pursuit of girls. The reference to his supposed ugliness also sounds authentic, with Saint-Exupéry working on feminine susceptibility by using methods he had exploited since childhood. An attitude of assumed or genuine sadness usually worked wonders, and many years later a woman friend wrote saying that she had fallen in love with him because 'you know how to suffer'.

In the case of Consuelo, what may have been an amusing flirtation for Antoine quickly turned into blinding passion and he expected his love to be returned in full. In her memoirs, Consuelo revealed that Saint-Exupéry was jealously possessive from the beginning. Although he was the most attentive person she had known, this was balanced by a tyrannical side in which he treated her like his exclusive property. In Buenos Aires, Saint-Exupéry expected her to be at his beck and call, especially when he returned from long flights, and throughout his life his demanding attitude never changed. She had to drop all her other friends at a moment's notice to be beside him at a restaurant or a show while he insisted that the only love worth living was when two people were devoted solely to each other.

As Consuelo had developed an artistic and original life-style and had her own circle of friends, it was asking the impossible for her to wait quietly at home while her husband went out on potentially fatal flying missions. This was the Vilmorin engagement in another form, and yet Saint-Exupéry had recounted in *Southern Mail* the unbearable tensions involved in trying to force a woman to abandon a precious environment and devote herself to a pilot.

'I tried to drag Geneviéve into a world of my own,' Bernis laments while his plane is refuelled at Cape Juby just before his fatal crash. 'Everything I showed her turned dull and grey.'

However, Consuelo's disillusionment with Saint-Exupéry's world was a long way off during the heady first days in Buenos Aires. He cut a dashing figure as an aristocrat with a castle in France, on the verge of fame and fortune as a writer and aviation executive, a worthy successor to the colourful Gomez Carrillo. For Saint-Exupéry, Consuelo's arrival had at last brought gaiety to Buenos Aires where prudish sexual convention lived side by side with international prostitution. Not long before Consuelo arrived, he had written to his sister Simone, whom he called 'my dear feathered toad', to tell her that the Argentinian capital was 'really boring', and later he described it as a 'gloomy place' in a letter to his mother.

As his job included inspecting fifteen airfields spread over a network of 3500 kilometres in one of the most dangerous areas of the world, he seized every opportunity to escape, and was often overcome by melancholy for Paris and its Left Bank literary cafés when he reluctantly returned to Buenos Aires. Despite a hectic work-programme, he had gradually found more time to work on his next book and his love-affair spurred him into new effort. Soon after meeting Consuelo he showed her eighty handwritten pages of what eventually became *Night Flight*, and by the time he returned to France the draft was 400 pages long.

This burst of literary energy owed much to his desire to impress Consuelo. She believed in Saint-Exupéry's genius and encouraged him in a way that no woman except his mother had ever done before, particularly after he had claimed that the eighty-page outline of *Night Flight* had been written as a love letter for her. Consuelo's life with Gomez Carrillo had sharpened her talent for literary criticism and she promised to put her own creative gifts at Saint-Exupéry's service, while he took equal pleasure from her ambition to sculpt, paint and write. In the enthusiasm of early infatuation and unstinting adoration, they seemed destined to become one of the great artistic couples of the twentieth century.

The Bride Wears Black

CONSUELO and Antoine were married seven months after their first meeting, but it was only on leaving him to return to France, according to her own version of events, that the young widow decided she was in love. Just before Christmas 1930, soon after Saint-Exupéry had proposed for the first time, she told him she had booked a passage home on a liner leaving Brazil for France in early January. He was disappointed because he had hoped to introduce her to his mother who was sailing to join him for a holiday. As it happened, the two liners crossed each other in Rio de Janeiro Bay, dashing Saint-Exupéry's hopes of presenting the woman he already called his fiancée.

This initial reluctance to fit in with Antoine's plans was the first warning that Consuelo was adamant about her personal freedom. Soon after returning to France, she even told a friend that the affair was over and then pretended her fiancé had been killed, but she pushed her doubts about a reunion aside when one of Antoine's former school-friends, Henri de Ségogne, knocked at the door of her Paris flat and said that Saint-Exupéry wanted her to welcome him when his homeward-bound ship docked in Spain.

Since their parting six weeks before, he had spent most of his time with his mother, flying her 1000 kilometres to Asuncion where she painted Paraguayan scenes. Mother and son spent a good deal of time discussing Antoine's hoped-for engagement and the unfavourable impact it would have within his aristocratic family, in which marrying a foreigner, according to one family comment, was considered at the time as unacceptable as marrying a Jew.

The exceptionally strong understanding between Marie and Antoine justified her speaking out openly about throwing away his chances of marrying a rich aristocrat. Apart from any other consideration, a wealthy marriage was the only way of saving the estate at Saint-Maurice-de-Rémens from going bankrupt. Even though Antoine was paying his mother a monthly allowance, she was living on an income of barely 10,000 francs, making it impossible to maintain the life-style of her aunt Tricaud.

Money, however, was a vulgar issue for Saint-Exupéry who usually spent faster than he earned. His impassioned praise of Consuelo's exotic personality and artistic talents swept away Marie's reluctance to the point that she became Antoine's most influential advocate after the couple were reunited in Spain and she personally prepared the ground for the wedding.

On rejoining Antoine, Consuelo was spared acquaintance with a new addition to Saint-Exupéry's long list of animal friends, which included a little monkey he gave her before leaving Argentina and a bird which whistled like a locomotive. He had bought a young puma in South America as a present for his sister Gabrielle and had asked his mother to care for it during the final leg of the sea-voyage to Marseille, which she undertook alone.

During the Atlantic crossing, Antoine had taken the wild animal for walks on the deck on a lead, but this was a less predictable pet than the tortoise he once led on a string at Saint-Maurice. After he disembarked, his harassed mother found the job of looking after the puma beyond her. When the animal bit a ship's officer on the leg, the liner's captain advised her to sell it to an animal-breeder returning to France with a cargo of chipmunks.

While the story had its funny side, it also showed how little thought Saint-Exupéry gave to some decisions. The puma was obviously an unsuitable pet even though Gabrielle lived in a château. Consuelo may have asked herself whether Antoine had given as little reflection to 'taming' her and attaching a tight conjugal leash.

[137]

Many of her friends told her she was making a mistake in think-ing of marrying someone she called a 'flying madman', whose only real prospects rested in a book which had not been finished. But any second thoughts disappeared during the journey with Antoine between Madrid and the French Riviera where they had intended to join Marie at Agay, Gabrielle's home. Instead, they stopped in Nice where Consuelo owned a house inherited from Gomez Carrillo. The setting on the Cimiez heights overlooking the Baie des Anges enchanted Saint-Exupéry and he settled there to write *Night Flight*.

His wish to please Consuelo played an important part in a sudden burst of concentration in which he locked himself up for days, writing, rewriting and correcting before reading the result to Consuelo. The 400 pages were whittled down to barely a third. He probably never worked harder in his life, because Gomez Carrillo had to be outshone. His fiancée's stories of her first husband's fame were not an exaggeration. In Guatemala City, the central park had been renamed in his honour.

These were idyllic weeks in which the couple believed in each other intensely. Consuelo devoted herself entirely to her future hus-band, cutting out the rest of the world and pampering him with his favourite meals like a contented housewife. She told Antoine she was 'totally happy'.

There was one exception to their reclusive life. Gomez Carrillo had been a close friend of the Belgian-born poet and Nobel prize-winner Maurice Maeterlinck, who lived near Villefranche in a villa as large as a palace. Any lack of confidence that Saint-Exupéry had about his own writing talent was swept away during a lunch with the morose sixty-year-old introvert who usually discouraged new contacts. The two men went down to the wine-cellar where they discussed the plot of *Night Flight*, and when they returned a consider-able time later, Maeterlinck enthusiastically endorsed the marriage plans. Consuelo's belief that hazard had thrown her into the arms of one of the geniuses of the twentieth century was confirmed without reserve by the poet, who was convinced that Saint-Exupéry would one day be France's greatest writer.

All Antoine's most attractive and persuasive qualities were on display that day, one of the brightest moments of Maeterlinck's premature old age. The euphoric young couple persuaded the misanthropic poet to join them on a drive high above Nice to the skiing resort at Peira-Cava.

If there is any doubt as to whether Consuelo and Antoine were really in love, there is a photograph of them walking arm in arm in the snow, their faces radiant with shared joy. Saint-Exupéry looks slim and handsome, while Consuelo, a tiny figure beside him, smiles up at him in adoration. Similar light-hearted sentiment shines through a letter Saint-Exupéry wrote a month after they were married. Calling her 'my golden feather', he solemnly undertakes to make her happy. 'I can no longer live without you,' he writes soon after rejoining Aéropostale in Toulouse in May 1931. 'You are the most adorable woman in the world – a fairy.' He is fascinated by her 'wild little soul' and appeals to her to come into his house and 'fill it with your wonderful confusion'.

Consuelo described the weeks they lived together in Nice as the 'maddest and most beautiful' days of their lives, during which they went to Agay to announce their formal engagement to Marie de Saint-Exupéry and discuss a date for the marriage. Yvonne de Lestrange was also staying at Gabrielle's château with André Gide, who offered to write the preface to *Night Flight* as a wedding present.

Hesitation over setting a date ended during one of Marie de Saint-Exupéry's occasional visits to the house in Nice where, worried about the couple's immortal souls, she pressed them to agree to a religious ceremony as soon as possible. On 12 April 1931, Antoine de Saint Exupéry and Consuelo Suncin de Sandoval were joined in matrimony for better and for worse by Abbé Maurice Sudour, the Bossuet headmaster who had sponsored Saint-Exupéry's meeting with Beppo de Massimi in 1926.

The wedding-day was blessed by beautiful weather, with the road to the chapel at Agay brightened by blossom and the first spring flowers. Ominously, the photographs taken afterwards in the château grounds were subdued as if the couple had returned from a funeral rather than a marriage. Saint-Exupéry stands like a forbidding peasant in his Sunday best, clutching his hat. Consuelo clings to the arm of the husband who towers over her. In her left hand she holds a bunch of carnations against her frail body as she looks unsmilingly at the camera. She is wearing a mantilla. Like her dress, it is black.

CHAPTER NINE

Happiness, Freedom and Duty

BEHIND the sombre faces at the wedding there was real cause for anxiety. Aéropostale and its subsidiary, Aeroposta Argentina, had overstretched their resources and had been put into liquidation a few days before. There was no certainty that Saint-Exupéry still had a job. Nothing was clearer ten days later when, at a civil ceremony, Consuelo and Antoine were formally married at Nice town hall.

The airline's owner, Maurice Bouilloux-Lafont, had made a fortune in South America but had been involved in dubious financial deals which brought the house crashing down. In the months that followed, the glamorous image of pioneering aviation was sullied by political intrigue, sordid infighting and the eviction from Aéropostale of Didier Daurat on trumped-up accusations.

The honeymoon idyll in the villa at Cimiez also collapsed with dizzying rapidity. Almost as soon as the Aéropostale scandal broke, Saint-Exupéry accepted a job as pilot on the Casablanca – Port-Étienne mail-run. He told his mother that he had asked to return to Africa so that Consuelo could spend time in a dry climate because she suffered from severe asthma.

Until his return to Agay to spend Christmas 1931 with his family, Saint-Exupéry lived outside the struggle over Aéropostale's future, gathering new material for *Wind, Sand and Stars*. Amongst this was the passage in which his plane 'slipped from the confines of this world' during a desert flight. His radio operator, Jacques Néri, had received inaccurate information on their position while flying northwards over Rio de Oro at night. Running out of fuel, they waited desperately for guidance from silent air bases in the desert until Casablanca broke in with an urgent message from a government official, but only to tell Saint-Exupéry that he was to be disciplined for flying too close to the hangars when he left on a southbound trip. In the book, his contempt for the stupidity of officialdom reflected his aversion for the bureaucrats who were closing in on Aéropostale before it was forcibly merged with other airlines to form Air France in 1933. By then, Saint-Exupéry's service to Patagonia had already been shut down.

Saint-Exupéry's account of the near-fatal adventure with Jacques Néri makes no reference to the distress of airmen's wives as they wait, apprehensive, for planes to return, although this is an essential theme in *Night Flight*. Fabien, the pilot who dies at the end of the book, has been wed for only six weeks. His young bride is waiting to welcome him home with a candle-lit dinner and anxiously telephones Rivière to find out if her husband has landed safely. Rivière's brusque resentment at her anguished call – 'mothers and wives are not allowed in the operating theatre' – leads the author to speculate on the suffering of a flyer's family.

Rivière considers Simone as an enemy because she 'champions a self-contained world with its own rights and duties', but finds it difficult to argue against what he calls 'Simone's truth'. When Rivière makes an attempt to justify himself she does not hear him. 'Her hands were bruised with beating on the wall and she lay fallen, or so it seemed to him, almost at his feet.'

Nothing in Saint-Exupéry's writing tells how he came to terms with Consuelo's anxiety, particularly after she moved to Casablanca to join the group of women waiting for their men to come back from the long haul along a hostile coastline. The use of Latécoère 26 aircraft had made the route much safer and there was much less danger from dissident Arabs. However, sandstorms, engine failures, crashes and kidnappings were not forgotten dramas. The radio operator Jacques Néri and two other flyers had recently been taken hostage after a forced landing.

For the women left behind, there was nothing reassuring about the fact that most aircraft now took off as dusk was gathering for a long night flight or that pilots were asked to fly longer and take shorter refuelling stops, returning home exhausted after days on the move. Even without the unease about Antoine's return, the weeks in Morocco must have been a bitter revelation for Consuelo. She had given up her Bohemian, artistic life in Paris for a city which Saint-Exupéry himself found oppressive. He detested the artificial social life of French colonists, the only escape Consuelo had from the company of other aircrews' wives during his long absences.

She learned the hard way what Louise de Vilmorin had guessed; that love often played a secondary role to Antoine's need to fly. This might have been bearable in Argentina, where she was among people who spoke her own language, but in Casablanca she was a foreigner in a society caught between French arrogance and Arab resentment.

Saint-Exupéry's absence was a worse form of tyranny than his demanding presence, leaving Consuelo considerable time to think about the poor rewards of being married to an airman who was not even sure whether he would get paid by his bankrupt firm. One of the few consolations was her husband's ardent correspondence, sent back to Casablanca or France by Aéropostale's regular service when Saint-Exupéry's flights crossed other aircraft at one of the desert bases. The quantity of letters caused some amusement among his colleagues and schedules occasionally had to be bent a little to be sure that his mail was not left behind.

The eloquence of the letters gave Consuelo hope that Saint-Exupéry would quit the airline and devote himself to literature, a possibility which was strengthened when a message caught up with him as he landed at Cape Juby on 4 December. *Night Flight* had been awarded the 1931 Prix Femina, a literary award of considerable prestige decided by an all-woman jury. The message was accompanied by permission to return to France to receive the prize, as long as he brought the mail with him from Cape Juby to Toulouse.

Twenty hours later he landed in France, living up to the image of the veteran pilot defying the elements. His face was covered with stubble and grime from the engine exhausts, while his overalls were dirty and torn. Incongruously, he was protected by an old raincoat tied round with string. After a hurried stopover to report an unevent-

[143]

ful trip, he changed into a crumpled suit and caught a train to Paris where he took a room in the Hotel Lutétia.

ONLY an aviation metaphor could describe what happened almost immediately afterwards. At the very peak of Saint-Exupéry's climb towards literary fame, he became caught in an emotional air-pocket which flung him down almost to the level of the unsuccessful lorry salesman he had been five years earlier. The publication of *Night Flight* brought him so much misery that he never wrote another novel. Unfavourable reaction among his Aéropostale colleagues shocked and hurt him, making him feel that he had committed a crime by writing about their heroism.

Although he was over-sensitive to criticism, Saint-Exupéry's consternation was partly justified. Many of his colleagues considered him an enemy. Old grudges from his Cape Juby and Latin American periods were unearthed. Internal conflicts had divided Aéropostale into pro-Daurat and anti-Daurat clans. After *Night Flight*, it was clear where Saint-Exupéry's loyalty lay even before he campaigned openly with Mermoz and Guillaumet to have Daurat reinstated.

Either through jealousy or to pay off old scores, some Aéropostale pilots and groundcrew joined in a chorus of claims that Saint-Exupéry was pretentious and had used their experiences for his own glory. Others defended him strongly. Mermoz sent a telegram saying how happy he was that Saint-Exupéry's talent had been recognized and that he deserved even better in the future.

Guillaumet was in South America and Saint-Exupéry made no attempt to contact him, fearing his friend's reaction. He did not write until Guillaumet returned to France on leave. With a touch of panic, Saint-Exupéry told him that he had been condemned by his comrades for writing 'this unfortunate book', and begged Henri not to let him down. He reproached himself for writing *Night Flight* and humbly asked his colleague to stay at his flat in Paris so that they could talk it over.

Guillaumet, a man with more common sense than imagination, must have wondered what the fuss was about. He had been one of the first to read the original draft in Buenos Aires but had shied away from giving his opinion. Instead, he pointed out that his wife Noëlle had cried over Fabien's death.

Within this strong fraternal relationship, the book probably did not cause even a momentary flutter of disapproval. When Guillaumet was sent to Casablanca, after Saint-Exupéry returned in August 1932 for a third West African posting, their friendship continued as before. Once, when Guillaumet went missing during a sandstorm, Saint-Exupéry said nothing to Noëlle and took her to the cinema. Every half-hour he slipped out to seek the latest news and told her only after Henri's plane had landed safely. The incident confirmed Saint-Exupéry's awareness of the terrible pressure suffered by any pilot's wife, not least Consuelo. Even so, despite his own well-known hyper-anxiety which caused him anguish when Consuelo was late for a rendezvous, there was never any question of his giving up flying.

While *Night Flight* was to become one of the most popular French books of the twentieth century, the controversy over its eulogy of duty and obedience resurfaced long after Saint-Exupéry's death when Daurat denied that he was the model for Rivière's philosophy. Soon after publication, some critics had found the authoritarian character too fascist. Later, the often chilling concepts of blind acceptance of orders and scrupulous respect for regulations were brought into question by the war. France's misplaced trust in Vichy, which considered order more important than justice, made many people uncomfortable over André Gide's interpretation of the central message in *Night Flight*. Saint-Exupéry, he said, had underlined the sentiment 'that man's happiness lies not in freedom, but in the acceptance of duty', a precept that led many Frenchmen to collaborate with the Germans.

The End of Saint-Maurice

AFTER receiving his literary prize, awarded primarily for the quality of his prose, Saint-Exupéry strung out his leave until mid-February 1932, sharing his time between Paris, the Riviera and Saint-Maurice-de-Rémens. His hopes for a secure future dwindled. The financial and political scandals surrounding Aéropostale intensified as the company staggered from one crisis to another. With as many powerful enemies as friends in the firm, Saint-Exupéry was forced to accept an almost humiliating offer as pilot on the flying-boat route between Marseilles and Algiers, sometimes acting only as co-pilot.

Within four months of taking up this job in mid-February, he asked for compassionate leave to help his mother move to a flat in Cannes. The château at Saint-Maurice-de-Rémens had been sold to Lyon city council as a country boarding-school and the rest of the estate had been virtually given away by his mother to her tenant farmers.

Accompanied by Consuelo, Saint-Exupéry went to assist Marie during a heart-breaking ceremony in which all the château's furniture was carried out into the street to be put on sale. For two Sundays running, dealers and private buyers picked their way through the souvenirs of Antoine's childhood, haggling over prices. By the time they had finished, all that was left was the heavy buffet, table, chairs and chandelier in the dining-room and the four long wooden chests in the hallway which had once served as toy-boxes.

The sale was one of the villagers' last glimpses of Consuelo. There were several small cafés at Saint-Maurice which no woman would enter except to force a wayward husband to return home. Marcelle Lefin, who was a member of Marie de Saint-Exupéry's church choir, remembered the amazement among customers when Consuelo walked casually into her father's bar, smoking a cigarette in a long holder.

'She read her newspaper, ordered a *pastis* and drank at the counter, just like one of the labourers,' Marcelle Lefin said.

THE atmosphere inside the scandal-ridden Aéropostale was so bad that Saint-Exupéry deliberately put off returning to Toulouse at the end of his compassionate leave and had to be ordered to return three weeks later. He seized on a chance to go back to the West Africa run and in August settled with Consuelo in an underfurnished rented flat in Casablanca. The couple made their first attempt to establish a

HAPPINESS, FREEDOM AND DUTY

joint life-style. Guests, mostly Saint-Exupéry's fellow pilots, dropped in at all hours of the day and night and were surprised to see a pot on the mantelpiece where the servants helped themselves to money for daily expenses. Anyone else in need could take what they wanted without asking.

Conflicting feelings of disregard for money and a desperate need for financial security recurred in letters to friends. Over the years, the tone developed into the familiar complaint of the disgruntled artist who resented having to earn a living from writing film scripts and newspaper articles instead of being allowed to concentrate on nobler forms of literature, such as the philosophical project *Citadello*, translated as Wisdom of the Sands.

'Cinema and journalism are vampires which stop me from writing what I would like to,' he wrote in 1936 to Nelly de Vogüé.

> For years I haven't been allowed to think in the only way that would suit me. I feel like a prisoner weaving reed baskets when I would be more useful elsewhere. The obscure but powerful act of dynamic energy needed for each script and each newspaper article is one less opportunity to write a book. What you tell me about *Night Flight* doesn't do any good but causes infinite pain. It's like the call of the organ's song, reminding me there are many other things I want to say.

His own carelessness with money was matched by Consuelo's extravagance. Unused to making economies, she continued the free-spending life-style she had enjoyed during her marriage to the wealthy Gomez Carrillo. Both Antoine and Consuelo had probably exaggerated their personal resources and, in Consuelo's case, her financial situation worsened when she was forced to sell the house at Cimiez to pay for damage caused by a car crash.

Inevitably, money problems contributed to friction in the marriage, but Saint-Exupéry pushed the question of insecurity aside during his campaign in favour of Daurat, which eventually precipitated his own departure from Aéropostale. In February 1933, with the backing of Guillaumet and Mermoz, he put his future on the line

[147]

by writing a strong letter of protest to the airline management and asking for unpaid leave of absence until the affair was sorted out.

In retrospect the decision was reckless. He soon found himself in serious difficulties, although he may have believed that a Hollywood contract to film *Night Flight*, starring Clark Gable and Helen Hayes, would solve his money troubles. Unfortunately, the deal was disappointing and attempts to find a new job with another airline were frustrated by his enemies in Aéropostale.

Daurat eventually offered help, repaying Saint-Exupéry's loyalty by persuading Pierre-Georges Latécoère to employ Antoine as a test pilot. After selling Aéropostale to Bouilloux-Lafont in 1927, Latécoère had gone from success to success with new plane-building programmes and needed an extra pilot to help run in forty torpedo-carrying flying-boats ordered by the French navy. The trials were carried out on a salt lake at Saint-Laurent near Perpignan.

Three years earlier in Brest, Saint-Exupéry had had trouble coping with special seaplane techniques and his first flights on the lake were marred by mistakes on touching down. But after 200 hours of flying at Saint-Laurent, he seemed to have mastered his tendency to misjudge the angle of approach and was asked to try out new Latécoère flying-boats destined for Aéropostale's Venezuela run.

Saint-Exupéry had fallen into a daily routine which resembled the life of a bachelor military pilot on active service. His evenings were often taken up with playing his favourite games, like chess and battleships and cruisers, or in visiting local restaurants. Consuelo had to stay in Paris, where she gradually renewed the friendships with artists whom she had met before her marriage. Apart from letters, Saint-Exupéry kept in touch by telephoning her regularly at midnight.

The couple met even less frequently than when Saint-Exupéry was on the Africa run but a chance for a long reunion arose in late December 1933 when he was transferred to Saint-Raphaël. He had been asked to finish tests on the navy's flying-boat order, a plane based on the Latécoère 28, the aircraft which Saint-Exupéry flew on his first meeting with Consuelo. She hurried down to Saint-Raphaël to join him at the Hôtel Continental, ready to spend the holiday season with him at Agay, a suburb of the Mediterranean resort, and at at Villefranche with Maurice Maeterlinck. Instead, the next few days turned into a nightmare in which Saint-Exupéry nearly died in a crash before being sacked for bad flying.

The most technical description of the accident which on 21 December 1933 came close to killing four people was given by the flight-mechanic, Gilbert Vergès, who spent more than thirty years in the aviation industry. Nothing before the trial flight gave any cause for concern, Vergès said. The Latécoère 28 which Saint-Exupéry tested four days before Christmas was one of the safest models in the world and fundamentally the same aircraft with which Jean Mermoz had set several world records. Except for the floats, there was little difference from this familiar and well-proved design.

As the Latécoère 28 had been thoroughly checked at the factory at Montaudran, the flight was intended to be a routine hand-over to the naval pilot who sat beside Saint-Exupéry in the front cockpit taking notes. Vergès and a civilian technician from Paris sat just behind.

'There was a machine-gun turret in the middle of the fuselage where I decided to sit on touch-down in Saint-Raphaël bay,' Vergès said. 'I realized that Saint-Exupéry was coming in at the wrong angle and hung on grimly. The shock was terrible, breaking off one of the floats.

'The plane turned completely upside-down. The naval officer sitting beside the pilot had opened a hatch above him and was thrown out into the sea. I scrambled out through the machine-gun turret.'

Vergès swam back to rescue the civilian technician, helping him into a navy lifeboat. Saint-Exupéry, who was no longer in the cockpit, was at first given up for dead. In fact, he was unaware that the plane was lying on its back and vainly sought the escape-hatch in the cockpit ceiling. Running out of breath, he crawled down the fuselage where he found a pocket of air. When this filled with water, he almost gave up hope until he saw a patch of light. Vergès had forced open a door near the front of the plane, but had given the pilot up for lost. Suddenly Antoine surfaced beside the rescue launch, vomiting sea-water.

In seeking an explanation for Saint-Exupéry's near fatal error,

Vergès suggested that he had insufficient experience with seaplanes and could not break the habit of flying as if he were touching down on land. 'He had a tendency to flatten out too late which hardly suited flying-boats because the floats were set at a special angle,' Vergès said. In other words, Saint-Exupéry simply forgot he was not piloting a land-plane.

The accident not only ended his contract as a test pilot; it also cut short the two-month holiday he had planned to spend with Consuelo at Saint-Raphaël. It took him several days to recover completely and for much of the time he had to be nursed by his wife. Like Louise de Vilmorin long before, Consuelo had to listen over and over to Saint-Exupéry's stories of 'terrifying and sublime moments between sky and earth'. He told her how he had thought of abandoning himself to drowning after swallowing a few mouthfuls of water. The prospect of sinking slowly into the sea and finding eternal peace had tempted him.

He repeated much the same sentiment to another test pilot, Bernard Dupérier, the future commander of an RAF fighter wing in wartime Britain.

'Saint-Ex told me soon after the crash that he had never suffered as much in his life as during the time he held his breath,' Duperier said. 'When he finally gave up and swallowed a few mouthfuls of sea-water he felt a sensation of contentment and relief.'

Although Consuelo had come within seconds of being widowed for a third time, she received no promise that her husband would give up flying and find a safer career. He was determined to seek another post, this time with the newly formed Air France, a state airline made up of five companies including Aéropostale. Consuelo would have no escape from the realities of life as a pilot's wife, in which short periods of happiness as a couple could not make up for long separations and intense anxiety. Over the next few months, she took increasing refuge in the company of her friends in the art world, drank a little too much and veered towards melancholy.

La Comtesse de Saint-Exupéry

ANTOINE could hardly have chosen a wife more likely to shock accepted family opinion than Consuelo. Like her husband, she was a natural eccentric with an excessively demanding personality whose impact on his friends and family varied enormously. Time and again, Saint-Exupéry himself said he wanted to break out of his tradition-bound background.

'My cousin used to talk repeatedly about his desire to be a non-conformist,' André de Fonscolombe recalled. 'Nonconformist, non-conformist – that word still resounds in my head.'

Some of Consuelo's critics linked the rapid decline in Saint-Exupéry's fortunes to the day he married Gomez Carrillo's widow, saying that marriage ruined his life. Others argued that her inspiration was crucial. Falling in love with Consuelo helped Saint-Exupéry to finish *Night Flight* and eventually provided a theme for *The Little Prince*. Credit also has to be given to Consuelo, an accomplished painter, for the improvement in her husband's draughtsmanship which he perfected while illustrating the fable. André de Fonscolombe said there was considerable complicity between them over many things. 'The drawings are an excellent example of her influence,' he added.

During their thirteen years of marriage, Saint-Exupéry spoke of Consuelo with both adulation and exasperation. In letters he addressed her as 'my darling little girl', 'my little chick' and 'my sorceress', while in *The Little Prince* he was full of tender compliments which made the rose sound more like a sweet, defenceless child than a full-grown woman.

Antoine was known to be pathologically anxious and friends felt that Consuelo kept her hold over him by exploiting his sense of responsibility. Saint-Exupéry would acknowledge a measure of emotional blackmail in *The Little Prince*, particularly with regard to her attacks of asthma: he said the rose 'would cough enormously and pretend to be dying.

'And I would have to pretend to take care of her because if I didn't she would let herself die to humiliate me.'

There was another view that Saint-Exupéry rediscovered in Consuelo the enjoyment he once found in Louise de Vilmorin. Louise's sister-in-law, Andrée de Vilmorin, agreed that Consuelo was 'pretty, gay and charming', but she was neither as clever nor as fascinating as Antoine's first love. 'Consuelo was sweet, a nice little creature,' she said.

Consuelo tape-recorded hours of reminiscences and wrote lengthily about her life with Antoine. She also published a book called *Oppède*, tracing her life in France during the first two years of the war when Saint-Exupéry was in the United States. In none of these recollections is there an echo of the slightly hysterical tone found in some of her letters when they refer to health problems and her fears that Saint-Exupéry was leaving her for another woman. Although she admitted being scatter-brained, she was also a woman who had learnt to take care of herself after a series of personal dramas.

In *Oppède*, released after the war, she wrote of her days fleeing the approaching Germans after the Fall of France. When her train stopped in Carcassonne, she went to buy some food but the train pulled out before she returned. Apart from her other lost luggage containing Saint-Exupéry's most recent love-letter, she particularly regretted the loss of a cape with a red silk lining.

Curiously, this story repeated an incident witnessed some time before the war by Charles Sallès at Tarascon, his family home in Provence. Saint-Exupéry arrived alone by car and went with Sallès to meet Consuelo at the station. Instead of returning with her, they came back with one suitcase which Saint-Exupéry had found in the crowded corridor. Consuelo had missed the train at Narbonne after getting off to buy a sandwich. Several other bags and a beautiful mink coat had been left in a luggage-rack and were never recovered. Consuelo had made a desperate call to the station master at Tarascon in the hope of finding the expensive fur, but she was in an exceptionally good mood when she turned up the following day after hitching a lift in an old van.

'She never made any mention of the mink coat again,' said Sallès.

Consuelo's Latin temperament and unpredictable behaviour were the subject of many recollections. As a teenage boy, Claude Werth often saw her when Antoine used to visit his father Léon in the family's small apartment in the rue d'Assas on the Left Bank. Werth remembered being half amused and half embarrassed by the way she dealt with inattentive shop assistants, proclaiming loudly that they should be aware that she was the Comtesse de Saint-Exupéry. He was also struck by her thoughtlessness, recalling the day she threw eau-de-Cologne on a waning fire and nearly set the chimney alight at the Werths' country home in the Jura.

Other friends remembered being exasperated because she kept them waiting for an hour or more while getting ready to go out, an anecdote which evokes a passage in *The Little Prince* referring to the rose.

'She dressed slowly, adjusting her petals one by one. She didn't want to come out all dishevelled like the poppies. She wanted to appear only in the full glory of her beauty. Oh yes. She was very coquette. Her mysterious *toilette* had taken days and days.'

Jean d'Agay, Antoine's nephew, was often apprehensive when he went to visit her as a schoolboy. She would keep him waiting on the doorstep a long time and then flounce off in a huff if he made a misplaced remark.

One of Consuelo's harshest judges was Simone de Saint-Exupéry, who castigated her in a collection of short stories called *Météores* which she published in French Indo-China in 1943. Transforming Consuelo into a Vietnamese bride on her first visit to France with her French husband, Simone retraced her version of Consuelo's visit to Antoine's beloved housekeeper, Moisy, at her retirement cottage in the Drôme. In a story called *Pèlerinages* – Pilgrimages – the barely camouflaged Consuelo is dismissed as an outrageous and capricious snob who despises all the childhood memories which Simone and Antoine hold dear and who deliberately offends Moisy.

In private conversation, Simone liked to speculate that Consuelo had ensnared her brother by sex alone as if Antoine was still an innocent boy when he married at the age of thirty-one. Behind her remarks was the resentment that many members of the family felt for a woman considered as an intruder, despite the friendship and loyalty shown by Marie de Saint-Exupéry to her son's wife.

Even those who felt a strong sympathy for both Consuelo and Antoine were aware of the strain in their marriage but felt that the

[153]

blame had to be shared. 'They were not an ideal couple, but then who is?' said André de Fonscolombe.

> They were not made for one another. Consuelo loved him a lot but she did not know how to make him happy. She was not the perfect wife for Antoine.
>
> Antoine was often unhappy but you can't say she was bad for him. He came from a very traditional background and she simply did not know how to adapt. It was not her fault when he could not write and he may even have written better because of her. People say you must be unhappy to write, don't they?

There is no doubt that the relationship between Antoine and Consuelo became extremely difficult about three years after their marriage when he felt increasing resentment at the time she spent at social occasions without him and she knew he was being unfaithful. From then on mistrust and recrimination worsened. In 1936, Consuelo wrote to Léon Werth's wife Suzanne that she was suffering from the 'bad rhythm which exists between Tonio and me and soon it will be the end because I have no more strength'.

Much of the misunderstanding between the couple resulted from a failure to reach a compromise in their pursuit of separate artistic ambitions. What Consuelo thought was tyranny, Saint-Exupéry saw as a husband's right. He expressed his bitterness in scribbled notes, often a little incoherent. His correspondence with Consuelo was so frequent, and the tone changed so often, that it sounded like a running matrimonial row, with hastily penned acrimony being followed almost immediately by reconciliation. His compulsive need to pour out his feelings with little reflection led to many hasty accusations. Some of these letters may well have reached Consuelo after she had already received an apology. A frequent complaint was that Consuelo neglected him and that this affected his will to write. Her selfishness angered him.

'Of course, I am full of rancour against life,' he told her in an undated letter. 'You never give me what I thirst for. You'd do better to be at home more often. Isn't there a shadow of hope? I am terribly hungry for help; the help of a woman . . . to make my dinner. To pour a cup of tea. To put a hand on my forehead. When I am dead, you will realize what you have lost. You make me hate life.'

Consuelo's detractors added to damaging gossip by saying that she was repeatedly unfaithful, a reputation handed down to later generations of the Saint-Exupéry family who believed Consuelo to have been the mistress of several writers. Convinced by these stories of infidelity, Antoine's cousin Yvonne de Lestrange, who had herself been marked by an unhappy marriage, added her weight to the pressure on Antoine to make a clean break. In one of his last letters to Consuelo, however, Antoine said that Yvonne's interference was wrong. He had abandoned a long-running extra-marital liaison so that he could rebuild their marriage: another written admission that no woman could replace Consuelo. Despite his claim that frequent rows affected his work, he admitted that his imagination dried up when Consuelo was not with him and he pleaded with her to forget old scores.

Antoine may have come to the conclusion that some of the spiteful exchanges and allegations that he referred to in letters of reproach were not well-founded. Just before the Fall of France the writer Maurice Sachs had an attack of conscience about a relationship with Consuelo, which had ended in 1937, and he wrote to Saint-Exupéry to apologize for causing so much damage. He had been flattered by her attention and had wanted to believe he was more important to her than he really was.

'But it is absolutely true that during the evenings and afternoons we spent together she talked to me mostly about you in such a way that I knew full well that she could love no one except you,' Sachs wrote.

Consuelo, he said, had turned to him because she was sad and bored. She drank a little and did not know where to put her feet in the shifting soil of this earth, but 'loved only you'. He remembered Consuelo above all for her 'grace and sweetness'.

Le Grand Coup

SOME of the tension in Saint-Exupéry's marriage could have been relieved by money. Writing had not made him rich enough to cope with personal extravagances like his Bugatti and private plane. Gallimard's original contract for *Southern Mail* in 1929 included the promise to publish at least six more books, but royalties from *Night Flight* were insufficient to convince Antoine that he could live by writing alone. Inevitably he was attracted by another familiar writer's dream: *le grand coup*, which would free him from financial restraints for ever.

Hopes of earning a good living from a regular pilot's job had collapsed with the crash at Saint-Raphaël, and he had to be content with an offer from Air France in April 1934 for a post with the company's information department. The salary was only 3500 francs a month, barely enough to cover the monthly purchases of his favourite brand of cigarette, Craven A.

The job included addressing conferences abroad and he was assured of an extra 1000 francs each time he piloted a plane for one of these meetings. During the first seven months of his contract, he earned more than 40,000 francs to add to his income from *Night Flight* and fees from articles in the weekly illustrated magazine *Marianne*.

There were three other possibilities of ending dependence on his inadequate salary: patenting a profitable invention, writing for the cinema or winning one of the big prizes on offer for a long-distance aviation record. Over the next few months he would try all three, and still be left with insufficient funds to pay his gas, electricity and telephone bills.

In December 1934 he registered his first patent, an aircraft landing system, and by 1940 thirteen others had followed. Sometimes he would hint that he was making a good income out of his inventions, but this was bluff because most of them were not finally registered until 1939 and 1940, too late for him to draw much benefit. His new ideas were linked to his pilot's experience and included blind-flying aids, rocket propulsion, safety systems and navigation equipment. These complicated but practical innovations, often inspired by his increasing interest in geometry and the sciences, were evidence of his

[156]

restless and unlimited imagination; but a more promising prospect of making money was offered by the cinema.

The American production of *Night Flight* had played for ten weeks on the Paris circuit in 1934. Although Saint-Exupéry's film rights had fallen below expectations, he was impressed by the spectacular flying scenes and felt that the essential atmosphere of civil aviation had been successfully brought to the screen for the first time.

By then he had nearly completed a scenario for a film called *Anne-Marie*, begun in South America in 1931. This script has been deliberately overlooked by some biographers, reflecting a feeling that Saint-Exupéry was far from pleased with this run-of-the-mill commercial melodrama. He told friends that he had little control over the film, directed by Raymond Bernard, whose father Tristan was one of the most successful playwrights of the day.

The plot has neither the delicacy of *Southern Mail* nor the moral arguments of *Night Flight*. Briefly, five test pilots are fascinated by the same woman, an aircraft-designer and pilot called Anne-Marie, played by the actress Annabella who later went to Hollywood and married Tyrone Power. By the end of the film, the test pilots have been outmanoeuvred by a sixth character known as the inventor, who saves Anne-Marie from crashing on a test mission at night during a blinding storm. The inventor cuts into a town's electricity supply, using the streetlights to send her a Morse-coded message directing her to an airfield.

Three of the test pilots, known as the peasant, the lover and the boxer, are based on Guillaumet, Mermoz and Marcel Reine, who shared adventures with Saint-Exupéry in the West African desert and Latin America. The other three male characters, the inventor, the thinker and the detective, are all facets of Saint-Exupéry, allowing him to manipulate the whole plot, win the girl and die in an accident.

Perhaps the oddest episode is a confrontation between the detective and the thinker. The detective, like Saint-Exupéry himself, is an ace conjurer, but so is the inventor, who spoils one of the detective's acts by revealing the trick. In real life, nothing angered Saint-Exupéry more than seeing his magical secrets exposed. Towards the end of a complicated intrigue, competition for Anne-Marie's heart narrows down to the thinker and the inventor. The thinker's most striking talent is writing love-letters, but he dies in a plane crash, leaving the field to the inventor. In the finale, the detective/Saint-Exupéry has the honour of pushing the inventor/Saint-Exupéry into Anne-Marie's arms with the remark: 'Kiss him. He's a man.'

The powerful sense of personal identification in all his writing from 'L'Évasion de Jacques Bernis' to *The Little Prince* opens up endless speculation on the meaning behind the film script. Nelly de Vogüé, who spent more time studying and editing his work than anyone else, pointed out that Saint-Exupéry always wrote the same story, and there are elements of some of his dominant themes such as interdependence and courage. Otherwise, *Anne-Marie* is a misfit in his literary output, not least because the story has a heroine who is daring enough to have been modelled on the pioneer French flyer Maryse Bastier. In another uncharacteristic twist, the inventor wins her heart by technical expertise rather than an act of courage or by moral example.

Maybe nothing should be read into the script except an attempt to make some money out of a popular art-form. Over the next few years Saint-Exupéry copyrighted other film scripts, which never reached the screen, but in 1936 he adapted *Southern Mail* for a highly praised production in which he did much of the desert flying as a stand-in for the star, Pierre Richard-Willm.

His greatest screen achievement, however, was unsigned. He wrote and directed a film called *Atlantique sud*, commemorating the 100th Atlantic airliner crossing between Africa and South America. The hour-long production was the most successful documentary ever shown on the French cinema circuit and was still being screened twelve years after its gala opening in 1936. He refused a credit but would have received little benefit anyway. The film was part of his salaried work for Air France, which included writing unacknowledged articles for the company's magazine.

SAINT-EXUPÉRY had returned to flying before finishing the script for *Anne-Marie* in May 1935, hoping to pick up a big cash prize for breaking a long-distance record. He first attacked the Paris–Saigon route, and although the attempt failed in a spectacular desert crash at the end of December, the adventure turned him into a national hero.

Looking back over the year, it seemed almost inevitable that it would end in disaster. A frenetic quality had marked the twelve months. He worked exceptionally hard, trying to cope with money problems that did not leave him enough to pay the 650-francs-a-month rent on the four-room apartment at 5 rue de Chanaleilles in Paris where he had moved in 1934. He had travelled to Moscow on an assignment for *Paris-Soir* and piloted his own plane around the Mediterranean for a series of Air France lectures. In the three months before his first long-distance attempt he covered about 15,000 kilometres, often visiting family or friends at Ambérieu or on the Riviera. Between times he had finished the script for *Anne-Marie*, written newspaper articles, prepared others for the *Air France Revue* and patented his first invention.

His compulsion for creative writing was undiminished, much of it being done in fashionable Left-Bank literary cafés and restaurants like Les Deux Magots and the Brasserie Lipp where he was often seen surrounded by a pile of crumpled, rejected drafts. Café life was more bearable than working in the cramped flat which the pacifist writer Henri Jeanson called a 'fly-cage'. Lack of space was compounded by Saint-Exupéry's untidiness while his concentration was upset by the constant coming and going of Consuelo's entourage. Meanwhile, his own social life continued at a high pitch. His friends worried about his poor appearance and health, caused by too much drink and heavy food. He became fat, looked tired and complained increasingly about his liver.

His chaotic life-style, which often led to his being absent for weeks on end, was at the centre of rows with Consuelo and he hit back with accusations that she neglected him or spent too much on clothes, jewels and entertaining. However, this tension was only an indirect cause of her decision to leave the flat in the autumn of 1935 and move into the Hôtel Pont-Royal, near Gallimard's offices in Saint-Germain-des-Prés.

At home, unpaid bills had piled up and it was no longer possible to live in the apartment. Gas, electricity and telephone were cut off and Saint-Exupéry was faced with civil suits over the non-payment of rent, and demands for unpaid income tax which led to his furniture being impounded. There was not even enough spare cash to buy dog-food. Consuelo's Pekinese, another of Antoine's gifts, had to be boarded with the concierge, who accepted responsibility only after he gave his gold watch as a guarantee.

Saint-Exupéry reacted to financial pressure by spending more. In April 1934, even before the job with Air France was confirmed, he bought himself a Farman 402 touring-plane for 20,000 francs. In September 1935, with bills pouring in, he took delivery of a new Caudron 630 Simoun at ten times the price of the Farman and piloted the aircraft on his trip around the Mediterranean.

In aircraft design, the two-seater Simoun was among the world's élite, a Bugatti of the air which still has a sleek, modern look today. From 1930 onwards the Caudron company had been building planes powered by specially developed Renault engines, and their performance was way ahead of that of most rival aircraft. By 1935 the latest model was capable of maintaining a cruising speed of about 280 kilometres an hour for 1200 kilometres, confirming its prominence in the international craze for breaking long-distance speed records. The Simoun's racing success had a commercial fall-out and the aircraft served as a fast workhorse for Air Bleu, a domestic French mail service set up by Beppo de Massimi and Didier Daurat after the collapse of Aéropostale.

Only one Simoun, though, has a secure place in literature: the bright red and cream model lettered F-ANRY, with a 180-hp engine, in which Saint-Exupéry made his attempt to cut the time between Paris and Saigon before crashing and nearly dying of thirst in the Libyan desert.

The prize for arriving in less than 99 hours was 150,000 francs, enough to settle his most urgent debts. He also contracted to write a series of articles for the daily newspaper *L'Intransigeant*, the commission coming from the editor, René Delange, one of his future biographers.

Because of the phenomenal success of *Wind, Sand and Stars* in which he recounted this adventure four years later, Saint-Exupéry eventually became a wealthy man, but the immediate result of the abortive Saigon excursion was another blow to his dreams of being financially independent.

Under the chapter-heading 'Prisoner of the Sand', Saint-Exupéry devotes about sixty pages of *Wind, Sand and Stars* to his accident in the desert. Nowhere is there a hint of the sloppy preparation which preceded the dangerous trip. When the Simoun hits the ground after nearly twenty hours' flying, just 3700 kilometres from Paris, the reader has an impression that some malevolent elemental force has intervened, playing an underhand trick, luring the pilot off course and robbing him of precious altitude.

In truth, the whole undertaking was a desperate, badly planned gamble put together hurriedly to beat a 31 December deadline. The expedition was prepared the night before to the background of Consuelo's nagging, although in Saint-Exupéry's account his wife (whose name was not mentioned) was accredited with only one remark. She interrupted an important pre-flight briefing to give him a bag containing a razor and a change of shirt.

However, a close reading of the chapter captures the sense of relief when Saint-Exupéry at last sinks into his seat in the Simoun's cockpit, a comforting space which he describes as a world unto itself and home for the pilot. 'The plane is a way of escaping from towns and their book-keeping and getting to grips with reality,' he wrote, perhaps his simplest statement of all on the fascination of flying.

When he climbed into the Simoun at Le Bourget, then Paris's main airport, he had just escaped the maddening atmosphere of the Hôtel Pont-Royal which had served as the flight headquarters; but except for his chat with the meteorologist, there is little in the book about the often comic hours before take-off.

Until settling into the pilot's seat, Saint-Exupéry had taken only a half-hearted interest in preparations. He could not be bothered with mechanical inspection and, at the last minute, the Simoun had been handed over to Didier Daurat's Air Bleu. Servicing was left to Antoine's in-flight engineer, André Prévot. Unwilling to concentrate on the minutely detailed pre-flight navigation plan, Saint-Exupéry called in a friend and former Aéropostale pilot, Jean Lucas, and gave him the entire responsibility.

Lucas said afterwards that he suspected Saint-Exupéry's main motive for the record attempt was a wish to escape from his worries in Paris. At Saigon he intended to meet his sister Simone, who worked in the local archives, and spend time touring Indo-China.

[161]

'When I used to meet Saint-Ex while I was in charge of the Aéropostale base at Port-Étienne on the Africa run, he was always relaxed and happy,' Lucas said. 'In Paris it was never the same. He still burst out laughing like a child but he was always haunted by a problem of some sort or another.'

To prepare maps for the 10,000-kilometre journey, normally the pilot's personal affair, Lucas had to work through the night in Consuelo's bedroom. She kept up a constant chatter that exasperated and disturbed him. When he reproached her, she was said to have slapped his face and Lucas responded by tucking her under his arm and smacking her bottom.

'That's what I call a man,' Consuelo was reported as saying in an account of the scene written by one of Saint-Exupéry's air force friends, Marcel Migéo.

Saint-Exupéry was probably not even aware of the incident. The hotel room was the centre of a constant bustle as old friends came to wish him luck or offer advice, distracting him from a serious study of navigational risks. These visits contradict an often repeated claim that Saint-Exupéry jealously separated his friends into compartments. His well-wishers represented a cross-section of every important period in his life. While Lucas led an Aéropostale contingent, Joseph Kessel and Gaston Gallimard were the centre of a literary crowd.

Antoine's friend from the Lycée Saint-Louis, Henry de Ségogne, a well-known mountaineer, drove him to Le Bourget at 4 a.m. on 29 December. Among those waiting in the cold for the departure, scheduled for 7 a.m., were Didier Daurat and the anarchist writer Léon Werth.

During the next few anxious days the Hôtel Pont-Royal became a crisis centre. After the plane was reported missing, there was an air of family reunion as Yvonne de Lestrange and Marie de Saint-Exupéry mixed with a flow of worried callers. Marie had arrived in haste from Cannes on 1 January 1936 and spent much of the time praying for her son's rescue. She would hardly have been reassured by stories of eleventh-hour hitches. Antoine, half asleep after a series of late nights during the Christmas festivities, forgot to pack the vacuum flasks containing coffee to keep him awake over the next four days. At the last minute an all-night pharmacy sold him two flasks, which were filled at a nearby café.

His flight problems began within hours of take-off. Soon after reaching the Mediterranean, the Simoun began leaking fuel and had to turn back to Marseille. An hour was lost while mechanics soldered the punctured tank before watching Saint-Exupéry leave on what he called his 'ultimate and culminating ordeal' in the Sahara.

CHAPTER TEN

Wadi Natroun

SAINT-EXUPÉRY'S plane crashed in the Egyptian desert east of the Libyan border at 4.46 a.m. local time on 30 December 1935 while travelling at 270 kilometres an hour. By then he thought he had already crossed the Nile, and neither his description in *Wind, Sand and Stars* nor his insurance report gave a satisfactory explanation of why he was nearly an hour's flying time short of his planned route nor why he hit the ground when his altimeter was showing a height of 400 metres above sea-level.

Saint-Exupéry had flown only three-quarters of the distance he thought he had covered before he dropped below the clouds to seek landmarks, a navigation error so enormous for an experienced long-distance pilot that it inevitably brings to mind an incident in which he lost all account of time only ten minutes after take-off and landed in a field because he believed he was running out of fuel.

The only mitigating factor was an undetected change in the wind direction which slowed down the Simoun. Although the pilot had been told at Benghazi four hours earlier that he could depend on a tail-wind, this had turned against him without being noticed. Normally he would have been alerted by radio, but he had decided against a communications system to save weight for extra fuel.

Caught in heavy cumulus, Saint-Exupéry deliberately lost altitude in the hope of picking up the lights of Cairo and found the desert covered in mist, giving a deceptive impression of height. The crash, he wrote in his official report, took him completely by surprise and he and his mechanic would have been killed if the Simoun had not landed on a plateau of round black pebbles which acted like a bed of ball-bearings. The plane slithered 'like a reptile' for 250 metres, while the pilot desperately tried to bring the aircraft under control before it came to a sudden halt in a stretch of sand after the right wing had been ripped off.

After his rescue, Saint-Exupéry returned by car to the site of the wreck so there is no doubt about the glaring miscalculation of his flight position only twenty hours after leaving Paris. Even allowing for the unfavourable wind and a possible faulty altimeter, some of the cause has to be attributed to a fatigue-induced breakdown in a veteran pilot's instinct. The febrile days leading up to the flight had taken their toll and the account in *Wind, Sand and Stars* gives the feeling, as the journey progressed, of a pilot sliding into euphoria as his worries disappeared behind him. In the blacked-out security of the cabin where his solid Man Friday, Prévot, slumbered in the co-pilot's seat, Saint-Exupéry quietly puffed his cigarettes and drank an occasional cup of coffee.

There was the minor irritation of a distracting cockpit lamp, which Prévot fixed, but otherwise, as Saint-Exupéry wrote, he was happy and 'could go on like this at the controls for ten years'. In this enclosed world where there was a unique relationship between man, machine and the elements, he agreed with Jean Mermoz that the joy of flying was so intense that it made the inevitable final smash-up worthwhile. Somewhere, all sense of the passage of time disappeared against the background of purring engines and a moonless sky.

If Saint-Exupéry the pilot could be blamed for the accident, Saint-Exupéry the writer made up for his faults by the most brilliant passages in *Wind, Sand and Stars*. His three days' wandering in the desert with the reliable but self-effacing Prévot is expressed with even greater emotion than the account of Guillaumet's rescue in the Andes. The mirages, the threat of death by thirst, the hallucinations, the comradeship and the arrival of the nomadic Arab saviour with a bowl of water are the classic ingredients of desert survival, while woven into this fabric is the constantly repeated assertion that the adventure is a spiritual experience. The whole of mankind emerges stronger from this terrible trial, and the divisions of race, language and creed are wiped out.

Retelling the ordeal other than by using Saint-Exupéry's own words would reduce the value of some of the best prose in twentieth-

[165]

century literature but, as with all of his adventures, there is an unrecounted sequel and some anecdotes that he left out rather than break the noble tone of the narrative. In the book, he wrote that all he saved from the wreck was an orange, a litre of wine and a few cupfuls of water. He described how he ripped up a parachute to gather condensation which, because of the fabric's chemical coating, nearly poisoned him and his mechanic. In Cairo he told a reporter the cost of the torn-up equipment: exactly 6203 francs, enough to have paid the rent at the rue de Chanaleilles for most of the year.

On returning to Paris, he went to see the playwright Marcel Achard and begged him to recall the words of a folk-ballad, *'Aux Marches du palais'*, a song Saint-Exupéry had often sung. In the delirium of advanced thirst he had forgotten the words and they were still blocked out of his mind.

His Aéropostale colleague Jean Lucas remembered that after his rescue Saint-Exupéry had suddenly understood the biblical tale of Jacob and Esau, who sold his birthright for a plate of lentils. When Prévot and Saint-Exupéry were found, the Arab nomads forced lentils down their throats to line their stomachs before letting them lap up water from the bowl as if they were calves. Like the two lost airmen, Esau had returned from the desert dying of thirst and sold his birth-right, not for the mess of lentils, but for the water he would be given afterwards. Looked at like that, Esau was less of a fool than the Bible appeared to suggest.

Most of the extra information on Saint-Exupéry's crash comes from a diary kept by the Raccaud family at Wadi Natroun, west of Cairo, where he was taken on 2 January 1936 after walking 180 kilometres, much of it retracing his own footsteps. Saint-Exupéry and Prévot had travelled eastwards by camel after being rescued, but they were so exhausted that their Arab saviours had left them at an oasis while help was sought at Wadi Natroun 20 kilometres further on.

Émile Raccoud, a Swiss, was manager of the Egyptian Salt and Soda Co. and lived with his wife and family in a desert setting as austere as that around the fort at Cape Juby. Late in the afternoon of 2 January, an Arab messenger arrived at the factory with a pen-cilled note from Saint-Exupéry, written on the back of a flight-plan.

The note asked for the guide to be paid two guineas for his trouble and for a car to be sent to fetch him and Prévot from the oasis. The two men stayed with the Raccaud family only long enough for a cup of tea and a glass of whisky before Émile Raccaud took them on a six-hour drive to Cairo, running out of petrol six kilometres from the pyramids. Saint-Exupéry telephoned the French ambassador from the Mena House Hotel at the foot of the pyramids to say that he was safe. When Consuelo received the news at the Pont-Royal in Paris at midnight, French time, she shrieked and passed out. Minutes later she was chattering happily and, with a crowd of her husband's friends, she went to the nearby Brasserie Lipp for a noisy celebration.

Saint-Exupéry did not hurry back. With Prévot, he returned to the isolated Raccaud homestead, an oasis of colonial well-being in the shadow of the soda factory. For more than a fortnight he relaxed in a soothing atmosphere, far from his debts, paperwork and emotional pressures. There was not even a telephone to disturb him.

Writing to Émile Raccaud from France three months later, Saint-Exupéry said how much he missed Wadi Natroun and its feeling of peace. 'Here the world looks less like a desert, but in reality it is more so,' he added.

The Raccaud family took photographs in which Saint-Exupéry looks like the Michelin Bibendum, almost bursting out of his suit, his bald head covered by a beret pulled down on his brow. In one of the pictures he stands beside the wrecked Simoun whose fuselage is in surprisingly good condition. Later, Émile Raccaud had the plane towed back to Wadi Natroun and then sent by ship to France. Nearly two years later, the factory manager was still involved in a wrangle with the insurance company over compensation claimed by the Egyptian Salt and Soda Co., which had paid out more than 500 Egyptian pounds to salvage the Simoun.

Yearning Eyes

Saint-Exupéry made several references to Guillaumet's escape in the Andes when describing his own desert adventure. Against all logic, he had gone eastwards simply because Guillaumet had also chosen that direction when leaving the Laguna Diamante. If Saint-Exupéry really believed he had passed the Nile, he was faced only by the wilderness of Sinai, but it was as if his best friend were leading him to safety. For both men, the will to survive came from their devotion to their wives. Guillaumet drew strength from the small photographs he carried of his wife Noëlle. Saint-Exupéry resisted the temptation to lie down and die by thinking of Consuelo's 'yearning eyes . . . as if a flame were searing me'.

'What flame could leap higher than this that darts up into the night from my heart?' The eyes were like a cry for help and he knew that every second of silence from him 'drove the knife deeper into someone I loved'.

These are passionate words, a public admission that Consuelo was the most demanding personal force in his life. It was a statement to be read and understood by the people who knew him best. Only they could be aware that between 1936 and the publication of *Wind, Sand and Stars* in 1939 the couple had virtually been torn apart by repeated separation. Only Antoine's closest friends suspected how difficult the marriage had been, so difficult that one day Saint-Exupéry told Consuelo that he 'needed a holiday from being a husband' – a remark quoted by his wife in a radio broadcast in 1954.

The crash in Egypt had done nothing to ease Saint-Exupéry's material problems, which would have made life easier with Consuelo. In February 1936 they moved to the Hôtel Lutétia in the boulevard Raspail. Suzanne Werth received a letter from Consuelo in which she said that the first night at the Lutétia was 'perhaps the end of everything and perhaps the beginning'.

'In a very reasonable way Tonio and I have talked about living separately,' she added. 'Life will be easier because he wants to meet his "*mignonne*" at his place. Well, so be it. It is sad to feel old and not to be loved by your companion and, anyway, Tonio's friends don't like me much. Let's hope I will be more at peace living alone, alone, if I can continue to live because I am very ill.'

A complete break was avoided by taking a spacious flat in the place Vauban near Les Invalides, where Consuelo had an atelier-apartment downstairs to meet her fellow artists and where she could call them on her own telephone line. But in 1938 the couple moved into separate buildings and she predicted the end of their relationship. In other tear-stained letters, in which she named her rival, Consuelo said the other woman had 'won the day' and that Saint-Exupéry would soon 'weep as he made me weep'.

Behind the often self-pitying tone in Consuelo's letters was the real and understandable distress of a woman in her late thirties who felt abandoned in a foreign capital. As Saint-Exupéry was to write in *The Little Prince*, his rose's only defence was a handful of thorns. Her health worsened because she felt that the appeals to her husband went unheard. He 'preferred great open spaces, wrecks and ghosts from the past', she wrote.

The possibility of stabilizing the marriage by starting a family was ruled out primarily by Saint-Exupéry's restless life. However, he used to joke about his childless union, saying that there was no way he could have a baby with Consuelo because the unfortunate child would have been accidentally left in a taxi.

There was no doubt that he loved to be surrounded by children. He spent hours playing with his nephews and nieces at Agay, telling them stories and singing them songs before they went to sleep, intriguing them with card-tricks and his brilliance at chess and draughts. Mireille d'Agay, a bridesmaid at his wedding, remembered his gentleness when he lifted her and held her close after she had fallen and hurt herself. He was such a hero at Agay, where he was known as Uncle Papou, that his two nieces treasured his empty cigarette-boxes as souvenirs.

Many other children were to remember his kindness, including Paul Claudel's granddaughter Marie-Sygne Claudel, who knew him when she was four years old in New York. He drew several sketches for her while telling her fairy tales. He was also close to the two children of his American publisher, Eugène Reynal, whose wife, Elisabeth, recalled how he once joined the children in dropping water-filled paper 'bombs' from the windows of their apartment on to passers-by.

Léon Werth's son Claude kept many adolescent memories of a youthful Saint-Exupéry, who was just as ready to play with toys as to start a philosophical discussion. When twelve years old, Claude was also given a special treat when Saint-Exupéry took him on a flight in the Simoun over the château at Ambérieu while telling him stories of his childhood.

One of Antoine's favourite games was to make paper helicopters and let them fly from high buildings, a pastime that attracted dozens of young Arab spectators while he was living in Casablanca. Later, in New York, he tried to send the helicopters into the open windows of flats below. On another occasion he filled a basket with paper planes at Henri Claudel's flat and launched them from the top of the Empire State Building.

While still studying in Paris he had told his mother that he had a strong wish for a family, but concern over whether he could protect his own children must have weighed heavily on his mind. His dangerous job was not the only consideration. He was beset by health worries, often attributed to the memory of his father's sudden death at forty-one, which left his wife to bring up five children alone. The early deaths of François and Marie-Madeleine were warnings of possible hereditary illness, but the loss of Gabrielle's baby son Melchior was more traumatic.

In both *Southern Mail* and *Night Flight* there are long references to the fatal sickness of a young child, and while this had some relevance to the plot in the first novel, it sounds like an attempt to come to terms with injustice when introduced almost irrelevantly in the second.

Apart from these misgivings, there was his inability to accept adult values. This was best expressed in *The Little Prince*, with its regret that the abrupt and irreversible transition from childhood to adulthood killed off the essence of sublime infancy. The theme was foreshadowed several years earlier when he wrote of similar feelings of sadness and hopelessness in an article for *Paris-Soir* in 1935 while travelling through central Europe. The rewritten passage appeared in the closing pages of *Wind, Sand and Stars*. In it, Saint-Exupéry was struck by the angelic face of a peasant child, asleep between his mother and father.

A kind of golden fruit had been born to these parents. This perfection of charm and grace had sprung from these dirty rags. I leaned over his smooth brow and those sweetly pouting lips and I said to myself, this is the face of a musician, this is the child Mozart with the beautiful promise of life to come.

Little princes of legend were no different from him; if protected, sheltered and cultivated, what could this child fail to achieve? When a hybrid rose is born in a garden, all the gardeners rejoice. The rose is looked after, tended and fostered.

But man has no gardener. This child Mozart will be shaped by the stamping-machine just like the rest of men. Mozart will take his pleasure from shoddy music in the foul odours of sleazy bars. Mozart is condemned.

The passage ends with the words: 'What torments me is not these hollows, these bumps or this ugliness. It's as if, in every man, there is a murdered Mozart.'

Nelly de Vogüé

EVEN if Saint-Exupéry's marriage had been a success, Consuelo could not have satisfied his need for pure cerebral reflection that developed rapidly in his mid-thirties. Her intelligence and artistic talent were instinctive, not analytical, and she was probably bored by her husband's tendency to pore over abstract problems instead of sharing her preference for romance, invention and humour.

About four years after his marriage, Saint-Exupéry began to depend more and more on an intellectual sympathy with Nelly de Vogüé, a business woman whose father, Maximilien Jaunez, had made a fortune out of a ceramics firm at Sarreguemines in eastern

France. Antoine met her when she was nineteen, just after she had married a naval officer, Comte Jean de Vogüé, a Bossuet contemporary and a member of an influential aristocratic family with manufacturing and banking interests.

Nelly's importance in Saint-Exupéry's literary career continued long after his death, as she inherited and edited the draft of *Wisdom of the Sands*, wrote a biography under the pen-name of Pierre Chevrier soon after the war and continued to sponsor the publication of Saint-Exupéry's work for the rest of her life. Without revealing the fact that she was one of Saint-Exupéry's favourite correspondents in the thirties, she also anonymously published many of the letters Saint-Exupéry sent to her from all over the world. To a large degree, public perception of Saint-Exupéry's character and literary worth can be credited to her because she was also the source of much of the unattributed information that appeared in subsequent biographies by other authors, one of which was even dedicated to her.

Apart from being a novelist herself, Nelly de Vogüé had the money, business acquaintances and organizing ability to straighten out Saint-Exupéry's money problems. She was also an attentive listener during the long explanations of social, scientific, economic and literary theories that occupied his mind so much in the pre-war years.

NELLY de Vogüé, born Hélène Marie-Antoinette Jaunez, was in her late twenties when her friendship with Saint-Exupéry strengthened. Before that, they had mixed in the same privileged social circles which gravitated around Louise de Vilmorin and Yvonne de Lestrange.

Nelly's passion was painting, which she had studied at the École des Beaux-Arts in Paris a few years after Saint-Exupéry had left. Her family's business interests, however, were paramount and she suppressed her artistic vocation to take a leading role in promoting French investment in the United States in partnership with René de Chambrun, son-in-law of the future Vichy Prime Minister, Pierre Laval. De Vogüé's friendship with Saint-Exupéry compensated for some of the cultural sacrifices she had made, and she saw herself as one of his Muses. She was fascinated by his exceptional and eclectic imagination and willingly accepted his bursts of intolerance. According to her, he despised anyone who did not think as he did or was incapable of developing a vision of the world that would enable one to escape from what he considered to be a pond of stagnant water.

'However, he was capricious himself,' she wrote in 1949. 'Either he would fall into silent meditation which appeared hostile or he would give in to fits of temper and absolutely infantile sulks. From his childhood he had kept the freshness of his emotions both in joy and in anger.'

The tantrums were not restricted to emotional or intellectual conflict. De Vogüé described one of the consequences of his legendary untidiness. Referring to his flat in the rue de Chanaleilles, she said that his presence could be recognized by the disorder in his bedroom.

Crushed cigarettes, books, toothbrushes, empty tubes and scattered pills were mixed up with shirts, ties and shoes. Saint-Ex's idea of tidying up was to spread out, and even though he did not own much, all the bedrooms in the world would have been too small to contain this display.

Only his papers enjoyed a privileged order. A bedroom would not have been his own without this fantastic arrangement of his things. If someone tried to tidy it up, he refused to go back there like an animal whose den had been violated.

As she dined with him often, de Vogüé was also a reliable source on Saint-Exupéry's favourite dishes, to the point of reciting them like a menu in her biography. According to her, he liked black pudding, curry, chocolate, carp roe, aïoli, steak tartare, pâté and ratatouille with noodles. On the other hand he hated green vegetables, saying that spinach and Brussels sprouts were rabbit's food. His disgust for green beans had been a joke since childhood, but on one occasion when Saint-Exupéry was on holiday his sister Gabrielle thoughtlessly served them at a meal at Agay. Antoine burst into tears and accused her of not loving him any more.

Of his favourite Paris restaurants, the best-known apart from the Brasserie Lipp was Androuet, the cheese specialist near the Gare

Saint-Lazare, although his refuge remained the Café Jarras next to Yvonne de Lestrange's flat, where he had gone since his days at the École des Beaux-Arts. Even when Saint-Exupéry was broke, the owner served him wine in his own parlour and often lent him money when times were bad.

Along with these glimpses of his everyday life, de Vogüé also wrote of Saint-Exupéry's writing methods after watching him on many occasions in France, the United States and North Africa. He worked in a sort of physical fever and total absorption, 'sweating, cutting, crossing out and fiercely attacking parts of a sentence'.

He rewrote the opening of the chapter entitled 'The Planet' in *Wind, Sand and Stars* thirty times and rejected sentences which he felt weakened his text, even when he considered them to be beautiful. When he threw rejected drafts into the waste-paper basket, he smiled like a little boy who had been naughty or like a man dismissing a *mignonne* with whom he had passed the night.

De Vogüé received many letters in which Saint-Exupéry discusses his growing non-literary interests. Much of the correspondence reads like the spontaneous outpourings of a mind trying to catch fragmentary ideas before they slip away. They sometimes have a didactic and patronizing sound as if the writer is already preparing himself to dismiss possible contradictions, and there is the same feverish tone that de Vogüé observed when he was writing the drafts of his books and articles.

By the time Nelly became a privileged correspondent, Saint-Exupéry was preoccupied by what he called his 'poem', the first formalized outline of what would eventually become *Wisdom of the Sands*. Some letters contain elements of this philosophical work which Saint-Exupéry hoped would be as important as Nietzsche's *Thus Spake Zarathustra*. However, some of his writing first published by de Vogüé sounds like a literary version of his conjuring tricks. Although it dazzles by virtuosity of language, it tends to become argument for argument's sake, with Saint-Exupéry struggling to find his way out of a self-constructed maze.

An unsigned typewritten letter with handwritten corrections which takes up eleven pages in the Chevrier biography was in fact sent to the physician René Planiol. Essentially it is a continuation of several conversations that had taken place between Saint-Exupéry and Planiol since they were introduced to each other in 1937. The letter begins with an attempt to explain the paradoxes contained in Saint-Exupéry's 'extended idea of relativity in the outside world and my idea of an absolute in spiritual and moral domains'.

Almost without transition, Saint-Exupéry discusses jealousy, thirst, democracy, racism, poetic creation, Descartes, Newton's gravitational laws and a dozen other apparently random subjects, sometimes illustrated by equations, before reaching a long litany of personal definitions on order in the universe, and on man's creative activity. His final analysis reads: 'The biological stages are: Electron, atom, molecule, cell, organism and conscience. The material stages are: Electron, atom, molecule, heavenly body, galaxy, universe.'

Despite the weightiness of the essay, Saint-Exupéry appears to be laughing at himself in the pay-off line of the 5000-word discussion when he adds: 'What does it matter if, once again, such reflections can be criticized?'

AFTER the financial mess ensuing from the crash in the Egyptian desert had been straightened out with de Vogüé's help, Saint-Exupéry set out to prove that his ill-prepared bid on the Paris–Saigon record was an aberration. 'I have an old account to settle with the desert,' he wrote in a letter to Nelly.

In 1937, equipped with a new red Simoun, he offered to pioneer a route from Casablanca to Timbuktu, an enterprise for which he received a 40,000-franc grant from the Air Ministry and further sponsorship from Air France. This impeccably planned journey of 9000 kilometres over desert restored his confidence in himself as a pilot and revived all the satisfaction of long-distance flying. In a letter written from Oran on 16 February 1937 and published by de Vogüé, he expressed his pride at an outstanding feat of desert navigation as he searched out recognition points which appeared to him like 'islands in the ocean'.

I was happy when the tiny square appeared 30 kilometres away in the desert after 500, 1000 or 1500 kilometres of emptiness. For hours, the engine beat like a heart but that wasn't enough. A fine punishment awaited me if I fell below my own opinion of myself.

I am coming back happy with my trip and myself. Mountains, storms, sands; these are my familiar gods to be met as equals.

The trip was the origin of another Saint-Exupéry animal anecdote which became even wilder with the telling. At Dakar he was offered a lion cub which he decided to bring back to France sitting alongside him in the co-pilot's seat. In the version he related to de Vogüé, the beast started to jump around the cabin while trying to maul the pilot. To calm it, Saint-Exupéry swung the Simoun on its back, knocking the animal partly unconscious as it hit the ceiling. The manoeuvre had to be repeated every time the lion recovered its senses until the plane made a refuelling stop at Casablanca.

In fact André Prévot, the in-flight engineer, tackled the frightened cub and kept it pinned down for most of the journey. At Casablanca Prévot had to be taken to hospital to be treated for deep wounds in his arms and hands.

Place Vauban

SAINT-EXUPÉRY succeeded so well in his ambition of being a nonconformist that accounts of him sometimes appeared to be describing different people. His work-programme, split between flying and writing, defied chronology and order. Sometimes it is difficult to imagine that the humanist thinker brooding over *Wisdom of the Sands* is the same light-hearted author who earned most of his income from reporting and from writing inconsequential film scripts.

While de Vogüé stresses Saint-Exupéry's often solemn, petulant and visionary temperament, other observers, such as the pacifist writer Henri Jeanson, draw an almost comic portrait, starting with an image of Antoine and Consuelo as a couple out of an imaginary Walt Disney cartoon, the bear and the tropical bird.

Jeanson wrote his reminiscences for the magazine *Constellation* in 1968, and while there were gaps in his memory which he covered by fantasy, he had an alert eye for the incongruous side of Saint-Exupéry's personality. Nowhere was this more evident than in the new flat on the sixth and seventh floors of a block in the place Vauban overlooking Les Invalides.

This luxurious penthouse apartment, rented between 1936 and 1938 for 25,000 francs a year, three times the cost of the rue de Chanaleilles, was in the heart of the elegant 7th *arrondissement*, but, as Jeanson pointed out: 'This was home to a Bohemian who had gone to the wrong address.'

While Consuelo guided porters carrying huge blocks of stone to her sculptor's atelier a floor below, Saint-Exupéry showed Jeanson around the vast flat where huge windows gave on to one of the most beautiful views in the capital. Inside, it was the bareness that struck Jeanson.

> From far, far away you could just make out a piece of furniture; an armchair, a piano, a garden chair, a little bench and a table in white wood. Saint-Ex's room was a masterpiece of disorder and a model of jumbled objects.
>
> You stumbled over the weirdest mixture of things; a trunk, a boot, some ties, a compass, electric razors, field-glasses, shirts everywhere, American magazines, an African mask, a sun-visor, a pair of pliers, some cigarette packets and a sunshade.

It was a strange ménage at the place Vauban where the couple lived out their semi-separation between bursts of affection and recrimination. Consuelo's most exasperating habit was to rush into the room 'like a waterfall' and interrupt Antoine while he was entertaining his friends with a repertory ranging from recitations of Mallarmé with an Italian accent to leading a spontaneous chorale of folk-songs.

'She was a seductive little animal . . . very amusing, very intelligent, very lively, very chattery, who could paint, write and sculpt happily,' wrote Jeanson.

[177]

Consuelo's intrusions were never greeted with much more than a mild reproach and despite the pressures that would lead to real separation in 1938, Jeanson was struck only by the tenderness that Saint-Exupéry always showed her in public. 'She was so fragile, so small and so unbearable . . . she surprised him, fascinated him and, in a word, he adored her.'

JEANSON, who wrote mainly for the satirical, pacifist weekly *Le Canard enchaîné*, also observed two other facets of Saint-Exupéry's life: cinema and journalism. Although the filming of *Southern Mail* had left Saint-Exupéry dissatisfied because he had only limited control over the screen transcription, he was persuaded by Jeanson to discuss a British plan to film the history of aviation going back to Icarus.

The project was never realized, but the initial preparation led to a meeting between Saint-Exupéry and the aviation pioneer Louis Blériot in Paris and a visit to London to talk with the film's producer, Alexander Korda. His one and only stay in Britain was marked by a chat with H. G. Wells, a night out at a cabaret with the painter Fernand Léger, and a visit to a down-at-heel London club where he met a French bar-hostess whom he had known in Dakar.

The club-owner tried to break up his conversation with the hostess as they reminisced over long-lost friends. According to Jeanson, Saint-Exupéry grabbed the man by his tie and demanded an apology.

'There was a scuffle, some punches were exchanged and a table overturned – just like a bad film. The bar-owner apologized and all was peaceful,' said Jeanson.

Jeanson also met Saint-Exupéry in 1937 when they were both special correspondents in Madrid, where Saint-Exupéry had been sent by *Paris-Soir*. This was his second Spanish Civil War assignment. While visiting a group of anarchists, Saint-Exupéry was treated to a display of grenade-throwing which had a frightening similarity to Russian roulette. After watching a militiaman test his nerve by holding on to grenades until the last split second before throwing them, Saint-Exupéry joined in.

'He was excited by the game,' Jeanson wrote. 'He tried it with a mixture of glee and clumsiness and I warned him that he would be shot if the other side saw him.'

Saint-Exupéry shrugged off the warning with the remark: 'So what – that's the game.'

In more serious vein, Jeanson remembered Saint-Exupéry's admiration for anarchists, 'not so much for their doctrines as their way of dying. Their elegant recklessness bowled him over.'

Later Saint-Exupéry wrote this tribute to anarchism: 'If your cellar or attic produces a fine human flora, favouring such human warmth, intelligence and heart, then let's save the cellar and attic.'

Saint-Exupéry's contempt for convention, however, stopped a long way short of an espousal of anarchy. By the time he went to Spain as a war correspondent in 1936 and 1937, his religious and political views had shaken off the reactionary conservatism of his social and family background and he was absorbed in a search to replace his lost ideals. He tried to reconcile violently opposing view-points by saying that their conflict could be attributed to a lack of mutual knowledge rather than to blind conviction. He blamed the upheavals created by extremist doctrines, such as fascism and com-munism, on a breakdown in communication and a failure to try and understand rival arguments.

In 1937 France was the scene of ideological clashes during the right-wing assault on Léon Blum's socialist-led Front Populaire. Saint-Exupéry wrote in his diary that the root of all the troubles was an ignorance of the facts, that neither fascist nor communist bothered to read each other's literature or tried to reconcile opposing theories.

At the same time, Saint-Exupéry never veered from his belief that a deep spiritual quality would save man from his own folly if he could discover the common goal which existed outside himself. This was illustrated by one of the best-known sentences in *Wind, Sand and Stars* – that 'loving is not looking at each other but looking together in the same direction'; the impression conveyed is that even the worst enmity can be bridged by 'essential words . . . the truth of truths'.

He recounts an episode in which a Spanish republican soldier and a fascist infantryman exchange greetings from the trenches in darkness and ask each other what they are fighting for. One answers

[179]

ANTOINE DE SAINT-EXUPÉRY

'Spain,' and the other, 'The bread of our brothers.' The conversation concludes with a mutual 'Good-night, friend' from two men who would try and kill each other when day dawned. In reference to their motives for fighting, Saint-Exupéry says: 'The words were not the same, but their truths were identical. Why has this high communion never prevented men from dying in battle against each other?'

Although the exchange between the two soldiers is narrated in great detail, the story is an allegory, intended to reinforce Saint-Exupéry's own arguments on the underlying brotherhood of man: an ideal that would have even greater significance for his readers when France fell into the darkness of defeat in 1940, torn between Gaullists and Pétainists.

The two Spaniards were called Leo and Antonio. Saint-Exupéry's closest friend was Léon Werth, an anarchist writer. They had spent hours debating from opposing political trenches, one speaking for France and the other for the bread of our brothers, yet the discussions had only strengthened their friendship, one of the most surprising in contemporary literature.

CHAPTER ELEVEN

Terre des Hommes

Léon Werth

LÉON Werth was twenty-two years older than Saint-Exupéry, and yet the relationship between the two men was described by Werth's son Claude as 'a brotherly friendship based on equality, not at all a father-son affinity'. This was not the only paradox. The man whom most friends believed to have been Saint-Exupéry's most trusted confidant was a Trotskyist Jew, committed to demolishing the privileges of the aristocracy.

In the rigid, class-conscious society into which he was born, Saint-Exupéry himself was often mistakenly written off as a communist, but his broadminded approach to social and political questions was far to the right of Léon Werth's. What joined them on an intellectual level was a tolerance of each other's views. They enjoyed a form of verbal chess, exchanging knowledge across a no man's land of differing family backgrounds and professional experience.

Werth wrote eighty pages of recollections under the title of *Saint-Exupéry, tel que je l'ai connu* – Saint-Exupéry as I Knew Him – in which he denied that he was a decisive influence on his friend. Saint-Exupéry himself had said in a published letter that when they argued he usually ended up by saying that Werth was right. 'What he meant was that despite our difference of views, we always started out on a common plane which was much higher than our disagreements,' Werth wrote. The two men were also emotionally attached and Saint-Exupéry became part of Werth's small family. He was a regular visitor to their Left-Bank apartment and their country home at Saint-

Amour in the Jura, only 60 kilometres from Saint-Maurice-de-Rémens.

Léon Werth and his wife Suzanne shared the problems of Saint-Exupéry's marriage, providing sympathy and comfort for both Antoine and Consuelo. Whenever he lost contact with Consuelo, who had a habit of disappearing without warning, Saint-Exupéry would turn first to the Werths. When they were absent from the rue d'Assas, he often left distraught messages, usually covered with sketches, on the drawing-room table. Consuelo also poured out her sadness and loneliness, particularly to Suzanne.

The friendship between Antoine and Léon started in 1935 after a formal introduction by René Delange, editor of L'Intransigeant. When it was suggested he should meet Saint-Exupéry, Werth reportedly replied, 'A Prix Femina – that's going to be boring.'

Saint-Exupéry might not have been too enthusiastic, either. Werth was nearing sixty and had a reputation of being ponderous and a little dry, an image that comes through in photographs of a schoolmasterly man with a solemn look, a pince-nez and a beak-like nose.

The meeting was arranged because of Saint-Exupéry's impending trip to the Soviet Union to which Werth had earlier been refused entry because of his attacks on Stalinism. Werth had been involved in unorthodox left-wing politics for more than twenty years, and they met at the height of Saint-Exupéry's own exploration of alternative political systems. As an example of nonconformity, Werth was an inspiring model. Behind the clouds of smoke from his pipe there was a natural rebel, a man as much an original thinker as Saint-Exupéry. While Saint-Exupéry was searching for a passage out of his traditional social and religious upbringing, Werth had been a free-thinker since childhood.

His Jewishness was a legacy of his middle-class parents rather than a religious conviction, but there had been no escaping the anti-Semitism stirred up by the Dreyfus Affair, which was at its height at the turn of the century when Werth abandoned tertiary studies and took on a series of small jobs, including portering in the Paris food-market, Les Halles. Until then, Werth seemed to be destined for a brilliant academic career after winning a national prize for philosophy while studying at a Lyon lycée.

Following his national service in the army, he took up journalism and befriended the writer and art critic Octave Mirbeau, who was twenty-eight years older. In the years up to the Great War, Werth himself became an influential art critic and in 1913 published his first novel, *La Maison blanche*, a semi-autobiographical work with a preface by Mirbeau. Although several other books were to follow, Saint-Exupéry's complicity seems to have been based more on Werth's refusal to align with convention, whether literary, political or social, than on his writing.

Werth served as an infantryman at the front in the Great War and returned as a committed pacifist. In 1919, in the midst of patriotic official ceremonies consecrating heroism and sacrifice, he published a scathing anti-militarist novel of his own experiences called *Clavel soldat* – The Soldier Clavel – which caused a scandal. In 1926 he visited French Indo-China and wrote a virulently anti-colonialist book called *Cochinchine*. His individualism alienated him from the orthodox left as much as from the reactionary right. Although Werth wrote for communist papers and was vice-president of the Anti-Fascist League in 1930, his criticism of Stalin offended the Communist Party and he was boycotted.

In 1935 the Soviet experience fascinated the French literary élite, not least André Gide whose *Retour de l'URSS* – Return from the Soviet Union – and its sequel, *Rètouches à mon retour de l'URSS*, started a rush of disillusionment with Stalinism. The political basis at the origins of the contact between Werth and Saint-Exupéry was, however, quickly overtaken by a genuine desire to share as much time together as possible.

Werth was too discreet in his short memoir to talk much of their personal closeness, but he gave some of the most enlightening descriptions of a man whom he called 'this character out of Balzac'. Perhaps the most perceptive remark was on Saint-Exupéry's inability to sustain a mood of happiness for long.

'Saint-Ex was at the same time the most transparent and anxious of men,' Werth wrote. 'He would abandon an apparently well-established feeling of joy in the middle of the road. He was loyal to everything except happiness.'

Despite this reference to ominous retreats into melancholy, most of the images recorded by Werth are amusing, at least to those who loved Saint-Exupéry for his faults as well as his qualities. One reminiscence referred to the soundness of his sleep, which ruined many early-morning appointments. Repeated shouting and shaking were in vain. On one such occasion, Saint-Exupéry raised his head, looked out of one eye and then returned to a 'kingdom of dreams, so closed and vast, that one was afraid of the tons of visions and unconscious thought that it could contain. While he fell back into another sleep, it was possible to believe that the whole world, sea, land and planets had been affected as well, falling into slumber and halting their course.'

Another time, Claude Werth was told by his father to ring a handbell in Saint-Exupéry's ear after other attempts to wake him had failed.

Léon Werth made an acute observation on Saint-Exupéry's fascination with card-tricks which, he said, were a method of dividing rationalist thinkers from 'those who were ready to place their confidence in a miracle and did not think that innocent wonderment was a fall from grace'.

Of all Saint-Exupéry's friends, Werth was perhaps the most ready to make a virtue out of his demanding personality, including his habit of telephoning in the middle of the night to sort out a mathematical problem or to ask to hear a tune he had forgotten. Often he would insist on an immediate meeting at a moment's notice when most people had gone to bed.

De Vogüé confirmed Saint-Exupéry's mania, saying that he used to reach for the phone at any hour of the day or night, often awakening his friends with a call from the other side of the world in the early hours of the morning. 'It was very exciting, but the conversation was so full of ideas that it took hours to get back to sleep,' she said.

His doctor, Georges Pélissier, said that Saint-Exupéry was so addicted to the telephone that he once saw him dial the same number about fifty times in the hope of contacting a friend. 'The telephone was an opportunity for extravagant spending,' he added. 'Saint-Ex telephoned as often as he lit a cigarette. If I was told that someone had been trying to call me from some unexpected part of the world like Casablanca, New York or Besançon I was sure it was him.'

Saint-Exupéry may have had difficulty maintaining a sense of joy, but this did not preclude him from constantly seeking amusement – taking the Werths to Luna Park funfair in Paris, for instance, or starting a singsong around the grand piano in their flat. Once, on a hot summer's day, he saw two West Indians in the street below and invited them in to sing Creole songs. Many evenings were spent in local restaurants debating with Saint-Exupéry on an endless range of subjects including science and economics. It was a measure of their sympathy that Werth never saw Saint-Exupéry react with the irritation he often showed to other people who would not accept his viewpoint.

'His conversational tone was always confidential, slightly soft, shunning any sublime varnish,' he wrote. 'He never changed this tone, not because he was polite or had learnt to control himself. He hated any polemic which was based on meanness or blind stubbornness.'

Georges Pélissier, however, felt that Werth was unlucky not have seen Saint-Exupéry when he was angry. The doctor described Antoine's wrath as a spectacular show like an unchained sea which would be followed by the 'adorably delicate nature of his repentance'.

The one subject over which there was never a shadow of conflict between Antoine and Léon was their shared love of the seventeenth-century philosopher Blaise Pascal – a love which, Werth said, they raised to the level of a cult. 'We believed that no one among French writers had used words with such power,' Werth recalled. 'Each word was a drop of blood. Saint-Exupéry himself played variations on Pascalian themes after which all literature appears savourless.'

Léon and Suzanne Werth had been among the privileged few to see Saint-Exupéry leave Le Bourget for the ill-fated trip to Saigon in December 1935. The replacement Simoun, F-ANXK, also became a familiar machine. Werth would often drive down from his country home at Saint-Amour in the Jura in his old Bugatti to pick up Saint-Exupéry at Ambérieu airfield, but was sometimes a passenger in the Simoun on flights across France.

On one occasion, Saint-Exupéry deliberately flew the plane towards a forest, only gaining altitude at the last second. 'I wanted to dazzle you a bit,' he explained. It was on these often hair-raising trips, in which Saint-Exupéry delighted putting the plane into a dive before accelerating heavenwards, that Werth observed the almost reverent attitude Saint-Exupéry assumed when he climbed into the pilot's seat. 'His movements were those of a gentle giant and he reached the pilot's seat with heavy gestures, installing himself as if he was about to meditate.'

Meditation did not save Saint-Exupéry from the worst accident of his career when the scarlet Simoun crashed in Guatemala in 1938. The consequences of that accident would weigh heavily on him for the rest of his life.

La Toile Souveraine

IN February 1938 Saint-Exupéry made an official attempt to pioneer a 14,000-kilometre air route from New York to Patagonia. The operation was backed by the French Air Ministry but, as with the Saigon record attempt, the aviator's principal motive was to escape vexations at home.

'His personal life was tormented at the time,' de Vogüé wrote. 'Certain conflicts were tearing him apart and he hoped that a spell of action would cut through disputes. The trip was instigated for reasons of interior necessity. The technical interest did not justify the risks.'

Weeks of persuasion were needed before official sponsorship was given and by that time Saint-Exupéry's private life had entered a new period of calm. According to de Vogüé, he would have called off the flight if preparations had not been so far advanced.

He and Consuelo had agreed to give up the flat at the place Vauban and live in separate apartments. Life together had become impossible. In later letters to her, Saint-Exupéry referred to 'so many, many, many nights of rows, screaming and insults' that had spoilt their marriage and complained that quarrels emptied him of the desire to work for weeks. By the end of 1937, Consuelo was so worried about the possibility that he would soon leave her for ever that she consulted lawyers.

Despite the rift, there was no sign that Saint-Exupéry's fascination with her was diminishing. In the six years between 1938 and his death, he dwelt many times on his inability to stop loving her.

'Consuelo, I am writing a love-letter to you this evening,' he said during a later break-up. 'Despite so many wounds, so many unheard words and appeals which die against the window of your soul it seems that I still have more love than ever found its way [to you]. There is something in you that I love, where joy is as fresh as April lucerne.' .

Even though many of his letters complained of her neglect, he also criticized himself. 'I cannot tell you the reasons why you should love me because there aren't any. The reason for loving is love itself.'

THERE was no group of friends to see Saint-Exupéry leave a snow-covered New York on 15 February 1938 at 6.30 a.m. His flight engineer was again André Prévot who had accompanied Saint-Exupéry and the Simoun, F-ANXK, during the Atlantic crossing on the liner *Île-de-France*. The plane was almost identical to the Simoun which had crashed in Egypt. Saint-Exupéry had been flying the aircraft since taking delivery in August 1936, seven months after his ordeal in the desert, and there had been no indication of technical problems. Like the Sahara crash, the accident in Guatemala, 32 hours and 5500 kilometres from New York, was caused by an inexplicable lapse in the pilot's instinct.

This time, Saint-Exupéry was not tired, having slept the night before the accident during the last American stopover in Brownsville, Texas; but he paid little attention to routine servicing when the Simoun touched down at Guatemala City soon after lunchtime on 16 February. Although Saint-Exupéry understood basic Spanish, he left Prévot to supervise refuelling. There was speculation afterwards that Prévot had overloaded the plane with petrol after confusing gallons and litres, a fatal mistake because Guatemala City was 1200 metres above sea-level and the thin air affected the Simoun's lift-off capability.

Although the initial error over fuel could have been Prévot's, there was no explanation of why Saint-Exupéry did not discover it when he checked the controls. Soon after starting the take-off run along the 1200-metre airstrip, he realized that the plane was carrying too much weight. Rather than hit a low embankment at the end of the runway, he made a last-second bid to gain altitude. The plane barely cleared the obstacle before plunging back to earth.

Photographs taken immediately afterwards show little more than a heap of broken metal scattered over more than 150 metres. The pilot and engineer were hauled semi-conscious from the wreckage. Prévot suffered a broken leg among other injuries. He never flew with Saint-Exupéry again. Apart from sustaining severe concussion, Saint-Exupéry broke his jaw and right wrist, while his left arm and shoulder were so badly damaged that he was unable to raise his arm fully for the rest of his life, an injury which prevented him from using a parachute.

He spent six weeks in hospital in Guatemala City. Four years later he recalled the accident in an interview in *Harper's Bazaar*, and spoke of it reawakening a long-lost memory of childhood. His wounds festered, causing him delirium for much of the time he was under intensive care. He continually called for '*la toile souveraine*', the sovereign cloth, but on recovering consciousness could not explain to the nurse what he had wanted. In Lyon a year later, while stepping out of the funicular railway car not far from the flat where he had spent much of his childhood, he saw an old poster advertising '*La toile du Bon Secours, souveraine pour les plaies et les brûlures*' – First Aid linen, the sovereign remedy for wounds and burns.

Consuelo told two British writers, Margaret Stewart and Richard Rumbold, that she flew to El Salvador from Paris before the accident because she had a foreboding that Saint-Exupéry was in danger. As soon as she heard of the crash, she made the short journey to neighbouring Guatemala where she refused to authorize amputation of his left hand.

'On the contrary, she called in a sort of witch-doctor,' the biographers said. 'She never hid the fact that she believed that her husband's recovery was due only to magic and he was ready to share this opinion. As for her presentiment of the accident, she put that down to a kind of telepathy.'

Her intervention did nothing to put off the impending estrangement. When Saint-Exupéry left for further medical treatment and two months' convalescence in New York on 28 March, Consuelo went back to El Salvador to visit family and friends. The couple never again had a settled life together until the period in 1942 when Saint-Exupéry wrote *The Little Prince*.

PHOTOGRAPHS taken on his return to Paris in the summer of 1938 show a slimmer and more handsome Saint-Exupéry. His appearance belies his chronic inability to dress smartly as he stands smiling at the camera in a new double-breasted suit and a grey silk tie. But behind his apparently relaxed appearance there were new anxieties.

In New York more fractures had been discovered, and his weeks of pain were worsened by nervousness which caused him to flinch at sharp sounds; he also complained of a constant buzz in his ears. Post-accident fevers continued for weeks until surgeons discovered a small green plant in the wound on his wrist. He insisted on leaving hospital before doctors were sure that there were no further complications. Over the next five years, during which Saint-Exupéry often suffered considerable pain and high fevers and spoke continually about the possibility of serious disease, doctors never agreed on whether he was prone to hypochondria or suffering delayed effects of his crashes.

The only positive result of the trip to America was an enforced stay in the United States, a country which had enthralled him from the moment he set foot there for the first time in February 1938 to prepare for the flight to Patagonia. He was to spend more time in the United States in the years up to his death than he spent in mainland France, but his published writings and letters give the impression of a continually changing love-hate relationship. He was both attracted and repelled by American consumerism, treating its products like toys and collecting electric razors, recording-machines, an electric organ and other gadgets. At the same time he abhorred all the subtle regimentation of an industrial society, seeing it as almost as grey and threatening as the Soviet Union.

In the long run the positive aspects overcame most of his distaste, not least because America fulfilled his impossible dream of becoming a rich man. His long convalescence in New York after the Guatemala catastrophe at last helped him to concentrate his mind on perfecting *Wind, Sand and Stars*, which would make him as famous in the United States as in France.

UNABLE to face writing another novel after the unfavourable reaction of some fellow pilots to *Night Flight*, Saint-Exupéry had been thinking for some time of arranging his magazine and newspaper articles for publication in a single volume.

In 1945, André Gide claimed to have initiated the project by suggesting a 'sheaf or bouquet' of original writing about aviation modelled on Conrad's *Mirror of the Sea*. On his advice, Saint-Exupéry had immediately read the collection of true stories of ocean life and later showed a selection of his own writing to Gide, who said it 'surpassed my dreams, hopes and expectations'.

As the talent-scout for Gallimard, Gide had influenced Saint-Exupéry from the mid-twenties. Just as Saint-Exupéry had been adopted by Werth's family, Gide counted on the friendship of the younger writer's relatives, although his contact with Saint-Exupéry was based mainly on professional respect.

Gide had been a friend of Yvonne de Lestrange before Saint-Exupéry's student days in Paris. He also enjoyed the company of Marie de Saint-Exupéry and they were neighbours in the Provençal village of Cabris during the Second World War. After fleeing to Algeria in 1943, Gide often dined with Saint-Exupéry following the latter's return from the United States and tried to convert him to Gaullism.

However, even Gide's extensive diaries give little information about his impact on Saint-Exupéry's literary style and humanist ideas. Without admitting it openly, Gide was probably a little in awe of the virile, adventurous younger writer with his aristocratic family.

The admiration Gide showed for Saint-Exupéry, a man thirty years his junior, was matched by his fascination with the quixotic and reckless André Malraux. In these relationships with writers whom Gide believed to be the most brilliant literary brains of the twentieth century, there was an element of adulation for men of action.

[190]

Despite the posthumous praise that Gide lavished on Saint-Exupéry, theirs was not an easy friendship; it lacked the simple readiness to accept opposing opinions that Saint-Exupéry shared with Werth. Saint-Exupéry was often disconcerted by Gide's moodiness and complicated personality, and in recollections set down after Antoine's death, Gide admitted that he was often at odds with him.

'On certain points and people, we just couldn't get on,' Gide wrote after the war. 'He ceaselessly returned to these differences in a mad charge with the stubbornness of an obstinate child. Then he immediately telephoned afterwards to say: I think I've upset Gide.'

Gide's idea of gathering together a sheaf of articles in a single volume was only one of a series of events that resulted in Saint-Exupéry's most popular pre-war book. After the Guatemala accident, he lived for several weeks in a New York East River apartment lent by Colonel William Donovan, future head of the wartime secret service unit that later became the CIA. Between visits to hospital, where surgeons still considered amputating his left hand, Antoine spoke of his plans to several literary contacts.

Jean Prévost, editor of the defunct *Navire d'argent*, was in New York on a university scholarship and introduced him to a publisher, Eugène Reynal, whose new associate, Curtice Hitchcock, had first met Saint-Exupéry in Paris. Exactly when a deal was struck is not clear, because a contract was not signed until Saint-Exupéry was approached by a literary agency on his return to Paris in the spring of 1938.

According to Rainer Biemel, the middleman in the negotiations, Saint-Exupéry was offered a pre-publication payment of 5000 dollars by Hitchcock and Reynal, the most he had ever received for a book. In addition, Gallimard offered enough money to cover the frequent advances made to Saint-Exupéry during the seven-year wait for the promised follow-up to *Night Flight*.

IN March 1938, Saint-Exupéry moved to a flat at 52 rue Michel-Ange in the 16th *arrondissement* while Consuelo set up an apartment and atelier in the 7th *arrondissement* near their former home at the place Vauban. Rue Michel-Ange was on the outskirts of the city near the Auteuil race-track and was the furthest Saint-Exupéry had lived from the centre of the capital. Communication with Consuelo, except by telephone, was infrequent and she took the split badly.

She wrote to Suzanne Werth saying that she had suffered for three years because of the impending separation. The heart-break was agonizing, she said, as if crabs were clawing at her stomach, and she believed that Antoine had left her for good so that he could entertain another woman at his new flat.

If the rue Michel-Ange was a love-nest, it had Saint-Exupéry's unorthodox mark on it. Like his other apartments, it was open house to a flow of friends and acquaintances who were welcomed by the Russian butler, Boris, a lugubrious former general in the Tsar's defeated army who previously oversaw the divided household at the place Vauban.

Discussing business in what became the campaign headquarters for the *Wind, Sand and Stars* project was not easy. The literary agent, Rainer Biemel, went to the rue Michel-Ange to spell out the terms of the American deal and had to watch while Boris served Saint-Exupéry a spoonful of olive-oil, a daily remedy for liver trouble. As Saint-Exupéry grimaced at the taste, Biemel told him he could buy cubes of frozen olive-oil from a restaurant in Marseille, a suggestion that was taken up. Later, friends frequently complained that their refrigerators were packed with frozen cubes of olive-oil whenever the author came to stay.

Having settled the question of the author's poor digestion, Biemel was given a demonstration of his latest gadget, a cartridge-loaded fountain-pen which avoided the problem of pressure leaks from conventional fountain-pens while flying. With these distractions over, Saint-Exupéry was persuaded by the agent to meet an American representative of the US publishing firm and hand over a pile of re-edited articles for translation.

Man-made Volcanoes

PREPARATION of *Wind, Sand and Stars* was the most challenging period of Saint-Exupéry's literary life. He was no longer just a pilot or a war correspondent relating his experiences in as dramatic a fashion as possible for magazine or newspaper readers. He was an author aspiring to perfection.

Long debates with Werth over writing style, in which they shared adulation for Pascal's 'drop-of-blood' prose, contributed to an almost paralysing search for excellence. Saint-Exupéry was reluctant to present a finished manuscript for the new book, knowing that his primary critics were relatives and friends whom he had spent years trying to impress with his intellect and writing skill.

His lack of self-confidence had been evident the year before when he promised at least eight articles to *Paris-Soir* about the Spanish Civil War on the strength of an 80,000-franc advance. He repeatedly delayed their delivery as he wrote and rewrote the text. Three articles were published more than two months after his return from Spain after several broken promises on deadlines to the editor, Hervé Mille. The delays were not caused by laziness but by an inability to let go of a manuscript until it was faultless. Saint-Exupéry's nerve cracked when he submitted the fourth article.

At 5 p.m. on the day before the piece was due to appear, he burst into Mille's office and asked to see proofs, supposedly to make final alterations, and then ripped them up in front of the astonished editor. To make sure the article would never be published, he stuffed the torn-up paper in his pocket and left without an explanation.

If the idea of unfavourable reaction to journalism could cause so much apprehension, the prospect of publishing a book was worse and he fell back on procrastination. Throughout the summer of 1938, Saint-Exupéry hunted for the ideal place to write: somewhere that would recall the gentle euphoria of the days in Nice with Consuelo before the completion of *Night Flight*.

He wasted time by visiting Gabrielle and his mother in Provence, before making another pilgrimage to his school at the Villa Saint-Jean at Fribourg to recreate the nostalgia which he had evoked in *Southern Mail* ten years earlier. With a new burst of hope, he took a cruise on Lake Geneva but left the ship without making much progress and tried another source of inspiration.

A brief visit to the château at Saint-Maurice-de-Rémens disheartened him even further and he drove on to the Drôme *département* in the south to visit Moisy, the housekeeper, in her tiny house at a village called Étoile.

The weeks away from his desk added only a few words to the planned book, and he finally made his way back to the rue Michel-Ange where he worked on the terrace of the apartment looking out over the Seine, helped by his cousin André de Fonscolombe. Saint-Exupéry spent more time cutting out long passages than adding new ones and he at last took the plunge and handed over most of the material for the French edition to Gallimard in late August 1938.

For the American version, he depended heavily on the advice of his translator, Lewis Galantière, who insisted on reinserting copy that Saint-Exupéry had taken out of the original version. Galantière also demanded additional sequences to fill in essential background to events and places that were unfamiliar to American readers. Because Saint-Exupéry stubbornly refused to learn English, often claiming that he did not want to pollute his writing with foreign idioms, he was less worried about critical reaction in the United States than in France and even left the final decision on a title to the American publishers.

For the French edition, the title was one of his principal concerns. After long reflection, he asked André de Fonscolombe for help. 'Find me a title and, here, I'll give you 100 francs if you do,' he said.

His cousin typed a list of twenty titles, most of them now forgotten. 'He seized on one of my ideas, *Terre des humains*, and immediately transformed it into *Terre des hommes*. He was like that; he always found the simplest word which changed everything. That was his gift. It was instinctive. By his choice of a word or expression he always wrote exactly what was right.'

Fonscolombe was given his 100 francs, but by the time the definitive title was chosen the book was already in proof form with its provisional name *Étoiles par grand vent*, Stars in the High Wind. While this was more poetic, Saint-Exupéry's final choice was a better reflection of the compelling humanist ideas the book was intended to convey through its connecting themes. The stories of the desert, long-distance flights and battles with the elements were not just brilliantly told adventurer's tales but were presented as the backdrop for Saint-Exupéry's message that man's condition was an eternal and sacred quest to surpass himself in an atmosphere of brotherhood.

The Second World War, which broke out within six months of

the book's publication, proved that his trust in a common human cause was an illusion, as Saint-Exupéry recognized in a letter to Consuelo in 1943 after witnessing the infighting among French exiles in New York.

'The world is all twisted, all twisted. And I'm going to be unhappy and suffer because there is no clear truth to give to men. And I, who so much love the truth, I will suffer for the truth without even being sure of my own.'

The optimistic message of *Wind, Sand and Stars* was, however, not wasted. Saint-Exupéry was unaware that his idealism, even though based on a naïve premise, gave hope to thousands of French people during the worst days of the war and in the sombre aftermath.

As time passes, the lasting achievement of *Wind, Sand and Stars* is the lucid use of language to convey a mood, scene, character or event with extraordinary economy. This often sublime imagery reflects the intellectual effort Saint-Exupéry dedicated to writing as an art. His progression as an author can easily be traced by comparing *Wind, Sand and Stars* with the original stories published in draft form as articles in national newspapers and magazines. Subsequent changes for the book show the workings of Saint-Exupéry's mind as he re-edits his own material for a work he correctly believes will stand the test of time. Editions of *Paris-Soir, L'Intransigeant* or *Marianne* in which he first wrote of his experiences are still easily available for comparison. Subsequent reflection on these events changed Saint-Exupéry's observant reporting into timeless literature.

His fascination with the precision of the written word was witnessed by friends who had to listen to him reading unfinished passages that might be changed yet again on another hearing. If debt and deadlines had not overcome his reluctance to offer work for public scrutiny, this process of rigorous self-criticism might have resulted in his published output being even smaller than it was.

Saint-Exupéry was preoccupied as much by tiny detail as by the broad sweep of personal conviction. Georges Pélissier, who served as both doctor and literary critic, was one of many people consulted before *Terre des hommes* was published. Saint-Exupéry flew to see him in Algiers soon after Christmas 1938 for what was primarily a discussion on grammar.

[195]

This was the last phase of a creative process often observed by Pélissier during a fifteen-year friendship. Saint-Exupéry usually wrote his first draft effortlessly before beginning a long and arduous process in which, in his own description, he separated the precious stones from the matrix.

'He had a religious respect for the purity of language,' Pélissier wrote in 1951, recalling how the author reacted when his sister Simone mischievously cabled from Saigon to point out the sole grammatical error in *Terre des hommes*. Pélissier believed that Saint-Exupéry should have been given the benefit of the doubt. 'Armed with my own knowledge, I tried to comfort him but it was no use. He remained inconsolable.'

Even after handing in his copy to Gallimard, Saint-Exupéry continued to pore over the text and produced another version of some episodes, with tiny variations, for *Paris-Soir*, in the late autumn.

Because he was again short of cash, he had offered to make amends for the Spanish Civil War articles he had failed to deliver in 1937. In October 1938 he contributed three essays on the threat of war, part of a series which included pieces by Colette and Winston Churchill. Between 8 and 15 November he submitted another six articles, all of them relating to incidents which were included in *Terre des hommes* on its release in March 1939. The *Paris-Soir* versions were published under the general title of '*Aventures et escales*', Adventures and Ports of Call.

Several extracts in *Wind, Sand and Stars*, which was two chapters longer than the French edition, never appeared in *Terre des hommes* because Saint-Exupéry's quest for perfection overshot the French publisher's deadline. The most striking omission, both from the aviation point of view and as an illustration of his cold courage, was his description of a battle with a cyclone off Patagonia when he tried to land at Trelew airfield. The French text was finally released in the magazine *Marianne* only two weeks before war broke out in September 1939.

The chilling last lines, with their references to Shanghai and Guernica, sounded like a terrifying prediction of the evil about to be unleashed across Europe. Saint-Exupéry expressed concern at the banalization of violent images resulting from the spread of cinema newsreels. He wrote that it would have been easier to arouse his readers' emotions by writing about an unjustly punished child than by recalling the ferocity of a South American cyclone which had nearly swept his plane into the Atlantic. Sickening events of war in Spain and China were being watched from cinema seats without the audience being tormented by the savagery.

'We can admire the twisting soot and ashes which these man-made volcanoes thrust slowly towards the sky without a feeling of horror,' he wrote. 'And at the same time we all know that along with the grain in the lofts, the heritage of generations and the family treasures, the flesh of burning children has been turned into smoke and is slowly fattening those black clouds.'

There could have been no more terrible description of the war to come while nations were sinking into hypnotized inertia at the rise of Nazism, but Saint-Exupéry added: 'The physical drama itself cannot touch us until someone points out its spiritual sense.' From 1939 onwards he set out to fulfil that spiritual mission himself by analysing France's humiliating defeat.

PART THREE

1939–1944

CHAPTER TWELVE

Flight to Arras

THE fame and wealth resulting from the success of *Wind, Sand and Stars* did little to diminish Saint-Exupéry's anxiety and self-questioning even though he was recognized as one of the best contemporary writers in a golden age of French literature. The Académie française awarded him the Grand Prix du Roman, despite the fact that the book was non-fiction, and it became a runaway best-seller in the United States. During the six months between March and September 1939, he was fêted on both sides of the Atlantic and his money worries disappeared almost overnight.

Even so, his emotional turmoil continued and minor events would overwhelm him. In a letter to a journalist friend, Sylvia Hamilton, written while living in New York after the Fall of France, he said that his vagueness and distraction led to 'missed trains, missed dates, lost addresses, unpaid bills, forgotten telephone calls, hurt friends, difficult reconciliations, writer's block and three dinner invitations accepted for the same evening'.

The six months preceding his call-up as an air force captain in September 1939 contributed to excessive restlessness. They were among the most harassing of his life and included two trips to the United States. On one of them, he was reunited with Henri Guillaumet who still flew for Air France on the Atlantic route.

Despite being grounded since the Guatemala crash, Saint-Exupéry persuaded Air France to let him fly as an observer with Guillaumet on an Atlantic record-breaking attempt in a new six-engined Latécoère flying-boat, the *Lieutenant de vaisseau Paris*. Among the eight-man crew was the radio operator from Africa days, Jacques Néri.

On the outward journey on 7 July, the plane refuelled in the Azores after taking off from its base at Biscarosse near Bordeaux. Saint-Exupéry then spent four days in New York where he toured bookshops displaying *Wind, Sand and Stars*, released ten days earlier. Leaving the United States on 14 July for the journey home, the flying-boat benefited from following winds to establish a record of twenty-eight hours for a non-stop Atlantic crossing.

A few days after his return to France, Saint-Exupéry made a second trip to New York to promote *Wind, Sand and Stars* now that it had become a Book of the Month Club non-fiction selection. He sailed in the *Normandie* and on the night of 28–29 July 1939 another Air France flying-boat, the *Ville de Saint-Pierre*, kept the liner company for several miles, flying low over the deck while the ship's lights were turned on and off as a welcoming signal. Again the pilot was Guillaumet and he sent a message of greetings to Antoine who replied by radio expressing his admiration for the seaplane crew. This was the last occasion the two friends shared in the same flying exploit.

The fact that Saint-Exupéry was earthbound on a ship while Guillaumet flew majestically above eloquently summed up their diverging fortunes as pilots. Saint-Exupéry would never have another chance to fly with an airline while Guillaumet, only two years younger, looked set on a long career as France's most famous civilian flyer.

In New York, Saint-Exupéry had to submit to a high-pressure book-promotion programme of interviews and signings, but the visit also gave him the chance to meet the US pioneer pilot Charles Lindbergh and his wife Anne Morrow Lindbergh, for whom Saint-Exupéry had written a preface to her book *Listen! The Wind*. Anne Lindbergh wrote in her diary of Saint-Exupéry's immediate physical impact on a stranger, remarking that he had an inscrutable sort of face, almost Slavic in its solidity, his eyes turning up a little at the corners. Saint-Exupéry spoke only in French, leaving it to Anne Lindbergh to translate for her husband as best she could.

'Stories bloomed from his conversation like monstrous flowers, leaving us spellbound, oblivious of where we were or what we were doing,' she wrote. The usually meticulous Charles Lindbergh was so captivated that he ran out of petrol on the highway while listening to Saint-Exupéry in the car. Antoine talked at length about his love for Provence and invited the Lindberghs to visit him, but the atmosphere of approaching war was so heavy that Anne Lindbergh noted in her diary that she knew they were living in a 'dream interlude' and that the invitation could never be taken up.

'We never saw him again but because of this brief interlude on the eve of hostilities, Saint-Exupéry became for me the lens through which I saw the war,' she added.

The strain of being away from Europe became too much for Saint-Exupéry. After repeated telephone calls to friends in France, he cut his US visit short and boarded the *Île-de-France* for Le Havre on 20 August, rightly convinced that war was imminent.

THE day after war was declared on 3 September 1939, Saint-Exupéry received his call-up papers and was told to report to the military air base in Toulouse where his career with Aéropostale had started thirteen years before. This time, the euphoria of adventure was replaced by the recognition that the aeroplane had become an instrument of mass destruction.

Unlike many other writers of his generation such as Céline, Montherlant and Drieu la Rochelle whose view of warfare had been shaped by vindictive European nationalism and the 1914–18 slaughter, Saint-Exupéry became aware of the more sinister threat of total war after witnessing indiscriminate bombings of civilians in Spain and meeting fanatical Nazis in Germany.

His Spanish war reporting often underlined the plight of children crushed by a mindless killing-machine, a theme which left him with an agonizing apprehension of the ravages awaiting the whole of Europe. These images would condition his choices during the war when he rejected Charles de Gaulle's Free French, but his revulsion for military violence pre-dated the Spanish war.

During the mid-thirties Saint-Exupéry spent considerable time with intransigent pacifists like Henri Jeanson, and might have considered conscientious objection in 1939 if he had not studied the Nazi system closely and decided that the use of force was inevitable when

[203]

facing a totalitarian regime. He made two visits to Germany to make up his own mind about Hitler's system. As a result, he was the first of a long tradition of military men to enter battle motivated by personal hatred of ideology rather than by blind and revengeful patriotism.

The first trip was in the high summer of 1937 when he flew to Berlin in the Simoun. His passenger, Nelly de Vogüé, described the voyage as an attempt to determine the sort of man Nazi doctrines produced. The research was far from theoretical. On landing at Wiesbaden, Saint-Exupéry was arrested on suspicion of spying after overflying a military airfield at Kassel. For the rest of the day, until diplomatic intervention brought his release, he was forced to stay with his plane surrounded by fifty adolescent air cadets. When he was finally allowed to take off, he dived the Simoun towards the group, passing just over their heads.

De Vogüé said that the young Germans raised their arms in the Nazi salute and the shouts of 'Heil!' could be clearly heard in the plane's cabin. Later, sitting in a bar beside the Rhine and drinking wine, Saint-Exupéry tried to convince a young German woman of the contradictions of Nazism, which he said would eventually destroy the traditional values it claimed to respect.

His belief in the inevitability of war became one of the main themes of his conversation after his return to France, particularly after hearing Léon Werth's denunciation of the 1938 Munich agreement. Disquiet over popular gullibility following promises of lasting peace led him to make another and much longer trip to Germany in February 1939, although he was still dealing with the proofs of *Terre des hommes* and arguing by letter with Lewis Galantière over the contents of *Wind, Sand and Stars*.

Travelling by car, Saint-Exupéry was constantly confronted by both military and political threats. However, he was less disturbed at being awakened by convoys of military vehicles passing his hotel than by watching columns of Hitler Youth marching in front of a café in Nuremberg. The waitress who served him was struck by Saint-Exupéry's look of concern. The woman approached him and said: 'My son is amongst them. They take them from you when they are very small. After that, they are no longer your children and there is nothing to be done.'

Much of the trip was organized by Otto Abetz, who became Berlin's wartime ambassador in Paris. He arranged for Saint-Exupéry and another French writer, Henry Bordeaux, to visit the Führerschule where young leaders of the Third Reich were trained. Saint-Exupéry was so sickened by the propaganda and discipline that he told Otto Abetz, 'The type of man you are turning out doesn't interest me.'

Later, he wrote that he hated Nazism because it would have sent Cézanne and Van Gogh to concentration camps while producing a population of submissive cattle. He knew that nonconformists like himself were doomed.

The regimentation and indoctrination of children, common to both Nazism and communism, is enough to explain Saint-Exupéry's contempt for authoritarian regimes, but his analysis of the inadequacy of France's Third Republic ended in confusion. His interest in domestic politics, like that of much of the French electorate, had been awakened by the riots of February 1934 when right-wing movements threatened to bring dictatorship to France. The events gave Saint-Exupéry his first chance to show contempt for a form of French extremism that drew much of its inspiration from the monarchist forces that he had so admired as a schoolboy. He was never tempted to join ultra-right-wing causes that linked the intolerant royalist supporters of Charles Maurras's Action Française and the Great War veterans' movement, Croix-de-Feu, led by François, comte de La Rocque.

Croix-de-Feu's anti-democratic crusade even caused a rift with Jean Mermoz, who had come out in support of the movement's populist leader. Saint-Exupéry's dislike for La Rocque was partly based on the count's empty and bombastic abuse of language. Antoine used to mimic him in mock speeches, to the annoyance of Mermoz who was still involved in the anti-republican campaign when he disappeared in the Atlantic aboard a flying-boat in 1936.

Saint-Exupéry's scorn for extremism also led to the only recorded row with his sister Simone. While out dining with relatives, Antoine was accused of writing in favour of the French conquest of Indo-China for a notoriously fascist and anti-Semitic newspaper, *Gringoire*. The article had been signed S. de Saint-Exupéry and he realized that it had been written by Simone who was working as an archivist in Saigon. According to André de Fonscolombe, who was present,

Saint-Exupéry was furious and rushed to the telephone to call her.

'You have no right at all to use my name in such a way,' he said. He was particularly upset because of his friendship with Léon Werth, who had condemned French Indo-China policy in a book and had been a target of *Gringoire's* hatred of Jews.

Although Saint-Exupéry shunned militant politics, he was intrigued by new radical theories of government and economic management, even keeping an open mind on communism until he dismissed the Soviet regime as totalitarian. His highly personal analyses of novel economic systems, with which he tried to impress Werth among others, had their roots in his association with Gaston Bergery, a maverick left-wing deputy who later rallied to Vichy. The pacifism of Bergery's group eventually became too rigid and unrealistic and Saint-Exupéry went his own way.

Nothing in Saint-Exupéry's writing shows a strong commitment to republicanism as such or an attachment to the ideals of the Revolution, although he cited his support for a democratic system as a reason for shunning de Gaulle's plans to establish an unelected government. His search for 'nonconformism' inevitably left him isolated and he never found an orthodox political conviction to replace his family's royalism, just as he never found a religious doctrine to replace Catholicism. None of the parliamentary parties of his generation interested him and he was repelled by ideology. Instead, he concentrated on drawing up a personal and sometimes eccentric code of principles which he intended to express in *Wisdom of the Sands*.

A study of this unfinished work shows how difficult it is to place Saint-Exupéry in an identifiable political framework, even though its main theme, featuring an all-wise paternalistic and unelected leader, might have been read as an oblique justification of Pétainism if it had been published during the Vichy period. There is no argument for shared rule in the book, which proposes a benign form of fascism dispensed by an hereditary ruler, but it is unlikely that Saint-Exupéry's values would have remained static had he lived to edit the final version himself.

He told friends that he would need at least ten more years to refine the ideas in *Wisdom of the Sands*, often referring to it as a posthumous work. Life's experience had already changed Saint-

Exupéry's class and social values enormously by the age of forty, but his early death would rob him of the chance to interpret the lessons he learnt in war.

A Leafy Retreat

AN agonizing period followed the break-up when the place Vauban flat was vacated. Despite Saint-Exupéry's complaint that his wife spent most of her time with friends he disliked, her letters often expressed acute loneliness, aggravated by health problems caused by asthma. Sometimes she killed time by taking trips to London or the Riviera but nearly all her correspondence reflected sadness and bewilderment that her husband was not by her side.

If there was a single cause for mutual incomprehension, it was an inability to understand each other's excessive emotional demands. Saint-Exupéry repeatedly referred to his own perplexity in what could well be the most profuse and beautiful correspondence from a well-known figure to his wife in the twentieth century. Towards the end of his life, when he had returned to the air force, Antoine wrote to Consuelo at least once a day, often long and passionate messages asking for reconciliation on any terms. Her infrequent replies, far too short by comparison with his own letters of twenty or more pages, only fed his anxiety over her safety or added to reports that she no longer cared for him.

His concern for Consuelo sometimes exasperated his women friends, but even in his correspondence with them he insisted on his passion for his wife and the torment caused by misunderstandings. In one of his wartime letters to Sylvia Hamilton he said that despite the fact that Consuelo's attitude saddened him, her motives were 'never futile, mischievous or low'.

Although he incessantly reproached Consuelo, there were several moments of happy conspiracy, especially when they decided to buy a country house soon after Antoine moved into the rue Michel-Ange. Consuelo told the story of the impulsive purchase in the same post-war radio broadcast in which she euphemistically referred to the separation as a request from Saint-Exupéry to take leave from being a husband.

While out on a drive in the Sénart forest, south-east of Paris, they stopped in the main square of a village called La Varenne-Jarcy. Across the road they spotted a sign offering a house for sale or rent. The garden was full of trees, giving the place its name: La Feuilleraie, the leafy retreat. In Consuelo's version of the event, Saint-Exupéry decided to buy the house when the estate agent, who was also the café-owner, showed them into a kitchen dominated by a crystal chandelier 'big enough for an opera-house'.

He signed a contract without knowing where the mortgage payments would come from, a problem which disappeared with the success of *Terre des hommes*. The house was Consuelo's home from 1939 until the French defeat and her daily company included a housemaid, a flock of hens, several rabbits and a dog.

By distancing Consuelo even further from his bachelor flat, Saint-Exupéry only deepened the torment of separation. Whenever he was in Paris during 1939, he went out to La Feuilleraie in his Bugatti or on a motor cycle to join her for the evening. He usually went to see Consuelo on impulse, sometimes turning back after seeing cars outside the house. She had re-created the gregarious Parisian life among her artist friends. On these occasions, Antoine usually scribbled a note in the café and sent it to her without calling.

Because she kept all his correspondence over the years, Consuelo's hoard of written messages included many hastily scribbled accusations of neglect and indifference. Many notes spoke of a long trail of missed appointments, of late-night disappearances and unanswered letters. Some expressed Saint-Exupéry's bewilderment that the woman he loved was not solely devoted to him and his work. As he recalled in one letter, Consuelo had once warned him that he was faced with an impossible task in trying to capture her unique personality, which she compared to a tangled nebula unable to concentrate into a single form.

*

ADDED to the emotional frustration was a frequently expressed disappointment that Consuelo showed only passing interest in his complex literary and scientific ambitions and particularly his *'grand livre'* the outline for *Wisdom of the Sands*. Other men and women had to fill his desperate need for an audience and hear the outpourings of his relentless imagination.

In this context, Nelly De Vogüé played a central role and much of the anonymously cited correspondence in her Pierre Chevrier biography and in the posthumously published *Écrits de guerre*, Wartime Writings, was sent to her. Her role as a sympathetic listener was decisive in his determination to go ahead with *Wisdom of the Sands*, while her business and political contacts were also important, notably after he was drafted into the air force.

From the moment he arrived at Toulouse, Saint-Exupéry campaigned to be sent to an active-service unit despite a preliminary medical examination which declared him unfit for training as a bomber pilot. There was a possibility of being transferred to a military VIP transport outfit commanded by Didier Daurat, but in a letter quoted by de Vogüé in which he asked for help to find an active posting, Saint-Exupéry said his former boss should not be contacted except as a last resort.

Even living in Toulouse's Hôtel du Grand Balcon, with its memories of the Aéropostale days, did nothing to relieve his fears that his usefulness as a professional pilot might be at an end.

'I am suffocating more and more,' he wrote. 'The atmosphere in this place is unbreathable. I have many things to say about these events. I can say them as a combatant but not as a tourist.'

One of his most useful allies was an air force general, René Davet, whom he had met during the Spanish Civil War. Davet remembered Saint-Exupéry saying that he hated life behind the lines and preferred to share danger with soldiers at the front, whatever side they were on. He rejected offers of bureaucratic backroom jobs when war broke out in France.

Although Davet had enough influence to overturn the initial medical report, Saint-Exupéry had to ask the Air Minister, Guy La Chambre, to intervene in the hope of a posting to a fighter squadron.

Instead, he was sent to a reconnaissance group to begin the first of two attachments to a high-level photographic unit numbered 2/33 in which he served from December 1939 to July 1940 and again from April 1943 until his death.

THE conditions of Saint-Exupéry's first posting – to Orconte among the Marne's bleak Great War battlefields east of Paris – partly fulfilled his longing for a retreat from secular worries and a return to the simple life and comradeship of Cape Juby. Sometimes he expressed a desire for a monastic existence, once telling Georges Pélissier that he would join the Dominicans 'if I had faith'. He was so pleased by the spartan conditions that he found on joining 2/33 on 3 December 1939 that he asked to be treated like an ordinary pilot officer.

This meant giving up the privileges and comfort reserved for his rank of captain which made him senior to his squadron commander. The fact that he was twice as old as most of the other flyers also entitled him to special respect but he did not even exploit his fame as a writer, preferring sparse accommodation and the communal life of an all-male mess even after the Académie française award was announced eleven days after his posting.

As at Cape Juby, the atmosphere at the air base during the freezing winter of 1939–40 reawakened the bitter-sweet nostalgia of childhood at Saint-Maurice and boarding-school at Le Mans and Fribourg. *Flight to Arras*, the book he would later write in the United States on his experiences during the Battle of France, reverts continually to childhood sensations. It was not just a matter of recalling comforting memories. One sequence described the pleasure of awakening in a freezing cold room at his billet in a farmhouse at Orconte. Comparing the room to a monk's cell, he recalled how he used to dash back to snuggle under the blankets after lighting a fire to unfreeze the water in the wash-basin.

Years later when they talked of Saint-Exupéry, airmen who served with him gave the impression of a middle-aged man reliving carefree school-days during the interminable weeks before the fighting started. René Gavoille, a future commander of the unit, said Saint-Exupéry was the life and soul of the party, dazzling the younger officers with card-tricks, anecdotes, folk-songs and word-games. He had another distraction to offer: hair-raising rides in his new car, a De Soto which he drove at 140 kilometres an hour over the pot-holed and cobbled roads of eastern France. His passengers remembered his disconcerting habit of slowing to near walking-pace or suddenly racing away, depending on the intensity of the conversation.

Most of the other pilots were career military men used to the dull everyday inaction of a peacetime defence force, but their reminiscences of life at Orconte and other air force bases also reflected dismay at the lack of high-command readiness which foreshadowed the débâcle to come.

Boredom, cold and anticlimax were the real foes. In December 1939, according to the group's campaign log-book, only one war mission was flown and that ended in disaster when a slow Potez 63 reconnaissance plane was shot down by an RAF Hurricane when returning from a photographic mission. The incident was a grim instance of incomprehensible military planning. The air force had just been ordered to reduce the size of the blue, white and red recognition roundels to the size of a soup-plate, diminishing the chances of identification. After the Potez had been hit and Saint-Exupéry had visited the injured pilot in hospital – an incident recounted in *Flight to Arras* – orders went out to enlarge the recognition signs.

The Potez 63 was too slow for its role and had a number of mechanical drawbacks, including machine-guns which froze at high altitude. In the spirit of make-do on which all French units had to rely to overcome administrative lethargy, the group was obliged to improvise. With the help of Professor Fernand Holweck, a scientist who often expressed admiration for Saint-Exupéry's inventive mind, the author worked alongside a research team to track down the cause of the fault. He found the answer, which had eluded engineers for months.

By the time he returned to the air base, it had been decided that the Potez 63 was no match for the Luftwaffe and the reconnaissance group was ordered to take delivery of a new plane, the Bloch 174, a twin-engined converted fighter-bomber which Saint-Exupéry would use on the mission that inspired *Flight to Arras*.

[211]

Under Attack

SAINT-EXUPÉRY'S 1 hour 40 minute mission to the northern city of Arras on 23 May 1940 was among the most dangerous of the 108 reconnaissance flights carried out by 2/33 up till that date. The belief, expressed in the book, that he was being sent on a futile sortie was wrong. This was the last chance for the Allies to discover a gap in the German lines as their tanks raced towards the Channel. The French army commander, General Maxime Weygand, had decided to make a stand on the Somme and needed to destroy a series of German bridgeheads in the Pas de Calais.

The operation depended on the exceptional flying qualities of the twin-engined Bloch 174. Faulty communications and poor intelligence had plagued the French army since the beginning of the war and the new plane was seen as a reconnaissance master-weapon. Built originally as a bomber, its speed of 400 kilometres an hour appeared to give it an advantage over German fighters.

The first of the planes, with their characteristic twin tail-fins, had been delivered to 2/33 in the winter of 1939 and the inaugural photographic sortie was carried out by Saint-Exupéry on 29 March 1940 in a mission which took him to Verdun and Bastogne in Belgium at a height of 9000 metres. What intrigued him most about the new plane was the Bloch's flight-deck, which was equipped with 103 dials, gauges and controls as against the one or two crude navigational instruments in the machines he had flown in Africa and South America.

Saint-Exupéry went on two other sorties in the three following days and then was not sent out over the enemy lines again until the Arras expedition on 23 May. In the meantime, he had received a medical check-up in Paris and had fought off a conspiracy by his friends to have him transferred to the safety of propaganda work or scientific research. He was in Paris when the Phoney War ended on 10 May and vainly tried to persuade the Prime Minister, Paul Reynaud, to send him to the United States to campaign for American intervention. René de Chambrun, son-in-law of the future Vichy premier Pierre Laval, was sent instead.

Consuelo with family friends. (*Frédéric d'Agay*)

Right: An undated photograph of
Saint-Exupéry and Consuelo in Nice.
(*André de Fonscolombe's private
collection*)

Below: Leon Werth. (*Claude Werth*)

Left: Saint-Exupéry and Consuelo arm in arm at a ski resort in 1931.

Below: Saint-Exupéry with Claude and Leon Werth at Saint Amour in the Jura.

Saint-Exupéry in Toulouse, 1933. (*Musée d'Air France*)

An illustration done for Marie-Sygne Claudel, drawn about the time he was preparing *The Little Prince* in New York. (*Lady Northbourne*)

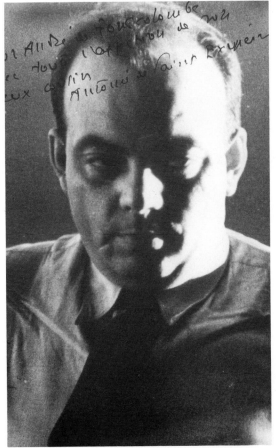

Saint-Exupéry aged about thirty-eight, probably taken after his crash in Guatemala. (*André de Fonscolombe*)

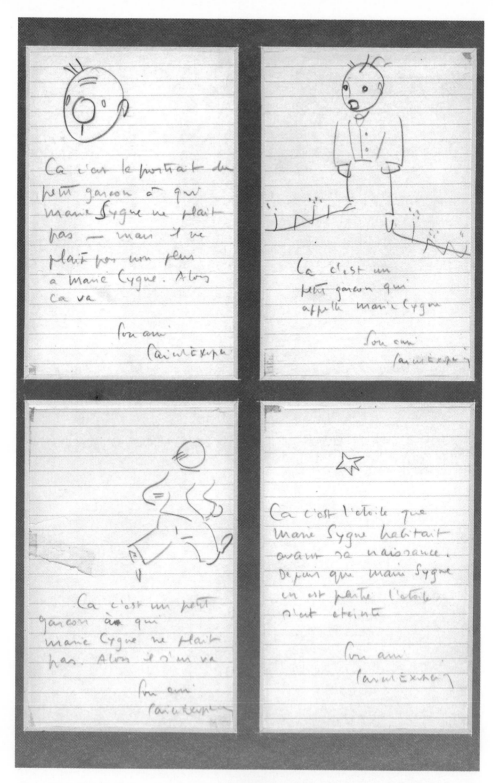

Saint-Exupéry's drawings for Marie-Sygne Claudel, accompanied by a brief text.
(*Lady Northbourne*)

Saint-Exupéry with colleagues
during the War.
(*ECPA, photo cinema video des armées*)

Above: A Lockheed P-38 Lightning similar to the one in which Saint-Exupéry died. His aircraft was unarmed. (*Quadrant Picture Library*)

Left: Consuelo with her bust of Saint-Exupéry.

Saint-Exupéry would have been refused permission to return to active service if it had been known that his health was poor. His old injuries caused terrible fevers while he was flying, but in his determination to stay in the air force he kept his suffering secret even when his temperature reached 41 degrees and his body was racked with rheumatic pains. To avert doctors' suspicions he pretended to have contracted malaria in Africa, and the truth was known only after his death on the publication of private letters.

Flight to Arras gave no hint of physical problems except in references to the enforced breathing of oxygen at high altitudes, although this was not a problem during much of the outward journey from the group's base at Orly, south of Paris. The unit's campaign diary showed that the mission was a hedge-hopping operation carried out at between 50 and 300 metres, close enough to the ground to be picked off by rifle-fire. Low cloud robbed the Bloch 174 of its usual height advantage, putting it at the mercy of German fighters. Saint-Exupéry had to depend on the plane's high speed and the protection of an exceptional escort of five Dewoitine fighters. In *Flight to Arras* he wrote that he was guarded by a full squadron of nine planes, but in fact four had been transferred to another base without his knowledge.

Unlike later reconnaissance aircraft, such as the single-seater P–38 Lightning in which he was to die, the Bloch was armed and had a three-man crew. Until the day before the mission, the presence of a machine-gunner sitting at the back of a long observation turret might have appeared superfluous because of the Bloch's speed and high-flying qualities. However, two planes from 2/33 had been destroyed by fighters on 22 May while on low-level missions to the same area assigned to Saint-Exupéry. One of the pilots was killed. The squadron leader, Jean Israël, was taken prisoner and spent the next five years in a German PoW camp where his most precious possession was a smuggled copy of *Flight to Arras*.

THE official account of the 23 May mission was written by Lieutenant Jean Dutertre, whose terse remarks take up much of the book. Saint-Exupéry gave no physical description of Dutertre, leaving only an

[213]

image of a nerveless young man unmoved by anti-aircraft fire which hit one of the petrol tanks. Photographs taken at the time show a solid and reassuring officer, ten years younger than his pilot. Like Saint-Exupéry, Dutertre was born in Lyon, joining the infantry in 1932 after graduating from the officers' school at Saint-Cyr. In 1938 he was posted to the air force as an observer and navigator, the role he filled on 23 May and again on a sortie on 6 June when Saint-Exupéry maintained the much safer altitude of 10,000 metres.

In 1976 the civilian pilots' magazine, *Icare*, asked Dutertre to write his own version of the famous reconnaissance flight. In it he recalled that Saint-Exupéry had maintained his course 'magnificently' as they approached Arras despite poor visibility and the threat of attack by a squadron of German fighters.

'Suddenly, I saw flowers or rather gigantic fires whose smoke mingled with the low clouds,' Dutertre added. 'The town blazed just in front of us and I felt almost reassured. It was Arras and half the mission had been achieved.'

Dutertre was fearful about being distracted by the spectacle of a city on fire instead of carrying out his job of observing enemy positions.

It was a superfluous worry because I discovered with a shock the sight of hundreds of panzers aligned like toys in a shop about 2 kilometres from the town centre, right in front of me. They were tightly bunched together like a herd in a field and appeared to be trying to outflank the town from the west. My instinct of self-preservation came into play and I shouted 'Turn right' to the pilot but it was too late. We passed over this wasps' nest at 700 metres. Behind us, the gunner had lost sight of the [German] fighters, but there was no real risk from them while we were flying over these tanks in action.

At about the same instant, anti-aircraft guns opened up and Dutertre counted thirteen seconds before a powerful explosion jolted the plane. Saint-Exupéry quickly corrected his course and took refuge in a cloud which provided cover for another twenty minutes as they escaped back to their base at Orly. Behind them a terrible battle had taken place between the Dewoitine fighter escort and six Messerschmitt 109s. The French planes had no chance and two of the five were shot down. The fighters' squadron leader, Joël Pape, was taken prisoner.

The other pilot, Jean Schneider, was a close friend of Saint-Exupéry and had been posted as a fighter pilot even though he was forty-four. As the Bloch 174 sped to safety, Schneider parachuted from his blazing plane and, despite being badly burned, returned to the French lines. Afterwards he was tormented by the belief that he had failed to protect Saint-Exupéry, thinking that his friend had also been shot down.

Antoine was equally morose, presuming that Schneider had been killed while guarding him from the German fighters, but then discovered by chance that the fighter pilot was being treated for burns at the American hospital at Neuilly in the Paris suburbs. Their reunion turned out to be their last meeting. Schneider escaped to join the Free French and was killed accidentally in November 1944 when the RAF plane in which he was travelling crashed in central France.

Israël's Nose

GROUP 2/33 was one of the most active air force units during May 1940 and the information it gathered might have changed the course of the Battle of France if its reports had been properly interpreted. The most important piece of intelligence was gathered on 12 May when Saint-Exupéry was still in Paris. An observer, Henri Chéry, a tank officer on loan to the air force, located a mass of heavy German panzers and other vehicles in the Ardennes before the decisive armoured offensive was launched through the forest. His observations corroborated a sighting which had been made the night before by another officer, René Gavoille, but had been dismissed as a hallucination. Several other crews from 2/33 were sent to confirm the news over the next few hours, although their sightings failed to convince the high command that they were sending infantry regiments into an armoured trap.

The frustration felt by 2/33's flyers was expressed by Jean Israël, Saint-Exupéry's squadron leader. 'We just got laughed at because it was well known in the high command that the Ardennes forest was impenetrable, at least until the Germans crossed it in force with their tanks.'

The two-squadron reconnaissance group was the first to know of the impending tank offensive and, a fortnight later, Saint-Exupéry brought back the news that the French had lost the last real chance of containing the German advance. On 31 May he was sent on a high-level mission to the northern city of Abbeville where the biggest tank battle of the 1940 campaign was taking place.

He was unaware that the French commander was Charles de Gaulle whose theories on concentrated tank attacks had been rejected by Philippe Pétain and most of the pre-war army command. The pitched armoured battle to destroy a German bridgehead at Abbeville had been going on for three days when Saint-Exupéry was ordered to overfly the area and report on Weygand's final hope of driving a wedge through thinly stretched German forces before they turned south for Paris.

The scene 10,000 metres below Saint-Exupéry's Bloch 174 left no doubt that the battle had been lost. De Gaulle had been given no time to draw up an orderly plan based on his pre-war theories and had lost 128 of his 187 tanks. The last offensive had failed about the time Saint-Exupéry set off from Orly to photograph the front lines, where the German build-up had restarted. The aerial pictures he took during this mission were recently discovered by a local historian, Henri de Wailly, but they were not clear enough to show how far they contributed to the almost immediate decision to start the French retreat southwards in the wake of the defeat.

By the time Saint-Exupéry returned to base after 2 hours 20 minutes' flying, de Gaulle and other local commanders had already agreed that the Scots Guards would take over from the shattered French cavalry for a last attack. The Guards also failed to dislodge the Germans and de Gaulle's remaining tanks had to be regrouped for the long withdrawal which ended with the 22 June armistice.

ALTHOUGH most of *Flight to Arras* was a precise reconstruction of a single mission, Saint-Exupéry allowed himself considerable author's licence, interweaving anecdotes from other sorties and events. The most obvious change was to give the impression that the flight took off from Orconte, which the unit had left long before, while the stories of the retreat actually occurred during the hazardous journey to the base at Orly.

As in most of his books, Saint-Exupéry gives little information about his heroes' background or physical appearance, although all the names are real. This makes one exception even more startling. Two pages are devoted to the nose of the squadron leader, Jean Israël. A future colonel and permanent secretary-general for the post-war Association des Amis de Saint-Exupéry, Israël is described in the book as among the bravest of the group's pilots. This passage led to one of the oddest political scandals of the Vichy years.

Saint-Exupéry insisted on the fact that Israël's nose turned red 'like a lantern' before a dangerous mission; the author's intention was to underline his comrade's Jewish origins and send a message of sympathy to his Jewish friends in France from his refuge in New York. In 1942, French Jews had become victims of harsh anti-Semitic laws which opened the way to mass deportation to Germany. But there was an element of pure mischief in the long and somewhat laboured reference to Israël's nose at a time when Vichy encouraged racial hatred with crude propaganda based on ugly caricatures of Semitic features.

In reality, Israël's nose, which Saint-Exupéry described as very big and very red, was much less spectacular. Contemporary photographs, even taken in profile, show a neat and only average-sized nose in a chubby, smiling face. If it did turn red before a mission, this was probably because it had just been broken in a plane crash.

Saint-Exupéry exaggerated to get a political point across, but the attack on Pétainist ideas went unnoticed immediately after the book was released in the Occupied Zone in October 1942, when the Germans gave Gallimard permission to print 2100 copies. Vichy's own approval had been signed by the novelist Paul Morand, who despised Jews.

For a week or two, Saint-Exupéry's irony was not commented

on in the press and the book was highly praised in the Pétainist *Nouveaux Temps* by another novelist, Pierre MacOrlan. But in January 1943 the climate suddenly changed. The Paris-based collaborationist newspaper *Je suis partout* condemned the book in an article signed by P.-A. Cousteau. Saint-Exupéry was accused of making Israël the 'most dazzling and sympathetic' member of his group.

'Of course, a man who is open-mouthed in admiration in front of his marvellous friend, Israël, and who boasts about Léon Werth being another friend, could be expected to believe that the sacrifice of France was acceptable,' the article added, referring to Vichy's claims that Jews had started the war for their own profit. 'When Jews ask you to believe something, there is no point in refusing.'

The *Je suis partout* article expressed astonishment that the book did not carry the *nihil obstat* of Georges Mandel and Léon Blum, two Jewish pre-war political leaders arrested by Vichy for allegedly contributing to the French defeat through neglect or pursuit of self-interest. Other anti-Semitic newspapers joined the outcry and the Germans withdrew their approval for the book on 11 January 1943. Within a few hours every copy had been withdrawn from the shops although attacks on Saint-Exupéry continued, with *Je suis partout* setting the tone for scurrilous papers like the *Cahier jaune*, *Au Pilori* and the *Cri du peuple*. *Je suis partout* wrote: 'Monsieur de Saint-Exupéry has always loved Jews with a sort of puerile vanity and ostentation, rather like one of those young recruits who are proud of catching a venereal disease and showing the results to the entire barrack-hut so the infection can be admired.'

Saint-Exupéry also attacked racial discrimination when he wrote *Wisdom of the Sands*. The Berber chief's gendarmes claim to have uncovered a sect whom they blame for the decadence of the empire. Using the imagery of Vichy, they support their case with a series of coincidences ranging from ugliness to cases of corruption among some members of the sect.

The Berber chief, whose contempt for the blind acceptance of duty by his police is one of the strongest themes of *Wisdom of the Sands*, mocks them by saying that there is an even more dangerous sect who can be recognized by a beauty spot on the left temple, although the worst of all are those with no beauty spot at all. After giving other absurd examples, the chief uses the logic of totalitarian states when he says: 'In the end, as we go from sect to sect, I condemn the sect of humanity as a whole because it is obviously the source of crime, kidnappings, corruption, gluttony and indecency.'

The chief says he might as well start a purge in the gendarmerie because they are men as well as servants of the kingdom. He finishes by ordering the police chief to arrest himself.

FLIGHT *to Arras* marked an important turning-point for Saint-Exupéry. The simple descriptive tone of the battle scenes and childhood memories in the first part of the book gave place abruptly to a long philosophical reflection on man's condition that foreshadowed his ideas in *Wisdom of the Sands*. The change of tone was not successful, and disappointed some of his fellow pilots in 2/33 who felt that the book lacked the coherence and polish of *Night Flight* and *Wind, Sand and Stars*. When he returned to his unit in April 1943, Saint-Exupéry explained that he had written under pressure from his US publishers' deadline and had not been able to perfect his ideas.

'My alchemy did not have time to work,' he said.

CHAPTER THIRTEEN

The Man Who Didn't Believe

IN the midst of the general panic of the French retreat when millions of refugees blocked strategic roads and compromised hopes of a counter-attack, 2/33 was suddenly moved from Orly to Nangis, a town north-east of Fontainebleau. It was from there that Saint-Exupéry flew the last two of the seven reconnaissance missions of 1940 that earned him the Croix de Guerre.

Nangis was only a few miles from La Feuilleraie where Consuelo was being drawn into the nation's mass hysteria as the Germans marched on Paris. On 3 June 1940, Saint-Exupéry drove to the house to find her hastily loading a little Peugeot with clothes and jewels. As she related it herself, he told the maid to take her mink coats back into the house while he buried the jewels in the garden. The priority was petrol and Saint-Exupéry filled the car with jerrycans, some of which were packed into suitcases which he had hurriedly emptied. Consuelo's ultimate destination was the Riviera and her subsequent, partly fictional, adventures were recounted in her 1945 book *Oppède*, the name of the Provençal village where she helped set up an artists' commune.

Whether Saint-Exupéry saw her again before he left France for good on 5 November is unknown. His own itinerary was chaotic and he rarely spent more than a few days in the same place. His unit stayed at Nangis for a week and then set up temporary headquarters on five other airfields before finding a fixed North African base in Tunis on 27 August 1940.

*

THE period between the armistice in June and his departure for New York at the end of 1940 was of considerable importance in Saint-Exupéry's decision to reject de Gaulle and remain loyal to Pétain. Nearly everything he saw in those few weeks reinforced his belief, evident since the first Nazi breakthrough, that France was too weak to confront the Germans and had to sit out the war until the United States came to the rescue.

The appalling failures of the command structure during the Battle of France convinced him that Nazi Germany was an irresistible power and that resistance would only result in mass civilian deaths. His judgement, like that of so many French in 1940, was affected by defeatist Vichy propaganda claiming that France had been sent to war totally unprepared by supposedly incompetent governments like the Socialist-led Popular Front of 1936.

Historians have since shown that France did have the military strength to face up to the Germans and that it was not simply a case, to use Saint-Exupéry's words in *Flight to Arras*, of 40 million farmers being defeated by 80 million factory workers. The French air force had far greater resources than appeared at the time but, as with the armoured cavalry, the military command threw the planes into the battle piecemeal and kept too many machines in reserve.

However, Saint-Exupéry's lack of confidence in a national will to fight was not restricted to the quality of armaments. He had predicted a collapse in morale as early as 10 May when Marshal Pétain was hurriedly summoned from his post as ambassador in Madrid and appointed Deputy Prime Minister. Although most people took the recall of the hero of Verdun as a sign of determination to carry on the battle, Saint-Exupéry was horrified.

'He's a pessimist and will do no good at all,' he told Jean Israël, a sentiment vindicated when Pétain was given the premiership on 17 June and immediately sought peace terms.

Every day of the humiliating retreat had decreased the chances of a miraculous recovery, though hopes among Saint-Exupéry's fellow pilots rose a little when 2/33 was ordered to fly to a new landing-field in colonial French North Africa; this base could have served as an assembly point for a fighting force from the vast empire. While the group commander, Henry Alias, flew a mixed fleet of planes to

Algiers on 19 June, Saint-Exupéry and the deputy commander, Olivier Penicault, were sent to Bordeaux's Mérignac airfield to collect four Bloch 174s. Mérignac was an extraordinary sight for air force officers who had been desperately asking for more machines in the past weeks. The airfield was covered by hundreds of warplanes, parked wing to wing, which had been held in reserve rather than used to stem the German advance.

Saint-Exupéry seized the chance to commandeer an obsolescent four-engined Farman capable of carrying more than forty people, large enough to transport stranded pilots and groundcrew from 2/33 and stragglers from other units as well. The plane was technically unfit to fly, but he obstinately worked alongside his mechanics throughout the night to make it airworthy. Turning away from working inside a motor, he was confronted by an ambulance officer, Suzanne Torrès, a former journalist married to an MP. An account of the meeting in her book *Quand j'étais Rochambelle*, When I was Rochambelle, gave some of the first insights into why Saint-Exupéry rejected the idea of joining de Gaulle and the Resistance movement before accepting the inertia and defeatism of Vichy.

Suzanne Torrès, who later married one of de Gaulle's friends, General Jean Massu, had arrived at Bordeaux determined to join the Free French in London. News had spread of de Gaulle's call for resistance on 18 June 1940 and Torrès was accompanied by an army captain who had been sent to discuss continuing the battle from North Africa. He received no encouragement from Saint-Exupéry, who tried to persuade the pro-Gaullist captain to forget his plans to fight on.

'In answer to the captain's enthusiasm, Saint-Exupéry put up technical arguments,' Suzanne Torrès remembered. 'There weren't enough planes, spare parts or petrol. He spoke gently and dispassionately and watched the expressions on the captain's face. I felt he regretted having to pour cold water on hopes that had been expressed with so much conviction.'

The argument did not have much effect. The young captain had an heroic war with Leclerc's Free French 2nd Armoured Division which fought its way from black Africa to the heart of Germany.

After flying the overloaded Farman to Algeria, Saint-Exupéry

[222]

often met Torrès in the bar of the Hôtel Aletti in Algiers, the centre of animated discussions among young officers determined to find a way of joining the Free French. According to Torrès, Saint-Exupéry listened in silence.

'Once he told me "What's the use of cooling their enthusiasm?",' Torrès recollected. 'He just wasn't a believer.'

Mers el-Kebir

SAINT-EXUPÉRY was demobilized while in Algeria on 31 July 1940 and sailed to Marseille in the company of another air force reserve officer, Paul Creyssel, who was a lawyer and MP in civilian life. For the next four months, Creyssel was a witness to Saint-Exupéry's hesitations in the aftermath of the defeat.

He had known the author since 1917 and they had been reunited in Algiers where they reported on the fighting capability of the air force to the North African commander, General Charles Noguès. Creyssel said that the semi-official inspection visits only increased Saint-Exupéry's pessimism regarding military morale. Creyssel was an unconditional supporter of Pétain, with whom he had served during the Great War, and helped convince Saint-Exupéry of the Marshal's integrity to the detriment of Charles de Gaulle. In conversations with an American biographer, Curtis Cate, Creyssel claimed to have observed Saint-Exupéry's disillusionment with de Gaulle while they were still serving with the air force in Algeria.

On 3 July, while the constitution for the new Vichy state was still in preparation, a British naval force destroyed a French fleet at Mers el-Kebir to stop it falling into German hands. More than 1100 French sailors died. Creyssel said that Saint-Exupéry was outraged by de Gaulle's broadcast condoning the British attack and gave no credence to the general's claim that Pétain's government was ready to hand over warships to the Nazis.

There was no written record of this conversation, but the events at Mers el-Kebir must have been a shock to Saint-Exupéry. Like most French people at the time, he believed in the Marshal's determination to resist the Germans but he was also haunted by a personal fear of being called on to join a force fighting other Frenchmen. His fraternal loyalty to the pilots of 2/33, who continued to serve the Vichy government from their base in North Africa until 1943, would have been enough in itself to make Saint-Exupéry refuse to join the Free French.

Very quickly, the nightmare of French soldiers fighting each other came true with the attack on Dakar by de Gaulle's forces in 1940, followed by fighting between Vichy and the Free French in Syria. The likelihood of France plunging into a merciless civil war like that in Spain was looming closer.

Creyssel's reminiscences gave an indication of Saint-Exupéry's state of mind only hours after his return to France from North Africa. Henri Guillaumet had also been mobilized and arrived in Marseille a few hours after Saint-Exupéry. Accompanied by Creyssel, they went to a bar where Antoine tried to console his friend whose home village had been occupied. Saint-Exupéry reportedly said that if France had continued to fight there would have been nothing left. Towns and cities would have been wiped out and the loss of life would have resulted in a blood-letting from which France would never have recovered. Nothing over the next few weeks changed his mind that de Gaulle's enterprise would only cause more unnecessary suffering.

Saint-Exupéry's personal analysis of a principal cause of the defeat coincided with the official line taken by Vichy and its main spiritual support, the Catholic church. The Church hierarchy publicly backed Pétain's call for a national revolution, blaming the Fall of France on pre-war moral decadence and the industrial revolution. Priests and politicians joined in campaigns for a new era of puritanism and a return to traditional family and rural values.

Despite his lack of interest in formal religion, Saint-Exupéry shared the belief that a spiritual revival was necessary if France were to recover her grandeur. After demobilization he retreated to the château at Agay, where his mother was staying with Gabrielle, with the intention of concentrating on *Wisdom of the Sands* as his own contribution to the revision of ethical guidelines. However, political choices could not be shunned. He was still tempted by an active role and regularly sought advice on the possibility of going to Britain to join the RAF, although he still opposed de Gaulle's leadership.

Many of his friends and relatives had either rallied to Vichy or responded to de Gaulle's 18 June appeal to defy the Germans and reject Vichy's armistice. Among the Gaullists was his cousin and friend from Paris student days, Honoré d'Estienne d'Orves, a navy commander. On 10 July 1940 he quit his ship in Alexandria to join the Free French in London.

D'Estienne d'Orves had been inculcated with the same social and religious values as his cousin and few cases gave a better illustration of the hazard of choosing sides in 1940. While Saint-Exupéry saw France's salvation in stirring the Americans out of their neutrality, D'Estienne d'Orves became a Resistance worker in London but was betrayed and arrested after being sent to France on a spying operation on 21 December 1940. Unlike Antoine, who said he was bound by a military oath to remain loyal to Marshal Pétain as army chief, his cousin defended his decision to reject Vichy. Just before he was executed by the Germans in Paris on 29 August 1941 he wrote to his family saying he had acted 'in the best traditions of our family' in defying Pétain.

D'Estienne d'Orves had spent his adult life in the navy, the defence arm most strongly characterized by blind allegiance to the Marshal. He had been personally touched by the loss of fellow officers at Mers el-Kebir. He was also a Catholic brought up in a royalist atmosphere, but he rallied spontaneously to de Gaulle who had been officially condemned to death as a traitor by a legitimate French government.

While D'Estienne d'Orves acted on the impulse of personal honour, Saint-Exupéry continued to search for arguments to prove that de Gaulle was untrustworthy. At the time, most of the French nation supported the Marshal and this was also the majority view among Saint-Exupéry's family and friends, who shunned the Resistance.

Nelly de Vogüé lived near Agay and her husband was among those who, perhaps involuntarily, helped Saint-Exupéry to make up his mind. Jean de Vogüé was a navy captain on the staff of Admiral François Darlan and had met de Gaulle in London. He advised

Saint-Exupéry against serving with him, describing the general as impossible to get on with. This warning did not prevent Jean de Vogüé from later becoming a leading underground fighter in a movement called Ceux de la Résistance, and as a member of the Conseil National de la Résistance where he served alongside Gaullists and communists.

Despite Saint-Exupéry's aim of working on *Wisdom of the Sands*, the man of action got the better of the man of literature and he made three or four trips to Vichy to discuss the possibility of a job. With Creyssel, he was interviewed by Pétain and may have been encouraged to believe that the Marshal was a secret resistance worker when he noticed a book on his desk, *La Prusse après Iéna*, Prussia after Jena.

The Marshal was not alone in giving the impression that he was playing for time like the Prussians after their lightning defeat by Napoleon in 1806. The Prussian resurrection and participation in the Battle of Waterloo was seen as an example by many members of the predominantly anti-German Vichy administration. Some were quickly disillusioned when Pétain met Hitler in October 1940 and agreed on close French collaboration with the Nazi war machine. Others backed Vichy until all France was occupied by the Nazis in November 1942. The rest stood defiantly by the Marshal even after he was sentenced to life imprisonment for treason in 1945.

Saint-Exupéry's loyalty to Pétain was counterbalanced by distrust of his administration. Nothing at Vichy convinced him that the fundamental military and political errors that had brought down the whole nation had been rectified in the Auvergne spa town where fratricidal conspiracy pitched political clans against each other. The presence of Pierre Laval as Pétain's Prime Minister and Dauphin was particularly offensive because he was widely seen as an opportunist politician who had seized on France's disgrace to further his own ambitions. De Vogüé, who was in Vichy at the time, recalled that Saint-Exupéry loudly greeted the arrival of Laval in the dining-room of the Hôtel du Parc with the remark: 'There's a scoundrel for you.'

By the autumn of 1940, Saint-Exupéry had refused tentative offers of posts with the new government and was unmoved by attempts to recruit him to a Vichy-based resistance movement led by men who thought that the Germans could eventually be defeated from within. His conviction that only the Americans could save France intensified after a visit to Paris with the pro-Nazi Gallimard author, Pierre Drieu la Rochelle. Through Drieu's influence, Saint-Exupéry was given a travel pass to visit the Occupied Zone to see friends like Yvonne de Lestrange and Jean Lucas.

Occupied Paris heightened the feeling of Nazi invincibility. The Germans treated him with suspicion and a sense of helplessness increased after he was interrogated. Saint-Exupéry was so afraid when caught in the open during a curfew that he literally ran through Paris to find refuge in a friend's apartment before going to the rue Michel-Ange to rescue his notebooks. De Vogüé watched the episode and compared his running style to that of an agile bear, saying it was difficult not to laugh while watching him jumping, panting and vociferating as he ran up the avenue du Président-Wilson.

'In highly nervous moments, he tended to dramatize everything,' she wrote. 'When he arrived at the friend's flat, his clothes were in a mess and his feet were covered in blisters. Afterwards, he started to laugh and said: "I'm not made to live in the Occupied Zone." '

Another important encounter added to his determination to campaign from abroad. In October 1940, after returning to the Free Zone where Vichy ruled without German supervision, he went to see Léon Werth, who had taken refuge at his country home in Saint-Amour in the Jura. Vichy had just introduced anti-Jewish legislation, which would force Werth to remain in hiding throughout the war. Werth was in favour of the plan to go to the United States and Saint-Exupéry tried to console him over the prospect of a long Nazi presence by saying that the Occupation could be compared to driving a locomotive into a small garden.

'The Germans have got here but now they don't know what to do next,' he said.

By the end of October 1940 he had returned to the Riviera where André Beucler, who prefaced *Southern Mail*, Raymond Bernard, director of the film version, and Gaston Gallimard were among those who were told that France's salvation depended on American intervention. Although Antoine constantly discussed alternative plans, the example of other writers in the Gallimard stable did not encourage resistance. Apart from Drieu who had gone over to the Nazis along with Robert Brasillach and Louis-Ferdinand Céline, most authors were ready to sit out the Occupation. Some participated enthusiastically in the Pétain cult, even backing Vichy's anti-Semitic legislation which led to the persecution and death of Jewish authors, including Benjamin Crémieux, the man who had introduced Antoine to Consuelo.

Among those who advised submission to Nazi rule was André Gide who wrote in his Journals that accepting enemy domination was not cowardly but wise and that there was no sense in beating against the bars of the cage. Of the literary men of action, only Joseph Kessel unhesitatingly rallied to the Resistance. André Malraux, whose war had been restricted to a tank battle in which the French vehicles broke down, had also decided to wait for the Americans and retired to the Riviera to write.

Faced by conflicting advice and few examples of unqualified heroism, Saint-Exupéry followed his own inclination. He finally decided to leave for New York just before visiting his mother at her village house in Cabris among the hills behind Cannes in December 1940. As a parting gift, he gave her a radio. Mother and son were never to see each other again.

The Death of Guillaumet

MUCH of Saint-Exupéry's recurrent melancholy was due to the deaths of family and friends. By 1940, the tragic list stretched from his father's disappearance only three years after Antoine's birth to the Battle of France when seventeen out of the twenty-three crews in his squadron were lost. Two of the priests who had played an important role in his youth died that year. Abbé Launay, who first recognized his literary talent, was taken ill soon after he retired to his native village near Le Mans as war broke out. The death of Abbé Sudour, the priest who helped Saint-Exupéry join Aéropostale, was attributed directly to the shock of the defeat. He collapsed while saying mass in Notre-Dame, dying soon afterwards in hospital.

There was to be no respite as Saint-Exupéry prepared to leave for the United States from Lisbon. On 1 December 1940 he received the news that Henri Guillaumet had been killed. His friend was at the controls of a Farman transport plane shot down by an Italian fighter over the Mediterranean nearly five months after the French surrender. At the time, the Italians were involved in a sea-battle with the Royal Navy and the French plane was mistaken for a British aircraft.

'Guillaumet is dead and it seems this evening that I no longer have any friends,' Saint-Exupéry wrote to de Vogüé. 'I am not complaining. I have never known how to feel sorry for the dead. But I took so long to find out about his disappearance and I feel weighed down by this horrible news. This is going to last for months and months. I am going to need him so often.'

He was shocked to realize that he was the last survivor of the pioneer team which flew the Casablanca-Dakar run.

> From the old days of the great era of the Bréguet 14 all those who passed that way are dead, Collet, Reine, Lassalle, Beauregard, Mermoz, Étienne, Simon, Lécrivain, Wille, Verneilh, Riguelle, Pichodou and Guillaumet. I have no one left on earth to share my memories. Here I am, a toothless and lonely old man, who has to chew over all that for himself alone. And from South America, no one left, no one . . .

The letter ended with an appeal for help as he hesitated over his idea of campaigning in the United States. 'There is a whole life that has to begin again,' he added.

Since leaving his mother in December and returning to North Africa for a last attempt to see whether the French military had the force and resolution to continue the fight, Saint-Exupéry had been beset by new doubts. One moment he again discussed joining the RAF in Britain, and the next wondered whether he should return to France and stay close to his family. He finally decided to leave for America after receiving a cable from his publishers asking him to come to New York to promote *Wind, Sand and Stars* and discuss a proposed book on the Battle of France. Saint-Exupéry was refused permission to cross fascist Spain because he had reported from the republican side in the Civil War and he had to take a ship from North Africa to Lisbon. From there he sailed for the United States with a mixed group of French exiles.

In December, allegiance to Pétain had been made easier by the sacking of Pierre Laval as premier, but on arriving in the United States Saint-Exupéry took the first opportunity to stress his reservations over the new government's analysis of the defeat. When his ship docked in New York on New Year's Eve 1940, he told a *New York Times* reporter that the French rout was the responsibility of the military high command, the senior officers whom Pétain had exempted from blame in his vengeful campaign against pre-war leaders like Léon Blum and Édouard Daladier.

Saint-Exupéry evaded questions on Pétain himself, a rule he kept in most wartime interviews. The Vichy authorities interpreted the silence in their own way and a month after his arrival in the United States Saint-Exupéry was appointed a member of the Conseil National du Gouvernement, an advisory body which included many eminent people who would later become enemies of the regime.

On the same day as the news was officially released, he turned down the appointment in a written declaration in English to the press, saying that he had not been consulted in advance. He was not a politician and intended using his influence to further French interests only through his writing. Despite this refusal, which failed to smother indignant rumours that he was on a secret mission for the Vichy government, the official Gaullist lobby stepped up an insidious and spiteful campaign of denigration that continued until his death.

From the outset, Saint-Exupéry was hurt by Gaullist propaganda hinting that he was either a traitor or a coward, but for most of 1941 his preoccupations were more personal than political and he abandoned his original intention to return to France as soon as possible. He was under pressure to finish his book on the flight to Arras and had to find a way of getting Consuelo out of France. Both plans took nearly a year to complete.

Saint-Exupéry's life and moods during 1941 have been best portrayed by his translator, Lewis Galantière, who wrote a long article in *Atlantic Monthly* in 1947. Galantière doubted Saint-Exupéry's ability to settle outside France. 'I have never met a man so little made for neutrality, emigration and exile,' he wrote.

Saint-Exupéry tried to ignore the fact that he was living in an English-speaking country. His friends were all French exiles or French-speakers, whose political allegiances spread across the entire range of contemporary French thinking outside the most extreme official expressions of Pétainism and Gaullism. His Parisian habits were quickly recreated after he moved out of the Ritz-Carlton hotel in February 1941 and into a twenty-seventh-floor apartment with a panoramic view at 240 Central Park South where his neighbours included Maurice Maeterlinck. Evenings were taken up by long dis-cussions in restaurants and bars or by card-tricks and games of chess.

Early-morning telephone calls to friends to read them his latest copy were renewed and there was not much point in visiting him in the morning as he often slept throughout the day after a night's work. Because of his reluctance to speak English, Saint-Exupéry would telephone friends at the last minute to find voluntary interpreters for his shopping expeditions in search of a new gadget. By far the most important acquisition was made with the help of Bernard Lamotte, an artist Saint-Exupéry had met in his Beaux-Arts days and who later drew the illustrations for *Flight to Arras*.

They were looking for an electric organ when Saint-Exupéry's gaze settled on a dictating-machine which recorded on discs. While the puzzled assistant tried to make sense of the conversation between the two Frenchmen, Saint-Exupéry pulled $700 out of his pocket and told Lamotte to ask for the machine to be delivered to his flat. From then on, he dictated his books and other work during the night so that a secretary could type out the manuscript during the day. The machine also brought out his sense of fun. He used to record songs, distorting his voice by slowing down the disc. Visitors were per-suaded to make impromptu recordings, only to hear them mischiev-ously played back in front of other people.

Despite a hectic social life and constant invitations to lecture on his war experiences, Saint-Exupéry was never happy in the United States, said Galantière. 'He was nervous with a tortured and tense mind and passed days and nights debating military and political communiqués and studying with physicians and engineers.'

In addition to his concern for Consuelo's safety, much of his unhappiness was due to bad health, which delayed completion of *Flight to Arras* and frustrated his publishers' hopes of bringing it out for the first anniversary of the armistice. Although nothing had appeared by July 1941, he alarmed his translator among others by slipping off to Hollywood to stay with the film director Jean Renoir.

The two men had become acquainted while sharing a cabin on the ship to the United States in the previous December, and Renoir had agreed to consider filming *Wind, Sand and Stars*. In an attempt to make a coherent narrative out of the disconnected chapters, Saint-Exupéry recorded an outline project on discs, using his recording-machine to describe his initial view of the treatment.

Unknown to Galantière, who was waiting to start work, Saint-Exupéry had also decided to go into hospital; but it was not until November 1941 that he finally wrote to explain delays in submitting the book. He told Galantière that he had been repeatedly struck down by an inexplicable illness for the past three years and the effects had worsened since his arrival in the United States. Without warning, he ran up fevers of 105°F. He had been informed by a Hollywood surgeon that he was suffering from complications following his first air accident at Le Bourget in 1923 and that a pocket of permanent infection had formed in the scar tissue. Saint-Exupéry told Galantière that convalescence was almost as painful as the operation and was accompanied by unbearable spasms, haemorrhages and more infection.

'Forgive me for the delay in my book,' he added.

Galantière was hardened to writers' excuses for not meeting deadlines and appeared to treat the letter with scepticism, because Saint-Exupéry sent a second note immediately afterwards complaining that his translator seemed to believe that 'I've one of those vague little illnesses suffered by neurotic girls'.

Galantière's disbelief was confirmed in the article for *Atlantic Monthly* in which he said that Saint-Exupéry was given five or six weeks by the publishers to settle down in New York, during which time he received the National Book Award for *Wind, Sand and Stars* at a banquet for 1500 people.

'Then we tactfully made him understand that it was time to start work,' said Galantière. When tact failed, the author was told it was his duty to explain the defeat to the American people who did not believe that France had fought actively enough. The suggestion made Saint-Exupéry 'absolutely furious' and he found a new excuse, saying he was being treated like a commercial literary product. When that storm subsided, the illness intervened.

By November the publishers' patience, tact and arts of persuasion had all run thin and the essential topical element for the commissioned book, the armistice, was nearly eighteen months old. That was the moment Saint-Exupéry chose to announce that the long-awaited manuscript was ready for publication.

The Night Worker

LEWIS Galantière, who also translated Jean Cocteau, Paul Valéry and François Mauriac, remarked that Saint-Exupéry never wrote without pain, destroying more than he kept, but as the director Jean Renoir was to learn he had no second thoughts about making his friends share the anguish. *Flight to Arras* would probably never have been finished without Renoir's tolerance and sense of humour.

Renoir, the impressionist painter's son whose films included *La Grande Illusion*, invited Saint-Exupéry to stay with him in Hollywood in July 1941 despite having suffered what he called 'the torture of the Dictaphone'. After buying the recording-machine, Saint-Exupéry used it to add to his already prolific correspondence and compulsive need for conversation.

'Instead of sending a letter he sent discs in which he spoke about everything from his books to his daily worries and sometimes finished off with reference to a card-trick,' Renoir recalled. 'The trouble was that the packets of discs were followed by a telephone call in the evening in which he wanted to discuss everything in the recording. The arrival of a packet of discs was a prelude to real torment.'

The recording-machine was no less of a nuisance when Saint-Exupéry moved into the Renoir household to write *Flight to Arras* without telling his publishers that work was progressing.

'His pockets were always full of bits of paper, sometimes covered with lines or drawings that resembled *The Little Prince*,' said Renoir. 'In the evening, he sorted out the papers and read them into his machine. He used to go on all night. We could hear him clearly and couldn't get any sleep.'

For Renoir, Saint-Exupéry was charming and attractive but an impossible house-guest. They rarely saw each other except over breakfast when Renoir had to beseech him to spend some time with his secretary who arrived in the morning after Antoine had gone to bed and left before he woke up in the late afternoon. She spent the day producing typescripts from the dictating-machine, including the film treatment for *Wind, Sand and Stars*, but sometimes burst into tears because she could not see Antoine to ask for explanations.

Jean Renoir's troubles continued when Saint-Exupéry went into hospital. He kept telephoning to ask the film director or his wife to interpret diagnoses or pass on complaints to the hospital staff. On one occasion it was to demand that carrots were withdrawn from the menu because the colour made him sad.

While in Hollywood, Saint-Exupéry also stayed with the exiled owner of *Paris-Soir*, Pierre Lazareff, who had tolerated his trying behaviour in the pre-war years.

'Every time Antoine gave us an article for *Paris-Soir* it was a real puzzle how to get it to the composing-room,' said Lazareff. 'You couldn't get rid of him. He was in the news-room until midnight changing the order of sentences or taking out a comma or word and completely disorganizing the whole shop.'

Although the porter was told not to let him past the newspaper's front door, Saint-Exupéry brought him bottles of wine to bribe his way in.

IN the rush to complete *Flight to Arras*, Saint-Exupéry found a new ally when he returned to New York in November 1941. Jean-Gérard Fleury, a journalist and aviation expert, had been introduced to Saint-Exupéry during his Aéropostale days. On their reunion, the author spent hours reminiscing about African and Latin American pioneering flights, dwelling on the warmth, courage and brotherly spirit of the pilots and saying how much he missed Guillaumet.

During the next six months, Fleury became part of Saint-Exupéry's disorganized life; memories of dinners with Jean Gabin and Marlene Dietrich at Bernard Lamotte's penthouse were mingled with others of hours spent listening to Saint-Exupéry's favourite record, Mozart's Fortieth Symphony, or watching him experiment with model ships and new methods of propulsion in his bath.

Fleury was writing a book of his own at the time, but he was not spared what Saint-Exupéry called 'la corvée du roman', being forced to listen to drafts of the novel. As well as receiving early-morning telephone calls, he was once awakened soon after midnight by a taxi-driver to be told that Saint-Exupéry wanted to see him immediately. Fleury was needed to comment on a new chapter of *Flight to Arras*. Despite warm praise, Saint-Exupéry decided to rewrite the section and his friend had to sit and wait until 5 a.m. to hear the new version.

Soon afterwards Lewis Galantière, whose full-time job was in banking, would become the main recipient of telephone calls at two or three in the morning when Saint-Exupéry wanted to discuss variations in his finished manuscript before it was translated.

'This man who wrote like a genius was convinced he could not write,' Galantière remarked. 'He needed to be constantly reassured by his friends.'

An historic event ended Saint-Exupéry's reluctance to let go of his manuscript despite his belief, as he told his friends in 2/33, that his alchemy had not been given time to work. On 7 December 1941 Pearl Harbor was bombed, giving new urgency to the release of a book on real fighting conditions. Publication was a vicarious return to the front line as Antoine's chances of going back to the battlefield in person receded.

During 1942 Saint-Exupéry began taking private lessons in English, a sign that circumstances were conspiring to force him to stay in the United States until the end of the war. His age and continuing poor health were obvious obstacles against a return to active service while his refusal to accept the authority of Charles de Gaulle ruled out a flying post with the Free French in Britain.

The prospect of an anonymous life in the services also had to be weighed against the comfort, revenue and prestige of living in America. He was the best-known and most highly paid of the French writers who had taken refuge in the United States and, in spite of his reluctance to engage in propaganda work, he had slipped into the role of a much-sought-after pundit through his writing, lectures and interviews.

A more personal reason for staying had arisen with the arrival of Consuelo by ship from Marseille in November 1941. Saint-Exupéry's desire to look after her in spite of their incompatibility was a prelude to his reflections on responsibility for his rose in *The Little Prince*. Over the next few months, their relationship often seemed like that of a worried and over-protective father and a wayward daughter, although Consuelo was then nearly forty years old.

The war and long separation from Antoine had done nothing to check her exuberant personality. Before joining the artists' commune in the Provençal village of Oppède, Consuelo had spent most of her savings living in Cannes's most luxurious hotel, the Martinez, or on treatment for asthma. A short period of deprivation when she lived in her artists' colony had been quickly forgotten after her husband had transferred funds to France to pay for a new wardrobe and a passage to the United States. When she arrived at the port of Hoboken in New York State, she was surrounded by luggage and announced that there was a lot more in the ship's hold.

Saint-Exupéry had no car and Jean-Gérard Fleury had been asked to chauffeur him to the port without being told that they were collecting Consuelo. Like so many people who had never met her before, Fleury was fascinated by her non-stop conversation, her flashing eyes, her South American accent and her expressive gesturing as she told of her life in Oppède and boasted of her childhood in El Salvador.

But this constant chattering and outrageous behaviour were among the reasons why Saint-Exupéry decided that they should continue to live apart. Instead of taking her to his apartment, he led her to an adjoining flat where she soon recreated the Bohemian life of Paris and Oppède. Her most regular visitors were the surrealist poet André Breton, with whom Saint-Exupéry was having a running row over the latter's attachment to Pétainism, and the Spanish painters Salvador Dali and Joan Miró.

The disruptive atmosphere of the days in the place Vauban was quickly re-established, with the voluble Consuelo often bursting into her husband's flat like the cascade evoked by Henri Jeanson. Antoine's friends marvelled at his patience, even though he was often visibly on edge. Henri Claudel, one of the Gaullist representatives in New York, remembered that when he and his wife were introduced to Consuelo, Saint-Exupéry pleaded: 'Now don't upset these people, I like them very much.'

The only time Claudel saw him reproach Consuelo angrily was when she revealed one of his card-tricks, but, if Saint-Exupéry's letters and notes of the time reflected his true feelings, there was a constant undercurrent of friction, disappointment and frustration in his relationship with his wife which he hid from all except his most intimate friends. In written messages, Saint-Exupéry constantly referred to his anxiety over Consuelo's unannounced absences or her failure to keep appointments even though she lived only a few yards away. The quarrels that had troubled the marriage in Paris were rewakened. Consuelo accused Antoine of acting like a prison warder while he told her in letters that the psychological shocks and the agonizing moments waiting for her to return in the early hours of the morning often left him drained, to face 'completely sterile days and days that left an impression of eternity'.

To add to the tension, Consuelo's extravagant expenditure brought back Saint-Exupéry's financial worries and by the end of 1942 he was again expressing fears that he would have no money to spend on himself despite his unprecedented royalties. However, until all of his correspondence with his wife becomes available, it will be impossible to say whether the reproaches in his letters were due as much to his own changeable personality as to the irritations of his wife's unique life-style. Maintaining a mood of contentment for any length of time had become an almost impossible task. Léon Werth's observation that Saint-Exupéry abandoned happiness and plunged into melancholy without warning was confirmed by many of his friends.

The strain of exile in North America did nothing to contain these abrupt swings of mood. His Canadian publisher, Bernard Valiquette, writing in Quebec's *Nouveau Journal* in 1962, said that Saint-Exupéry's unpredictable humours remained the most lasting impression.

'He moved from the most noisy form of joy and the maddest gaiety to almost complete stubborn silence. He was extraordinarily talkative but he also knew how to isolate himself completely in the middle of a group to reflect sadly on dead children, mothers deprived of their sons and the horrors of war.'

The Limits of Pétainism

SAINT-EXUPÉRY'S forebodings of the terrible consequences of a civil war in France were a consistent theme in his writing and conversations. His friendship with pacifists like Léon Werth and Henri Jeanson, and his experience of the terror in Spain and of the national humiliation after the most crushing defeat in France's history, were primary causes of his attachment to the passive attitude of Vichy expressed through Philippe Pétain's collaborationist policies.

To this has to be added a contempt for divisive party politics and public quarrels which alienated him from the most virulent Gaullist officials in New York. In a letter to Sylvia Hamilton, written in 1943 after he had given his backing to de Gaulle's rival in North Africa, General Henri Giraud, Saint-Exupéry described Gaullism as the 'politics of hate'.

De Gaulle took his refusal to join the Free French as a personal slight. But there are numerous recorded accounts, many from committed Gaullists, which show that Saint-Exupéry's adhesion to Pétainism fell short of ideological support for the reactionary right and was primarily humanitarian.

His rejection of the Free French movement might have been less unequivocal if the Gaullist leaders in New York had treated him fairly, according to Bernard Dupérier, a Gaullist RAF pilot and future MP, who played a key role in ensuring de Gaulle's return to power in 1958: 'It's probable that if some of the pseudo-Gaullists comfortably installed in America had forced themselves to speak to Saint-Exupéry instead of condemning him, they would have helped him to find a way out of the dilemma which kept him in New York.'

During a morale-raising trip to America in 1943 Dupérier discovered that local Gaullists could not find words hard enough to stigmatize Saint-Exupéry's conduct. Damaging allegations that he was secretly working for the Pétain administration were brought out into the open by the Gaullist *Voix de la France*, which described him as 'a friend of Vichy', while the France-Forever movement implied that he was a coward for fleeing to America and failing to join the Free French.

As one of Saint-Exupéry's reasons for opposing Gaullism was the need for reconciliation among the French, he was faced with an impossible choice in New York. From the moment he arrived, he was saddened by the quarrels of French exiles who, according to Jean-Gérard Fleury, 'tore each other apart with bare teeth with a whisky-glass in their hands'. Fleury added that Saint-Exupéry 'was disgusted by the politicization of Gaullism and by the fact that Gaullists asked him to join them only as a writer and become the docile spokesman for their doctrinaire beliefs in London.'

Because he never spoke to de Gaulle himself, Saint-Exupéry formed his opinions from experience of subordinates who themselves were divided into various chapels. These contacts did nothing to calm his suspicion that de Gaulle intended to head an undemocratic, fascist-style government, although Saint-Exupéry did say in a 1943 letter that he would have joined the general if he had proclaimed himself head of a foreign legion and not the chief of an alternative administration.

When speaking to Lewis Galantière, Saint-Exupéry was clear about his attitude towards de Gaulle's ambitions. He told the translator that national unity counted above all things and that de Gaulle was calling for a fratricidal combat. The general had ceased to be a soldier and had become a political leader.

'I would have joyfully followed him against the Germans but I could not fight against the French,' he said.

However, Saint-Exupéry never disowned Pétain or criticized him publicly, telling many friends that collaboration was needed to save France from chaos. The Marshal was the guarantor of French national cohesion, he told Robert Boname, a French aviation expert, in 1942: 'If he did not exist, he would have had to be invented.'

In July 1942, the Swiss novelist Denis de Rougemont recorded a conversation in his diary in which Saint-Exupéry said that Pétain had saved the substance of France. He then outlined an eccentric theory of his own which he elaborated over the following months. According to this, if the Marshal had revolted openly, the Germans would have stopped axle-grease reaching the railways, bringing food supplies to a halt.

'As for the Gaullists over here, [he said] they were not making war against the Nazis but against the lift-boy at the Waldorf or the chef at the Ritz who refused to be part of their faction and whom they treat as traitors,' de Rougemont added.

Despite frequent association with many of the more tolerant Gaullist officials like Henri Claudel, Saint-Exupéry refused to change his mind. As the months of exile dragged on he became ever more explicit in his defence of collaboration, even though doubt was spreading in the Vichy camp. During a visit to Canada in April 1942, he told Montreal newspapermen that the only watchword for France was 'Survival'.

'Famine gnaws at the vital springs of childhood, tomorrow's generation,' he said during a press conference. 'My country has already lost 250,000 children last year because of malnutrition. The Nazis want to wipe out France just as they annihilated Poland.'

Nine months later, in January 1943, Saint-Exupéry had refined his arguments on the supply of axle-grease to the point where he could shake the convictions of the Gaullist RAF pilot Bernard Dupérier. Because of a friendship that dated back many years, Dupérier defied the general's officials while on his morale-raising visit to New York and secretly went to see Saint-Exupéry at his flat in the hope of persuading him to join the Free French.

Since the beginning of the war Dupérier had been in the habit of taking notes, thus providing a rare verbatim account of Saint-Exupéry's ideas on collaboration, which appeared to have been unshaken by the Nazis' total occupation of France in November 1942 as a reprisal for the invasion of French North Africa by the Allies.

Saint-Ex was getting ready to go out for lunch and as he dressed I told him how much he was admired by the French 'boys' in the RAF. In turn, I had to listen to an extraordinary performance in which Saint-Ex took the parts of the accused, the judge and the defence counsel.

I felt that he had been refining and rehearsing everything for months, particularly the central theme that Marshal Pétain was obliged to collaborate to ensure the supply of axle-grease for trains. Saint-Ex told me that the only source for the grease was in German hands and if it was withheld there would be starvation.

Saint-Exupéry painted a terrifying picture of hungry townspeople pouring into the countryside and causing desolation before expounding further justifications for collaboration which included reluctant support for a man he despised, Pierre Laval. Without him as Prime Minister, the Nazis would have imposed a pro-German Frenchman like Jacques Doriot or a gauleiter, Saint-Exupéry claimed. The argument was identical to Pétain's own reasoning which he had used to explain his refusal to leave France after the Germans took military control of the Free Zone.

'Saint-Ex never let me get a word in,' said Dupérier. 'He continued in the taxi which took me to my hotel. The eloquent flow almost threw me off balance and I was so nervous that he would eventually sweep me up with his opinions that I did not take up his invitation for lunch the following day.'

Like many ordinary Gaullists, Dupérier bore no grudge against Saint-Exupéry and said he was certain that his heart and mind were on the side of those who continued to fight.

'But as he didn't join them, he had to find a way of satisfying his own conscience and elaborated extravagant theories like the preposterous one about the supply of axle-grease,' Dupérier explained. 'Faced with this great man who had lost his way, the non-combatant Free French in New York resorted to insulting him. They seemed to think this was a proof of their own patriotism.'

Saint-Exupéry's persistent loyalty to the Marshal might have been shaken by a conversation with Léon Werth who had developed a fierce hatred of Pétain while living as a hunted Jew in his country home at Saint-Amour, unable to send letters for fear of being arrested. While the exiled Saint-Exupéry had little but distorted propaganda from which to judge the Pétain administration, Werth was in touch with the dangerous day-to-day reality of collaboration and wrote contemptuously in his diary of the Marshal as representing treachery disguised as virtue.

To Werth, the Vichy leader's grandfatherly attitude, deceptively honest blue eyes and soporific national revolution were a trap for ordinary people. 'He is too old to be killed, but he should not be allowed to escape military degradation in front of his troops.'

CHAPTER FOURTEEN

Le Petit Prince

SAINT-EXUPÉRY'S enforced twenty-eight-month stay in the United States deprived him of a vital source of stability in his life, contact with his mother. From his school-days, he had turned to her time and again for moral and emotional support. A constant exchange of letters over the years sealed their unshakeable complicity, providing mutual tenderness and encouragement.

Much of the correspondence revealed Saint-Exupéry's need to envelop himself again in the cosseted and sometimes imaginary world of childhood watched over by an ever-understanding maternal figure. The two years in the United States not only broke physical contact. The mail service was unreliable and the few letters that reached Marie were often little more than brief notes that took censorship into account. When the Germans occupied all of France in November 1942 and the United States withdrew its embassy from Vichy the precarious postal link between mother and son disappeared altogether.

Saint-Exupéry's books showed that in moments of distress he often reached back in time to his earliest consolations. An example, which he never wrote about, occurred during a depressing period while he was in hospital in Los Angeles during the summer of 1941. If any moment can be pinpointed as providing the seed for *The Little Prince* it was these hours of acute loneliness in a huge isolation ward. Illness had often been a time for reflection. In 1930, writing to his mother from Buenos Aires, he told her that he learnt of the immensity of life not from the Milky Way, the skies or the sea, but in the spare bed of her room where he slept when he was unwell as a child.

'It was wonderful luck to be ill,' he said. 'We each wanted to be there in turn. It was a limitless ocean to which the flu gave us access.'

In the Los Angeles hospital he drew on the memory of that pool of innocent comfort, keeping only one book beside him, a copy of Andersen's fairy-tales. His mother had related them to him in infancy and, as he recalled in an interview with *Harper's Bazaar*, this was the first story-book he ever read.

The French actress Annabella, who had starred in his 1935 film *Anne-Marie*, lived in Hollywood at the time with her husband, Tyrone Power, and visited Antoine in hospital where she saw the book on his bedside table. In the weeks that followed, she also went to see him in a two-room flat he was renting while medical treatment was completed. There, in her own words, 'he conjured up a dream world', part of a creative process that led to the birth of *The Little Prince*.

In the next few weeks, illness, political battles, conjugal quarrels and writing pressures intensified his need to restore a childlike perspective of the world. On his return to New York, Saint-Exupéry telephoned Annabella to read some of the chapters of his own fairy-tale which slowly took shape through 1942.

The physical characteristics of the little prince had existed in embryo since Saint-Exupéry's childhood. The outline can be seen in hundreds of illustrations on letters to friends and some images are recognizable forerunners. The drawing of his solitary and bewildered child-hero standing on the pinnacle of a mountain with his back turned was similar to a drawing in a letter to Guillaumet after the latter's escape from the Andes in 1930. But the exact moment when *The Little Prince* was conceived as a publishable book is unclear. Saint-Exupéry's American publisher, Curtice Hitchcock, claimed to have commissioned it after seeing Saint-Exupéry sketch a golden-haired little boy on a restaurant table-cloth in 1941.

Although in Hitchcock's account the deal appears to have amounted to little more than encouragement to Saint-Exupéry to write a children's story in time for Christmas 1942, the outline had long been established in the author's mind and he had probably touched on some elements of the story during his regular meetings with the publisher's small children whom he often visited. Sylvia Hamilton, a journalist who knew Saint-Exupéry well in New York, said he told her the fairy-tale when they first met early in 1942 before he had put anything on paper. She suggested to him that he should draw pictures for the book himself rather than ask a professional artist like Bernard Lamotte who had illustrated *Flight to Arras*. Her influence received an acknowledgement when Saint-Exupéry gave her the original manuscript which she later sold to the Morgan Library in New York.

Several other people were involved during the months it took to produce the finished version with the author's paintings. Among them was Denis de Rougemont who posed for the picture of the little prince as he lay on his stomach among flowers, weeping over his estrangement from the rose. Some people were not even aware of their contribution, like the lamplighter recaptured from the days at Saint-Maurice-de-Rémens.

Identifying the inspiration and models for the book, which drew heavily on Saint-Exupéry's visual memory, is an endless puzzle, but an interpretation of the text has more poignant significance because of its disguised references to his personal life. Read in conjunction with the notes for *Wisdom of the Sands*, which were well advanced at the time the fable was published, the first half of the book reveals the frustration of a search for truth by a man who had abandoned or been deserted by so many certainties.

The Little Prince is almost a reproach to himself for taking on the impossible task involved in writing *Wisdom of the Sands*. In the fable, Saint-Exupéry asserts that only children can see the line between honesty and deceit, that the key to all understanding lies in innocence. Yet his philosophical work amounts to a contradictory attempt to provide firm answers to the most important moral issues by using adult reason and experience.

Set alongside the weightiness of *Wisdom of the Sands*, *The Little Prince* could be considered mistakenly as little more than a diverting conversation between the author and juvenile readers credited with an intuitive ability to read a message inaccessible to adults. The fable took him barely three months to complete while he insisted that he needed a further ten years to complete *Wisdom of the Sands*. However, the care Saint-Exupéry put into *The Little Prince* showed that this was the project closest to his heart for most of 1942.

[245]

In a book called *Saint-Exupéry in America*, his English teacher Adèle Breaux remembered seeing his desk covered with illustrations while discarded drafts filled the waste-paper basket. After showing her rejected drawings of the little prince, Saint-Exupéry told her: 'It is a little ridiculous because I don't know anything about drawing or painting. What I know about them dates from my childhood and I can assure you that my talent at the time did not attract anyone's attention.'

In 1942 Saint-Exupéry was often consulted by the War Office in Washington, where his work sometimes included interpreting air-reconnaissance photographs. Breaux asked when he found time to write.

At night, mostly. That's when I prefer to write. Often the day is taken up by conferences, meetings and visits. I rarely start writing before 11 p.m. and I always have a tray with big cups of very strong black coffee. I am free and can concentrate for hours. I can write for hours without feeling tired or sleepy and I never know when I am going to give in to sleep.

I drop off without realizing it and I wake up in daylight with my head on my arm. That's the only way I can work. Once the book is started I am possessed. When I am writing I am sure the work is good. When I'm finished I'm sure it's worthless.

The Rose and the Thorns

THERE is no mystery about who is the hero of *The Little Prince* in which Saint-Exupéry, as the adult pilot, talks with the blond-haired child who was Antoine himself before he left the magic garden at Saint-Maurice. Nor is there any contradiction between most of the themes in the fable and Saint-Exupéry's consistent preoccupation with friendship, responsibility and a search for values to replace his lost religious faith.

What distinguishes *The Little Prince* from his other works is the fact that Saint-Exupéry used a story to write of his inner distress over his marriage to Consuelo and the emptiness of liaisons with other women. Throughout the period the book was being written, Antoine and Consuelo were making one last effort to live together in harmony. Much of the dialogue appears to echo their conversations on fidelity during the summer and early autumn of 1942.

To escape the summer heat of Manhattan, Saint-Exupéry had rented a clapboard house at Westport on Long Island Sound. Consuelo moved in with him and then followed her husband during two other moves, one to Northport, also on Long Island Sound, and finally to Beekman Place, a four-storey New York house overlooking the East River where they lived from Christmas 1942 until Saint-Exupéry's departure for North Africa on 10 April 1943.

The couple had rarely spent as much time together since the idyllic days at Nice just before their marriage in 1931. Some accounts of these last few months make it seem like a relatively uneventful period, an impression contradicted by Saint-Exupéry's letters and an interpretation of passages in *Wisdom of the Sands*.

Denis de Rougemont and the French novelist André Maurois both provided pictures of devotion and harmony within a predictably unconventional framework. Rougemont spent many weekends at both Westport and Northport where Saint-Exupéry rented a large manor called Bevin House which bore a distant resemblance to the château at Saint-Maurice. The Swiss writer was also a neighbour at Beekman Place where he was constantly telephoned in the early hours of the morning by both Antoine and Consuelo to arbitrate on literary or conjugal matters.

At the time, Saint-Exupéry's preoccupations ranged freely over scientific, political and defence questions. Apart from his books and his brilliant conversation, he was constantly describing often unworkable inventions and drawing up plans to shorten the war. Rougemont commented in his diary: 'He gives me the impression of a brain which can no longer stop itself thinking.'

Saint-Exupéry had an insatiable need for conversation and Rougemont often had to put up with early-morning readings of *Wisdom of the Sands*, or with being kept awake long after going to bed at Northport while a chain-smoking Antoine argued on a variety of disconnected subjects in the middle of the night.

André Maurois, a Pétainist despite his Jewish origins, spent several weeks at Bevin House where there were usually many other guests. In his diary he recorded long evenings playing chess and cards with Antoine. On one occasion he was awakened in the early hours of the morning with shouts of 'Consuelo, Consuelo!'

Saint-Exupéry, writing in his study, had woken his wife to ask for scrambled eggs. This happened twice on the same night. After the second time Saint-Exupéry insisted that Maurois go for a walk and talk in the garden, the centre of a huge wooded estate. Maurois had hardly fallen asleep again before he heard Saint-Exupéry shouting for his wife once more. 'You or Maurois have got to play chess with me,' he said.

Maurois's image of Consuelo as a home-loving and dutiful housewife does not coincide with previous portraits, but she was now over forty and more dependent on Antoine's support than ever before. She had been assured of his devotion in a prayer which he had written for her to say every night.

Lord, I don't want to bother you too much, just accept me as I am. I may seem vain in small things but I am always humble when it's important. I may seem selfish in small things but I am capable of giving everything, even my life, when it's important. I may often seem impure in small things but I am only happy in purity.

Lord, make me always be the woman my husband knows me to be.

Dear Lord, help my husband because he truly loves me and without him I am alone. But I pray that he will die before me because, although he seems so strong, his anguish is too great when he no longer hears me in the house. Lord, above all, save him from this anguish. Always enable me to make a noise in the house, even if I've got to break something every now and again.

Give me the strength to be faithful and avoid seeing those he despises or who resent and detest him. That only makes him unhappy because he has made his life in me. Lord, watch over us. Amen. Your Consuelo.

By the time the prayer was written, Consuelo also felt less

insecure in her marriage. The rival she so much feared in Paris had stayed in France and although this woman made at least one visit to New York to see Antoine before his wife arrived, the affair was in its final months. Consuelo may have been unaware that her husband used to see the journalist Sylvia Hamilton who said there was rarely a day when he did not call round. Hamilton later published letters in which Antoine apologized for leaving her with *'beaucoup de chagrin et beaucoup de peine'*, much heart-break and pain.

Whether or not Consuelo knew about this friendship, she must have been consoled by the message of devotion and the promise of love in *The Little Prince*. As Saint-Exupéry was always seeking opinions about his writing, he must often have turned to his wife while the work was in preparation. Saint-Exupéry had consulted her about his books since *Night Flight* and, according to Rougemont, she had personally decided on *Pilote de guerre* as the French title of *Flight to Arras*. Saint-Exupéry's admission to Adèle Breaux that he knew little about painting made it all the more probable that he asked Consuelo, an accomplished artist, for advice on the drawings for his children's fable and he may have used her as a model. His English teacher said that the graceful costume and yellow scarf of the little prince brought Consuelo immediately to mind when Antoine first showed her the paintings when she visited Bevin House.

After the war, when there were quarrels about Saint-Exupéry's royalties and family resentment at the influence Consuelo had exercised over her husband, there were many attempts to deny or camouflage the fact that Antoine had been writing for his wife. Eventually she was forced to provide proof that she was the little prince's flower. Although she refused to publish any of his other letters, Consuelo showed friends a passage from one which proved beyond doubt that the book was written for her. Among those who saw it before she returned it to a safe in Nice along with hundreds of other letters was the air historian Edmond Petit.

'You know, the rose is you,' Saint-Exupéry wrote. 'Perhaps I haven't always known how to look after you well, but I have always found you pretty.' In another letter, Saint-Exupéry told his wife that his greatest regret was not to have dedicated *The Little Prince* to her.

With that evidence in mind, any number of theories can be drawn up about the real meaning of Saint-Exupéry's references to the dangers to his flower of grazing sheep, the handful of caterpillars on the rose's stem and the solitary plant's four thorns. The rose's pleas for protection from the sheep and the little prince's decision to leave his planet inevitably evoke Consuelo's lonely exile in war-torn Europe after Saint-Exupéry took refuge in the United States.

But whether the metaphors have any sense beyond the most obvious significance is less important than Saint-Exupéry's recognition that he loved Consuelo, that the world would have been dark without her and that he would stand by her for ever because of their shared experiences.

'If someone loves a flower which exists in a unique example among millions and millions of stars, that should be enough for him to be happy when he looks at them,' says the little prince. 'He tells himself: My flower is somewhere out there. But if the sheep eats the flower, it's as if all the stars have suddenly gone out for him.'

The torment caused by the rose's vanity, her demands for attention, her extravagant fears of non-existent tigers, her horror of draughts and her coughing to distract the little prince from noticing a white lie can all be seen as personal observations. No doubt Consuelo read the drafts and recognized these barely disguised rebukes, but this could have detracted little from her husband's admission that he had misunderstood her often irritating claims for attention.

'I should have judged her by her acts and not by her words,' the little prince says. 'She wrapped herself around me and enlightened me. I should never have fled. I should have guessed at the tenderness behind her poor ruses. Flowers are so contradictory but I was too young to know how to love her.'

The admission of incomprehension is reciprocal. The little prince is taken aback when the rose says she is sorry for being so difficult just before he sets out on his adventures to other planets. He cannot understand this 'calm sweetness'.

'But of course I love you,' the flower tells him. 'You didn't know anything because I was wrong. But you are as stupid as I am.'

From the moment the little prince leaves his flower, his travels parallel the vain search for interior peace that can be traced in Saint-Exupéry's adventurous life, his abandonment of Consuelo when he left for the United States and his discovery that relationships with other women were usually meaningless. The meeting with the fennec or desert fox at last makes him understand that the mutual need engendered by the trying years with Consuelo had bound them together for eternity.

'It's the time you have wasted on your rose that makes your rose so important,' the fox tells the little prince. 'Men have forgotten this truth. You become responsible for ever for that which you tame. You are responsible for your rose.' Death, with its implied return to innocence and the truths that grown men forget, concludes one of the strangest love-letters ever written.

The sentiments expressed in *The Little Prince* are complemented by numerous tender and remorseful references to marital love in *Wisdom of the Sands*. Saint-Exupéry's Berber chief leaves his sleeping wife and searches for an impossible treasure elsewhere. 'But sleep and be reassured by your imperfection, imperfect spouse,' he meditates. 'You are not an ambition or a reward, a jewel venerated for itself of which I will soon tire. You are the way, the means and the carriage.'

While there is still argument over whether these unfinished and unedited notes should have been published at all as a completed book, they contain startlingly clear moments of self-confession. In the loosely connected parables written in biblical style, the narrator admits to taking the wrong road in a rush to seek other women during aimless voyages. Comparisons are drawn to a frenetic search for a treasure from which he draws 'neither, glory, wealth nor love' and to collecting honey from hive to hive instead of recognizing that the real feast is elsewhere.

'But I want to perpetuate love and there is no love except where the choice is irrevocable because it has to be limited to love,' he wrote in a reflection on conjugal fidelity and the emptiness of casual liaisons. 'The pleasure of the ambush, the hunt and the capture is not love.'

In the fastnesses of the night and during his long and solitary flights, Saint-Exupéry became enmeshed in a search for ideals which he translated into fable and parable or repeated in letters. *The Little Prince*, written in his wife's presence, should have been the culmination of this self-examination, providing the justification for a tired couple approaching middle age to lay down the emotional weapons that had caused so many wounds.

Unfortunately, the book provided only a respite in the troubled relationship which was again near to collapse by Christmas 1942 when the couple had a fierce row. Within weeks of *The Little Prince* reaching the publishers, the atmosphere had become so bad that Saint-Exupéry told her in a letter that his only hope of inner peace lay in death.

Two days before leaving the United States in April 1943 to rejoin his air force unit in North Africa, Antoine referred to renewed quarrelling and the onset of despondency. The issue was again over Consuelo's expenditure on clothes. Because money was so short, he was unable to order a regulation air force officer's kit and had to make do with a slightly ridiculous dark blue stage uniform made for the Metropolitan Opera.

'I've spent the day in torment,' he wrote to Consuelo after his last-minute search for air force clothes.

> I haven't a shirt without a hole for North Africa – nor socks, nor shoes nor anything. I asked myself how am I going to find a few sous? Then you come back in new dresses. I only wanted to know the price, that's all. I am terribly discouraged.
>
> I think you will be happier without me while I think I will at last find peace in death. I desire and wish for nothing except peace and nothing has any importance apart from what awaits me.

CHAPTER FIFTEEN

Heaven's Pilgrim

ON 31 July 1944, thirteen months after leaving the United States in an Atlantic convoy, Saint-Exupéry failed to return from a long-range photo-reconnaissance mission over southern France. The 2/33 group campaign log-book recorded that he took off from Corsica for the Savoy region and had not come back to base four hours later when his sortie should have been completed. By 2.30 p.m. all hope of his returning was abandoned.

> With him we lose not only our dearest comrade but the one who gave us the greatest example. If he came to us to share the risks despite his age, it was not just to add vain glory to an already magnificent career, but because he felt the need within himself. Saint-Exupéry is one of those men who are great before life itself because they know how to respect themselves.

This first posthumous tribute is followed by the hope that Saint-Exupéry might have survived his eighth high-level flight in the fastest and most modern of Allied fighter-bombers, an American P–38 Lightning. The diary entry reflected on the possibility that he could have taken refuge in Switzerland with a damaged plane, gone into hiding with the Maquis in Savoy or been taken prisoner.

As no one ever found his plane, just as no one discovered the aircraft of Mermoz and Guillaumet, speculation over Saint-Exupéry's fate has increased over the years. Lindbergh put forward the theory that the Lightning disintegrated in high-level flight. Other pilots were sure he had crashed into a remote area of the Alps above Nice.

Although the most believable evidence indicated that Saint-Exupéry was shot down over Agay or Nice, his group commander René Gavoille thought that he could have plunged into the Mediterranean after passing out because of an oxygen fault.

Among those who knew of Saint-Exupéry's tendency to melancholy there were inevitable rumours of suicide, an idea which caused anger in the Saint-Exupéry family where it was considered preposterous that a man born a Catholic could deliberately take his own life. His literary executor, Frédéric d'Agay, summed up family feelings: 'If you don't believe that Saint-Exupéry gave his life in a spirit of self-sacrifice like a chivalrous knight then you know nothing about the man.'

The possibility that Saint-Exupéry had thrown in his hand in the face of professional and personal pressures was considered by his mother, Marie de Saint-Exupéry, who told friends that her son could well have taken refuge in a monastery to escape his worldly problems. But the vague hope that he was alive and working on *Wisdom of the Sands* did little to dispel Marie's grief, and she wrote a poem called 'Easter 45' in which she noted her sorrow that her son did not even have a grave.

> But his hunger for light was such
> That he ascended like a pilgrim of the stars.
> Pilgrim of heaven, has he arrived
> At the beacons of God? Ah, if I knew
> I would cry less under my veil.

There is no note or record of any conversation in which Saint-Exupéry talked of ending his life. On the other hand, there are many letters where he expresses an indifference to death and views the eventual prospect with relief. During his stay in North Africa during 1943 and 1944 he often wearied of an existence in which bodily and spiritual burdens were liberally heaped on him either by chance, by age or by spite. When he was confronted with the high probability of dying in a plane at the end of July 1944, just thirty-two years after his first flight with the Wrobleski brothers at Ambérieu, he may not have had the strength of will to make the superhuman effort to survive.

He knew that his air force flying days were numbered because he was too old for war missions. His health was worsening and his pessimism over the post-war world was acute. He might have struggled on if he had been able to turn to his mother for comfort, but with mainland France still enemy territory his last correspondence was limited to letters smuggled across the Mediterranean by Resistance workers. Not much came back to North Africa apart from grim reports which included the bad news that the château at Agay had been blown up by the Germans as part of the Riviera coastal defence plans.

An incalculable final psychological blow was the continued separation from Consuelo and her inability to provide him with the reassurance that one day they would grow old together in peace. He yearned for this prospect in his constant flow of messages to Beekman Place, their last home in New York, and yet his lack of confidence in his wife continued to torment him in the days before his death.

The most public assault on his sensitivity was the revengeful attitude of the Gaullist movement which did not give up its campaign against Saint-Exupéry even after he arrived in Algiers on 4 May 1943 following a three-week sea-journey in a troop transport. In articles and open letters from New York, Saint-Exupéry had repeatedly expressed his belief that differences between Vichy and the Free French had to be wiped out if national unity was to be restored. But he underestimated de Gaulle's determination to destroy Philippe Pétain's influence by what Saint-Exupéry saw as a vindictive purge of non-Gaullists.

Antoine himself became one of the lesser targets of this political war, although at first his life appeared to be again on a normal course when he arrived in Algiers and went to stay with Georges Pélissier, the doctor and amateur literary critic he had known for nearly twenty years. Within twenty-four hours he had also met his pre-war instructor from the Brest maritime aviation school, Lionel-Max Chassin, and had borrowed a plane for a reunion with the pilots of 2/33, then based at Laghouat.

Unfortunately, Saint-Exupéry's wish to return to a fighting role meant asking approval from General Henri Giraud, future joint chairman of the national liberation committee based in Algiers. The fact that Giraud was the central figure in President Franklin D. Roosevelt's scheme to block de Gaulle's rising power was eventually to turn to Saint-Exupéry's disadvantage. Giraud personally asked General Dwight D. Eisenhower, the American Commander-in-Chief in North Africa, to approve Antoine's return to 2/33. But the French general's authority was already on the wane within three weeks of Saint-Exupéry's arrival. De Gaulle had moved his headquarters from London to Algiers before taking full control of the French provisional government and ousting Giraud. For Gaullists, Giraud was a friend of Vichy, and this made his supporters equally untrustworthy.

If Saint-Exupéry had concentrated on what he could do best – flying and writing – instead of continuing to criticize the Gaullist movement, he might have saved himself from absurd petty persecutions, including the banning of *Flight to Arras* by de Gaulle's provisional government even though it was secretly circulating in France in editions published by the Resistance movement. De Gaulle also struck Antoine's name out of a speech delivered on 30 October 1943 to honour writers who had gone into exile rather than collaborate, and had refused to help Saint-Exupéry get back on active service, reportedly dismissing the author as 'that man who could play card-tricks'.

Because *Flight to Arras* had first been banned by the Nazis, Saint-Exupéry may well have felt that his most outrageous judgements of de Gaulle's authoritarianism were justified. Two of his letters reflected his contempt for the general's plans to exploit his personal prestige to restore France's world role. Saint-Exupéry told his US publisher Curtice Hitchcock that Gaullism carried with it the threat of dictatorship and national socialism. He then put his thoughts on a quasi-official level by writing to the American representative in Algiers, Robert Murphy, saying that the salvation of France could not rest on a bloody purge launched by fanatics of what he called '*le parti unique*', in other words the Gaullists.

Saint-Exupéry's provocative claims were a reflection of his bitterness at being called a coward by Gaullists in New York. His need to wipe out this stigma explained much of his determination to fly on some of the most dangerous missions of the war in a machine that represented a supreme test of skill and endurance even for the fittest and youngest of men. The only way to buy back his honour was to fly into the face of death.

His conscience would have been enough to drive him beyond his own limits even without the goading of Gaullist persecution. In a letter to Sylvia Hamilton, he admitted his 'heavy remorse' at having lived in New York while his countrymen were fighting and dying. 'Why can't they let me lead a pure life flying a warplane?' he lamented.

Only an official grounding order from the highest authority or the end of the war could have saved Saint-Exupéry from what seems to have been an inevitable and self-chosen fate, dying a glorious death in the face of an armed enemy rather than being ground down by acts of political revenge.

The Death Wish

SAINT-EXUPÉRY was well aware of the frustrating and futile life that awaited him if his usefulness as an active-service pilot was brought to an end. From July 1943 until 6 June 1944, after just one photographic mission over southern France, he had been grounded. His elation at returning to battle came to an abrupt end and a period of despondency ensued.

'Those eight months which followed [the grounding] were without doubt the most painful he had ever lived,' wrote Nelly de Vogüé who visited him in Algiers. He suffered the 'paroxysm of anguish and despair', although only his intimate friends understood the gravity of his suffering.

How different life had looked after his first flight over southern France on 21 July 1943 which had followed seven weeks of training on the Lightning, a complex piece of machinery capable of flying at 650 kilometres an hour. Practice flights were intended to build up endurance as much as skill, because reconnaissance pilots had to carry out solitary missions lasting up to six hours at 10,000 metres, a far more exhausting test than in the Bloch 174.

[257]

The physical strain of long-distance flight in a poorly heated, unpressurized cockpit with constant reliance on an artificial oxygen supply was increased by intense enemy activity. At the time, the Germans still held Sicily, Sardinia and Corsica from where the Luft-waffe operated fighter patrols to intercept Allied planes from North African bases. Fit young pilots returned exhausted from similar photographic raids, but Saint-Exupéry also had to put up with pain at high altitude where low pressure played havoc with old fractures and spinal rheumatism. Even so, he flew back to his unit's new base at La Marsa in Tunisia on 21 July 'radiant with joy', in the words of one of his comrades, Jean Leleu. 'In his eyes you could see his spiritual joy at having at last resumed his place in the struggle and being able to pursue in action the ideal that had inspired his life as a writer.'

Saint-Exupéry celebrated at a dinner in a small Algiers restaurant where the guests included the film actor Jean Gabin and Pélissier, who recalled how Antoine exulted in the sensation of overflying the coastline between Toulon and Marseille even though he was met by anti-aircraft fire. Hardly a week later, Saint-Exupéry's second outing to southern France was cut short by engine trouble before he reached the Mediterranean and he crash-landed on the airstrip at La Marsa. A pile-up the end of the runway was attributed to his failure to follow braking instructions and he was suspended from flying.

To judge from an unposted letter he wrote before the accident to General René Chambe, the provisional government's Information Minister, Saint-Exupéry's happiness over a return to active service was changing to disillusionment well before he was grounded – another instance of Léon Werth's observation that his friend was never happy for long.

I have just made several flights on a P–38. It is a lovely machine. I would have been happy to have such a present for my twentieth birthday but today I realize with sadness that at forty-three and with 6500 hours of flying behind me I can no longer find much pleasure in this game. [The plane's] nothing more than an instrument for moving from one place to another and, as in this case, of war.

The letter ended in pathetic bewilderment at growing materialism in a world at the mercy of a self-serving consumer society. Saint-Exupéry said he felt he was drifting towards the darkest time in the world, adding: 'It's nothing to me if I am killed in the war. Of what I loved, what will remain? As much as of fellow beings, I am talking about customs, irreplaceable rituals and a certain spiritual light.'

The plaintive letter, which included a second insistence that he couldn't care less if he died in battle, was published after the war under the title. '*Que faut-il dire aux hommes*?' – What Can We Tell Mankind? – a melancholic question in a text full of unease at changing values and fears of post-war chaos.

This self-questioning pursued him after his suspension from flying. During the next few months, his closest friends were aware of persistent low spirits despite a superficially gay and intense social life. Much of his time was spent in an incredibly untidy little room in Pélissier's flat in Algiers, a city which had always made him miserable. He felt trapped in the small living-space, describing it as a monk's cell without religion where he was forced to contemplate the 'total absence of days to come'.

In published letters, he repeatedly expressed incomprehension over his fellow Frenchmen's refusal to live in an atmosphere of love and forgiveness. 'Hate, everything is under the sign of hate. Poor country.'

Without the observations of de Vogüé and Pélissier, the unhappiness of these eight months would probably never have been known. Algiers was the temporary capital of France and many of Saint-Exupéry's old friends and acquaintances who joined him there spoke of apparently joyful parties and dinners where Antoine played his role of conjurer and story-teller.

Chess took up hours of his time and among his regular partners was André Gide, who had brought him news of his mother and sister in Provence. Their uneven friendship was severely tested by Gide's attempts to convert Antoine to Gaullism. But they continued to meet for chess as often as possible despite the older writer's tendency to cheat, a weakness revealed to Antoine by the writer Max-Pol Fouchet, who saw Gide rearranging pawns while Antoine's back was turned.

Books were still one of Saint-Exupéry's main refuges from gloom, although Pélissier said that Antoine read more for technical reasons than for distraction. When his ban had been lifted and he flew to Tunis in July 1944 to act as godfather to the child of his commanding officer, René Gavoille, fellow pilots could not drag Antoine away from a detective novel he was reading. 'He read it in the jeep,' the group's campaign log-book noted.

> He read it on the airstrip while everyone waited for him to get into the plane. He read it in the plane when someone went to get his earphones which he had naturally forgotten and he refused to let the book be torn from his hands before taking off under the pretext that he had some pages to read and he took off with the novel on his knees. We all thought he would start reading again after take-off and the story would end with a brutal contact between the plane and something very hard.

A dinner he was due to attend was held up for an hour while the guests watched Saint-Exupéry's plane circle over Algiers as he finished the last pages.

'We don't know what he was reading,' Pélissier said. 'But it's fair to think that Saint-Exupéry continued less out of interest in the story than in the technical problem of construction. His Poe-like imagination analysed books, their development and their clumsiness while finding a solution to the puzzle.'

Saint-Exupéry's own writing concentrated on *Wisdom of the Sands*. On 7 September 1943 a Free French captain from New York, Léon Wencelius, turned up at Pélissier's flat with a pigskin suitcase containing 700 typewritten pages of the philosophical work that Saint-Exupéry had entrusted to Consuelo. The suitcase was a present from his wife and contained several love-letters.

From then on, Saint-Exupéry's only important preoccupation in the long sleepless hours of the night, with the exception of his correspondence to Consuelo, was an attempt to perfect his parables of the Berber chieftain in his desert citadel. Even though he told friends that the book would not be finished for at least ten years, he had begun to give his personal philosophy a more coherent shape, drawing on personal experience, the Christian teaching of his childhood and the harsh lessons of life in the Sahara.

As he had no secretary to type out his notes, much of what was written in Algiers proved to be illegible, providing a conundrum for de Vogüé, Wencilius and Simone de Saint-Exupéry when they edited the unfinished work after the war. However, a typewritten passage dictated in New York provided evidence that Saint-Exupéry rarely went beyond his own immediate experience in the search for both anecdote and analysis. The Berber chief laments the torment of an aching back which the doctors did not know how to cure.

'Now, I am like a tree in the forest under the axe of a lumberjack and God will bring me down in my turn like a crumbling tower,' Saint-Exupéry wrote. Apart from the reference to persistent pain from old injuries, the reference amounted to a prophecy. On 6 November 1943 he fell in an unlighted staircase and severely bruised his spine.

In the weeks to come, the consequences of the fall became the subject of a thick wad of correspondence with Pélissier, some of it pushed under the doctor's bedroom door after he had gone to sleep. In a book called *Les Cinq Visages de Saint-Exupéry* – The Five Faces of Saint-Exupéry – Pélissier took thirteen pages to describe Antoine's reaction to the accident in which he disputed his doctor's refusal to believe that the vertebrae were fractured. The hand-delivered correspondence circulating inside the flat only ceased when Saint-Exupéry reluctantly accepted the doctor's original diagnosis of extensive bruising and Pélissier's refusal to prescribe a long period of rest in bed.

The 'absurd affair', as Antoine called it, is riddled with the curious humour of a hypochondriac. In letters to Pélissier, he says that he wants to be seriously ill and would prefer to be suffering from operable appendicitis rather than a benign stomach complaint.

This wish for a real illness, which would have provided him with a valid reason for being rejected by the air force, seemed to have been granted as soon as he accepted that the back pain was not as grave as he thought. He was sure he had cancer of the stomach and was sent for a series of X-rays. On 24 February 1944 he was told by

Pélissier that he was suffering only from severe heartburn caused by taking too much medication and eating too much spiced food.

With no escape, Saint-Exupéry again began lobbying for a return to active service and finally won his case in April 1944 after a personal approach to the American Mediterranean air force commander. Hardly three months later he was killed.

The Mantle of Love

IN late 1943 Saint-Exupéry wrote a moving plea to Consuelo in New York, begging her to be 'all in blossom' for his eventual return from the war. He had just received a letter from her which he showed to André Gide who found it 'extraordinarily moving'. The contents of Consuelo's letter are unknown but Antoine's reply leaves no doubt that it was another call to forget their past differences. After receiving the message, he told Gide that he was going to break off his affair with the other woman who had caused Consuelo so much heartbreak when they lived in Paris.

In twelve tightly written pages, Saint-Exupéry, who calls Consuelo 'my little chick', expresses his need for her influence as a Muse. Consuelo had been close to him when writing his most successful imaginative works and the inspiring effect of her presence was made explicit through a parable contained in the letter.

> Darling, I want to tell you about an old dream that I had during the time of our separation. I was in a field and the earth was dead. And the trees were dead. And nothing had either smell or taste.
>
> And suddenly, although nothing had apparently changed, everything had changed. The earth was again full of life and the trees lived again. Everything had taken on a smell and taste which was too much, too much for me.
>
> And I knew why. And I said: 'Consuelo has been reborn. Consuelo is there.' You were the salt of the earth. Just by coming back, you reawakened in me the love for all things.

Consuelo, I then understood that I would love you for eternity.

In his life and writing, Saint-Exupéry transformed dull and tragic events into occasions full of colour and comfort. Consuelo's letter had been enough to wipe out the tension of the last few weeks in the United States. She had again become the object of gratitude and adulation. It was for Antoine to assume the burden of contrition.

'Consuelo, thank you from the bottom of my heart for having made so much effort to remain my companion,' he told her. 'Now that I am at war and completely lost on this immense planet, I have only one consolation, a star which lights the house. *Petit poussin*, keep it pure.'

The continued separation weighed heavily throughout the weeks that followed as Antoine poured out his love to his wife in a flow of correspondence which amounted to at least one letter every day. All these messages were cherished and preserved by Consuelo who allowed little of importance to be seen by other people, even refusing to sell letters to pay for hospital treatment and tax arrears in old age.

It would have been an impossible task for anyone except a writer as prolific as Saint-Exupéry himself to have sent back enough reassurance to a man known for his hyper-anxiety and often morbid imagination. As Saint-Exupéry's absence grew longer, Consuelo usually replied only by short notes on postcards rather than by letters. Not long before he was killed she excused herself for being a poor correspondent, claiming that it was difficult to write because she had a broken finger.

Long periods of silence while awaiting Consuelo's replies from New York, and the fear that she had deserted him, often plunged Antoine into gloom and bursts of recrimination. These worries were evident in the days before his death when his air force comrades noticed the damaging effects of her enforced absence. Exhausting hours alone in a cramped cockpit, dependent on an inadequate oxygen supply, could only have added to the mental torment of a man who spoke so bleakly of the future.

He was much too old to fly Lightnings, supposedly restricted to pilots under the age of thirty, and the accumulated fatigue of eight high-level missions over France added to senior officers' worries about his will to survive. Visitors to the Corsican base were also struck by the strain being put on Saint-Exupéry, who would not admit to problems in coping with missions that lasted six hours. The American photographer John Phillips, who took the last pictures of Antoine in his Lightning, told him that modern fighter planes were like young women, that 'neither are made for ageing men'.

Originally Saint-Exupéry had been given permission for only five sorties and should have been rested long before his last flight, but it was difficult to exercise any authority over a man who ignored orders that clashed with his personal quest for honour – a quest which had already earned him three Croix de Guerre. Even after Saint-Exupéry made a serious navigation error which took him over Italy where he was chased by German fighters, the only effective form of rebuke from his commanding officer, René Gavoille, was to refuse to speak to him. Nor had anyone the courage to tell Saint-Exupéry that he would soon be taken out of active service because of age and fatigue. It was finally decided to employ a ruse and inform him of plans for the imminent invasion of Provence, because Allied headquarters had issued strict instructions to ground all military personnel who had advance knowledge of the August attack.

But the plan to tell Saint-Exupéry had still not been put into effect on the morning of his death, even though enemy air activity had been stepped up in anticipation of the invasion. The day before, the Luftwaffe had shot down the American pilot of a Lightning reconnaissance aircraft almost within sight of Saint-Exupéry's Corsican base. The plane had plunged into the Mediterranean accompanied by nothing more than a brief and agonizing shout of distress.

This picture of his fellow pilot's violent release from a planet which Saint-Exupéry viewed with unbearable sadness accompanied him as he prepared for his last flight and during the long haul up the Rhône Valley. Death under the cannons of a German fighter must have seemed as swift and sweet as the little prince's encounter with the poisonous snake.

Perhaps only an act of love, the total devotion which he had sought all his life, would have given Saint-Exupéry the strength to return safely from his final mission. Since leaving New York, the balance of his relationship with his wife had changed. He was no longer the apprehensive little prince trying to amuse a capricious flower. He had become the lost and bewildered boy of his own creation wandering in a hostile wilderness, craving the affection that would break the thin thread drawing him towards despair. Antoine needed a selfless guardian angel to re-create the security and consolation he had felt long ago in his mother's arms.

He had once prayed for Consuelo to assume the maternal role that Marie de Saint-Exupéry had filled in the château at Saint-Maurice forty years before. 'Dear Consuelo, be my protection,' he wrote from an overcrowded barrack-room on a desert air base not long before he died. 'Make me a mantle of your love. Your husband, Antoine.'

No one will know what Saint-Exupéry thought when he finally met the violent death which had eluded him so often. His radio had been silent long before his plane hit the sea.

EPILOGUE

The Search

HALF a century after Saint-Exupéry's death, the exact circumstances remain a mystery. For a long time it seemed probable that he had been shot down by two German FW–190 fighters which had taken off for an armed reconnaissance mission from a base at Orange an hour before the Lightning reached the coast. In 1972 a German military magazine, *Der Landser*, published what was thought to be a genuine letter from a pilot, Robert Heichele, to a friend, describing how he and a sergeant pilot pursued a Lightning P–38 on 31 July 1944 and saw the plane crash into the sea off Agay after being hit by cannon-fire.

Heichele was badly burned three weeks later in a landing accident and was killed when an ambulance he was travelling in was hit by gunfire from a Resistance group near Lyon. The twenty-one-year-old German flyer was buried in France.

The letter has recently been dismissed by most researchers as a hoax, but details in the account coincided with some findings by military and civilian historians and it may well have been based on a true, unpublished report. After a long examination of Luftwaffe files and the questioning of many French eyewitnesses, it was decided to conduct a search in the Baie des Anges off Nice in the autumn of 1992. An area of ten square kilometres was examined by sonar and mini-submarines but failed to find any debris.

More than forty local people had testified to sightings which confirmed the belief that the plane had been shot down off Nice just after midday, a theory supported by an adviser to the investigating team, Daniel Decot, a former fighter pilot and military researcher who had spent twenty years looking for evidence.

The fact that the plane was not found in the Baie des Anges does not mean it did not disappear into the Mediterranean. A plane hitting the sea would break into 10,000 pieces. After examining all available reports and documents I believe the most probable theory is that there was a battle with one or two German planes.

I am pessimistic about the full truth ever being revealed although investigations will continue. Unfortunately, the Germans don't want to admit that they shot down the author of *The Little Prince*.

After Saint-Exupéry's death, Consuelo bought an old house above Grasse with a view of the sea after doctors told her that the climate would ease her asthma. She continued to sculpt, producing life-size statues of Antoine and the little prince, and her paintings were shown in several exhibitions. She remained on good terms with Antoine's mother who continued to live in nearby Cabris until her death in 1972 at the age of ninety-seven. In 1992 the village school was officially named after Marie because of her kindness towards children and old people.

Consuelo did not marry again and lived until 1979. Her body was taken to Paris and buried in the Père-Lachaise cemetery alongside the writer Enrique Gomez Carrillo in accordance with his will. His bronze death-mask on the tomb was sculpted by Consuelo.

Bibliography

WORKS BY ANTOINE DE SAINT-EXUPÉRY
(ALL PUBLISHED BY GALLIMARD, PARIS)

Courrier Sud (*Southern Mail*), 1930

Vol de Nuit (*Night Flight*), 1931 – Prix Femina

Terre des Hommes (*Wind, Sand and Stars*), 1939 – Prix du Roman, Académie Français

Pilote de Guerre (*Flight to Arras*), 1942

Le Petit Prince (*The Little Prince*), 1943

Citadelle (*Wisdom of the Sands*), 1948

COLLECTIONS OF ESSAYS AND LETTERS:

Ecrits de Guerre (*Wartime Writings*), 1953

Lettres de Jeunesse (*Early Letters*), 1955

Un Sens à la vie (*A Meaning of Life*), 1956

Lettres à sa mère (*Letters to his mother*), 1955, revised 1984

RECOMMENDED BOOKS ABOUT SAINT-EXUPÉRY OR
PIONEER AVIATION

Cate, Curtis: *Antoine de Saint-Exupéry*, Paragon House, 1970

Chevrier, Pierre: *Antoine de Saint-Exupéry*, Gallimard, 1949

Chevrier, Pierre: *Saint-Exupéry*, essai, Gallimard, 1959

Delange, René: *La Vie de Saint-Exupéry*, Seuil, 1950

Delaunay, Henri: *Araignée du Soir*, France Empire, 1968

Dupérier, Bernard: *Chasseur du Ciel*, Perrin, 1992

Estang, Luc: *Saint-Exupéry*, Seuil, 1956

Kessel, P: *La vie de Saint-Exupéry*, Gallimard, 1954

Migéo Marcel: *La Vie de Saint-Exupéry*, Flammarion, 1958

Pélissier, Georges: *Les Cinq visages de Saint-Exupéry*, Flammarion, 1951

Roy, Jules: *Saint-Exupéry*, La Manufacture, 1990

Rougemont, Denis de: *Journal d'une époque*, Gallimard, 1968

Tavernier, René: *Saint-Exupéry en procés* Pierre Belfond, 1967

Werth, Léon: *Saint-Exupéry, tel que je l'ai connu*, Seuil, 1950

OTHER USEFUL BOOKS OR PUBLICATIONS:

Archives Nationales, Saint-Exupéry exhibition catalogue, 1984

Confluences (revue), articles about Saint-Exupéry, 1947

Carrera, Mario: *Microbiographia de Enrique Gomez Carrillo*, UCA editores, El Salvador

Estienne, d', d'Orves, Rose et Philippe: *Honoré d'Estienne d'Orves*, France Empire, 1990

Icare (revue) 1974–81

Lars, Claudia: *Tierra de infancia*, UCA editores, El Salvador

Nous (magazine, Collège de Notre-Dame-de-Sainte-Croix), May 1971

Rémens de, Simone, (Saint-Exupéry), Météores, Taupin (Hanoi), 1943

Saint-Exupéry de, Consuelo: *Oppède*, Gallimard, 1945

Index

Abbeville, battle at, 216
Abetz, Otto, 205
Achard, Marcel, 166
Action Française, 41, 44–5
Ader, Clément, 47
Aéby, Robert, 69–72
Aeroposta Argentina, 116, 141
d'Agay, Frédéric, 29, 254
d'Agay, Jean, 153
d'Agay, Mireille, 169
Air Bleu, 160
Air France, 156–60, 201
Alias, Henry, 221
Allégret, Marc, 81
Almonacid, Vicente Almandos, 116
Ambérieu-en-Bugey, 15–16; flying at, 47–9; pilots' school, fête for, 50–1
Annabella, 157, 244
Anne-Marie, 157–9
Apollinaire, Guillaume, 81
Aragon, Louis, 81
Atlantique Sud, 158

Base d'Aviation 278, 48
Beach, Sylvia, 81
de Beauvoir, Simone, 68
Bergery, Gaston, 206
Bernard, Raymond, 227
Beucler, André, 113–14, 227
Bibliography, 6–7
Biemel, Rainer, 191–2
Blériot, Louis, 47, 49, 178
Bloch 174, 211–13
Blum, Léon, 179, 218, 230
Boname, Robert, 239
Bonnevie, Louis de, 55, 60, 93

Bordeaux, Henry, 205
Bossuet private school, 65
Bouilloux-Lafont, Marcel, 116, 141, 148
Brasillach, Robert, 228
Breaux, Adèle, 246, 249
Brest, aerial navigation school at, 112–13
Breton, André, 81, 236

Camus, Albert, 29
Cape Juby, 94–111
Carambaceres, Luro, 117
Carvenas, Captain Ricardo, 132
Catholic Church: lay republican state, struggle with, 35; Vichy, support for, 224
Caudron 630 Simoun, 160
Céline, Louis-Ferdinand, 228
Ceux de la Résistance, 226
Chambé, General René, 258
de Chambord, Comte, 19
la Chambre, Guy, 209
de Chambrun, René, 172, 212
Chapays, Marguerite, 17–18
Chassin, Lionel-Max, 112–13, 115, 255
Château Malescot, 30
Chéry, Henri, 215
Churchill, Charlotte, 39
Churchill, Major Sydney, 61
Cisneros, Hidalgo de, 101
Claudel, Henri, 170, 237, 240
Claudel, Marie-Sygne, 169
Cocteau, Jean, 233
Collège de la Ville Saint-Jean: atmosphere at, 58; German

language and culture, emphasis on, 56; location, 55–6; open-air activities, 56; teaching at, 56

Collège de Notre-Dame-de-Sainte-Croix: Antoine's schoolmates at, 36; daily routine, 37; detention, 37, 39; discipline at, 38; excursions, 37–8; garrison, used as, 35–6; location, 34; playground activity, 37; priests, 35; reactionary conservatism and royalism, sanctuary for, 41; spartan atmosphere, 36; sponsors, 35; sport at, 38; timetable, 36; unhappiness of Antoine at, 38–9; uniform, 35

Conseil National du Gouvernement, 230

Crane, Helen, 39

Crémieux, Benjamin, 129, 228

Creysell, Paul, 223–4, 226

Croix-de-Deu, 205

Cyprien, 17

Daladier, Edouard, 230

Dali, Salvador, 236

Darlan, François, 225

Darlan, Admiral François, 65

Daurat, Didier, 83–7, 90, 92–3, 96, 98, 106, 111, 125–6, 141, 144–5, 147–8, 160, 162

Davet, René, 209

David, Félicien, 33

Debussy, 33

Decendit, Paul, 125

Decot, Daniel, 266

Decour, Lucie-Marie, 94

Delange, René, 160, 182

Delaunay, Henri, 100–2

Dietrich, Marlene, 235

Donovan, Captain William, 191

Doriot, Jacques, 241

Dreyfus, Alfred, 19

Drieu la Rochelle, Pierre, 227–8

Dunant, André, 38

Dupérier, Bernard, 150, 238, 240–1

Dutertre, Lieutenant Jean, 213–15

Eisenhower, General Dwight D., 256

Escot, Jean, 29

d'Estienne d'Orves, Honoré, 75, 113, 225

Farman, Henri, 90

La Feuilleraie, 208, 220

Fitzgerald, Scott, 81

Five Children in a Garden, 12–13

Flamand, Annette, 50, 58

Fleury, Jean-Gérard, 234–6

Flight to Arras, 210–11, 218; anecdotes in, 217; anti-Semitic criticism of, 218; category of, 3; change of tone in, 219; childhood games, memories of, 14; childhood memories, description of, 13; Gaullists, banned by, 256; mission inspiring, 212–15; physical problems, no hint of, 213; publication of, 218

flying: accidents, reports of, 51–2; airline pilot, Antoine as, 67–8; Antoine's career in, 83–4, 87, 92 et seq.; automatic pilot, 99; exploits, reporting, 47–50; first trial flights, 47; French vision of, 51; long-distance, strain of, 257–8

de Fonscolombe, Alice Boyer, 12

de Fonscolombe, André, 33, 151, 154, 194, 206

de Fonscolombe, Charles, 27, 33

de Fonscolombe, Emmanuel, 31, 33

de Fonscolombe, Baron Fernand, 32

de Fonscolombe, Hubert, 13

de Fonscolombe, Jean-Baptiste, 34

de Fonscolombe, Madeleine, 32

La Fontaine, Jean de, 44

Foreign Legion, 93; nomadic Saharan tribes, guerilla war with, 95

Fouchet, Max-Pol, 259

Free French, 224, 238

Front Populaire, 179

Gabin, Jean, 235, 258

Galantière, Lewis, 194, 204, 230–3, 235, 239

Gallimard, Gaston, 81, 113–14, 162, 190, 194, 227

Gaulle, Charles de, 216, 221, 223–5, 238

Gaultier, Paul, 37, 45

Gavoille, René, 210, 215, 260, 264

Gide, André, 81, 106, 113, 139, 145, 183, 190–1, 259, 262
Giraud, General Henri, 255–6
Giraud d'Agay, Pierre, 73
Gomez Carrillo, Enrique, 129–32, 136, 138, 267
Green de Saint-Marsault, Adelaide, 32
Green de Saint-Marsault, Victoire, 32, 62
Gringoire, 205–6
Guerrero, Francisco Mena, 130, 132
Guillaumet, Henri, 84, 89–91, 98, 100–1, 104, 116, 144–5, 147, 157, 201–2, 224, 244; Andes, crash in, 119–23, 168; death of, 229
Guillaumet, Noëlle, 122, 124, 145, 168
Guynemer, George, 48

Hamilton, Sylvia, 201, 207, 238, 244–5, 249, 257
Heichele, Robert, 266
Hemingway, Ernest, 81–2
Hitchcock, Curtice, 191, 244, 256
Holweck, Professor Fernand, 211

Irzaguin, 103, 105
Israël, Jean, 213, 216–18, 221; nose, 217

Jacques Bernis's Escape, 81–2
Jaunez, Maximilian, 171
Jeanson, Henri, 159, 176–9, 203, 237, 238
Joyce, James, 81

Kessel, Joseph, 65, 88, 97, 100, 162
Korda, Alexander, 178
Kouprine, Xenia, 132

Lacrouze, Marius, 50
Lamotte, Bernard, 231, 235, 245
Lars, Claudia, 131
Latécoère, Pierre-Georges, 84–5, 90, 92, 116, 148
Latécoère airport, 92
Launay, Abbé Auguste, 41–4, 228
Laval, Pierre, 172, 212, 226, 230, 241
Lazareff, Pierre, 234
Lécrivain, Emile, 93

Lefebvre, Jean-René, 98–9, 123
Lefin, Marcelle, 145
Lelièvre, Jean-Marie, 47
Lestrange, Joseph de, 32
Lestrange, Yvonne de, 68, 80–1, 106, 139, 155, 162, 172, 174, 190, 227
Lindbergh, Anne Morrow, 202
Lindbergh, Charles, 202, 253
Little Prince, The, 236; analysis of, 245, 249–52; Consuelo as inspiration for, 151; distress over Consuelo, reflecting, 246–7; genesis of, 244–6; hero of, 246; hidden language, explanation of, 4; love letter, as, 4; physical characteristics, 244; posthumous success of, 2–3; time of writing, 4
Lucas, Jean, 161–2, 166, 227
Lyautey, Marshal Louis, 93
Lycée Saint-Louis, 62–4

MacOrland, Pierre, 218
Maeterlinck, Maurice, 138, 148, 231
Malraux, André, 29, 75–6, 190
Mandel, Georges, 218
de Massimi, Beppo, 83, 86–7, 92, 160
Massu, General Jean, 222
Mauriac, François, 233
Maurois, Andre, 247–8
Mérignac airfield, 222
Mermoz, Jean, 90, 94, 100–1, 104, 116–17, 126, 134, 144, 147, 149, 157
Mille, Hervé, 193
Mirbeau, Octave, 183
Miró, Joan, 236
La Môle, 31
Molina, Alfonso Quinonez, 131–2
Monnier, Adrienne, 81–2
Montessuy, Father, 16–17, 19–20, 49
Monts du Bugey, 11
Morand, Paul, 218
Morocco, French forces in, 95
Mouthier, Louis, 48, 50

Nangis, posting to, 220
Négrin, Elysée, 125
Néri, Jacques, 141–2, 201
Night Flight: accident in, 125; American production of, 157;

category of, 5; critical acclaim for, 129; criticism of, 144–5; Daurat, portrayal of, 85; draft of, 135, 138; film contract, 148; misery, bringing, 144; Prix Femina, winning, 143; Robineau, portrayal of, 115–16, 124; story of, 142; success of, 5; writing of, 114
Noguès, General Charles, 223
Nouakchott, 104
Nubalde, Paul, 99

'Odyssey of a Hat, The', 42–3
Olivarès, Gaston, 52

Paris, occupied, 227
Pascal, Blaise, 185
Pearl Harbor, bombing of, 235
Pélissier, Georges, 116, 184–5, 195, 210, 255, 258–61
Penicault, Oliver, 221–2
Pétain, Philippe, 216, 221, 223, 226, 230, 238–40, 242; Morocco, in, 95
Petit, Edmond, 249
Phillips, John, 264
Planiol, René, 174–5
Poncet, Anne-Marie, 57
Potez 63, 211
Power, Tyrone, 157, 244
Pranville, Julien, 125–6
Prévost, Jean, 81–2, 113–14, 191
Prévot, André, 161, 165–7, 176, 187–8

R'Guibat, 103, 107
Raccaud family, 166–7
Reine, Marcel, 107–8, 111, 116, 157
Renoir, Jean, 232–4
Reynal, Eugène, 169
Reynaud, Paul, 212
Richard-Willms, Pierre, 158
Riguelle, René, 104–5
Rio de Oro, 95–6, 141
la Rocque, Comte François de, 205
Roubes, Raoul, 119
Rougemont, Denis de, 239–40, 245, 247
Rumbold, Richard, 188

Sachs, Maurice, 155
de Saint-Exupéry, Amicie, 61

de Saint-Exupéry, Anais, 37, 40, 45
de Saint-Exupéry, Antoine: absent-mindedness, 99, 112, 201; air force, joining, 68–70; Air France, job with, 156–60; airline pilot, as, 67–8; America, in, 229–32, 247–9; ancestry, 29–31; anger, 185; animals, gift for taming, 101–2; baptism, 12; birth of, 12; Buenos Aires, transfer to, 114–23; call-up, 1939, 203, 209; Cape Juby, success at, 102–3; card-tricks, fascination with, 184; centre of attention, as, 24; cerebral reflection, appetite for, 171; character of, 24; childhood home, 11–15; children, fondness of, 169; conscription, 64; crashed plane, recovery of, 105–6; creative writing, passion for, 25; death of, 3–4, 253, 264–7; demobilization, July 1940, 223; description of, 23–4, 202–3; domestic politics, interest in, 205–6; eccentricity, 118–19; fatalism, 60; fate, speculation over, 253–4; favourite foods, 173; Fernand, clashes with, 39–40; financial help, 71; first fiancée, 74–8; first flight, 46, 51–2; flying career, 83–4, 87, 92 et seq.; flying, works, inspired by, 5; flying-boat crash, 149–50; flying-boats, testing, 148–50; Fonscolombe characteristics, 32; Free French, refusal to join, 224, 238; Gaullism, opposition to, 238–41; Gaullist criticism of, 239, 255–7; Gaullist propaganda against, 230; Germany, visits to, 204–5; grounding, frustration at, 257; head of family, as, 24; height, 55; hypochondria, 29; last mission, 264; letters from, 79–80, 172; letters to Consuelo, 207–8, 262–3; Légion d'honneur, 98; Léon Werth, relationship with, 181–6; literary craftsmanship, 5; literary output, 88–9; literary talent, encouragement of, 41–2; long-distance flying, 160–7, 175–6, 186–8, 201–2; loss of

home, sadness at, 5; marooned airmen, search for, 107–8; marriage, 129, 136–41; marriage, breakup of, 4, 191–2; meeting Consuelo, 133–4; military flying career, 71–2; minorities, defence of, 45; money, carelessness over, 147; mood swings, 237–8; mother, influence of, 21–2, 26, 243–4; musical talent, 33; natural ambassador, as, 96, 98; naval academy entrance examination, cramming for, 62–5; need for money, 156, 160; need to fly, 143; nicknames, 40; non-literary interests, 174; office work, 78–80; Orconte, posting to, 210–11; paper helicopters, making, 170; passion for aviation, 48–9; patents, 156; personal problems, 5–6; pet rat, 45–6; Place Vauban, flat in, 177; poor health, 213, 232, 261–2; poor marks, 39–40; preparatory school, 36; private life, discretion concerning, 28; Prix Femina, going to collect, 143–4; reading, constant, 260; recording-machine, purchase of, 231, 233; relationship with Consuelo, 151–5, 168–9, 178, 186–7, 207–8, 237, 247–52, 255, 262–3; responsibility, avoiding, 124–5; sadness, increasing, 259; schooling, 34 et seq., See also Collège de la Ville Saint-Jean; Collège de Notre-Dame-de-Sainte-Croix; scruffiness, 70; Simone, argument with, 205–6; spiritual guidance, 34; suicide, possibility of, 254–5; telephone, addiction to, 184; title and social connections, using, 70; travelling salesman, as, 80, 83; untidiness, 173, 189; Vichy administration, attitude to, 226–7; women, romantic view of, 73; works, conciseness of, 5; writer, reputation as, 4; writing methods, 174

de Saint-Exupéry, Consuelo, 6; advice about books, giving, 249;

America, in, 236–7, 247; anxiety over flying, 142–3; appearance, 130–3; background, 131; birthdate, 130; Casablanca, in, 142–3, 146–7; disillusionment, 135; eccentricity, 151; first marriage, 132; intrusions by, 177–8; last years of, 267; life, writing about, 152; marriage, 129, 136–41; marriage breakup, 191–2; meeting Antoine, 133–4; money, spending, 147, 236–7, 252; relationship with Antoine, 151–5, 168–9, 178, 186–7, 207–8, 237, 247–52, 255, 262–3; sadness at marriage breakup, 207; Saint-Maurice, at, 145; sculpture, experimenting in, 132; storytelling, 131; temperament and behaviour, 74, 152–3

de Saint-Exupéry, Fernand, 29–30, 33–4, 37, 55; Antoine's clashes with, 39–40; authority of, 39; Marie, clashes with, 39

de Saint-Exupéry, François, 11–12, 49; character of, 23; death of, 59–60

de Saint-Exupéry, Gabrielle, 12, 137; character of, 23; marriage, 73, 88; son, death of, 170

de Saint-Exupéry, Georges, 32, 62

de Saint-Exupéry, Jean-Antoine, 30

de Saint-Exupéry, Jean Viscomte, 12; death of, 27–8; life of, 28–9; marriage, 32

de Saint-Exupéry, Marie, 16, 37, 162; ancestors, 31–2; Antoine, influence on, 21–2, 26, 243–4; Antoine's marriage, opinion of, 137; contemporary piano music, taste for, 33; death of, 267; early youth reminiscences of, 22; faith, 21; Fernand, clashes with, 39; flying, worry about, 71; grief over Antoine's death, 254; last visit from Antoine, 228; marriage, 32; music and painting, interest in, 21; painting, 34; Red Cross work, 58; Saint-Maurice-de-Rémens, inheriting, 70; tragedies, 26; widowhood, 21

de Saint-Exupéry, Marie-
Madeleine, 12, 14, 17, 70, 83;
character of, 23; death of, 87
de Saint-Exupéry, Raymond, 30
de Saint-Exupéry, Roger, 35, 55
de Saint-Exupéry, Simone, 12, 14,
48, 88, 95, 135, 196; argument
with Antoine, 205–6; Comtesse
de Tricaud, accounts of, 17;
Consuelo, criticism of, 153; diary,
keeping, 16; story-teller, as, 23
Saint-Maurice-de-Rémens, 4, 7,
11–12; description of, 15; dining-
room, 13; garden, 14; Marie
inheriting, 70; photographs at,
23; sale of, 146; war, after, 59; war
memorial, 15
de Saint-Simon, Comte Claude, 33
Sallès, Charles, 55–6, 64, 79, 94, 110,
152
Salvez brothers, 52–4
de Sandoval, Consuelo Suncin. *See*
de Saint-Exupéry, Consuelo
Sartre, Jean-Paul, 29, 68
de Saussine, Renée, 79–80
Schneider, Jean, 215
de Ségogne, Henri, 136, 162
Serre, Edouard, 107–8, 111
de Sinéty, Odette, 73
Sorto, Manuel, 130
Southern Mail: category of, 5;
childhood memories, description
of, 14; film of, 178; film
production, 157; Geneviève,
character of, 73, 76; outline of, 78;
publication of, 113; reviews of,
113–14; uneven construction of,
89; Ville Saint-Jean, evoking, 57;
writing of, 97
Spanish Civil War, 178–80, 193, 203
Stewart, Margaret, 188
Students, post-war, 68
Sudour, Abbé Maurice, 65–6, 83,
139, 228

Tarfaya, 94
Thénoz, Alfred, 51–2
Thibaut, Georges, 51–3
de Tivera, Miguel Primo, 96
Torrès, Suzanne, 222–3
de Trélan, Alix Bloquier, 30

de Tricaud, Gabrielle Comtesse, 13,
16, 32; description of, 16–17;
eccentricities, 17; republicanism
treatment of, 18–19; royalism, 19;
servants, 17; small boys and
animals, no time for, 17

Valéry, Paul, 81, 233
Valiquette, Bernard, 237
Vasconcelos, José, 132
Védrines, Jules, 50
Vergés, Gilbert, 149
Vichy administration: anti-Semitic
legislation, 228; Antoine's
attitude to, 226–7; Catholic
Church, support of, 224; defeatist
propaganda, 221
Vilmorin, Andrée de, 152
Vilmorin, Louise de, 74–8, 130, 143,
152, 172
Vogüé, Comte Jean de, 172, 225–7
Vogüé, Nelly de, 60, 147, 158, 171,
204, 225, 257, 259, 261; Antoine's
literary career, role in, 172;
friendship with Antoine, 172–4;
marriage, 172; painting, passion
for, 172; role of, 209

Wadi Natroun, 166
Wahl, Antoine, 56
Wells, H.G., 178
Wencelius, Léon, 260–1
Werth, Claude, 152–3, 170, 184
Werth, Léon, 48, 152, 154, 162, 170,
180, 191, 193, 206, 218, 227,
237–8, 241–2, 259; books, 183;
Jewishness, 182; Munich
agreement, denunciation of, 204;
relationship with Antoine, 181–6
Werth, Suzanne, 168, 182, 185, 192
West Africa territory, conquering,
93
Weygand, General Maxime, 212,
216
Wind, Sand and Stars: American
promotion of, 202, 229–30;
American version, 194; Christmas
night images, 108–9; death of
child, description of, 170–1;
desert crash, account of, 161,
164–5, 168; French version, 196;
Grand Prix de Roman, award of,

201; images in, 90; impact of, 120; locations, switching, 92; material for, 141; National Book Award for, 232; optimistic message of, 195; preparation of, 192–7; rewriting, 174; success of, 5; title, choice of, 108, 194; writing, quality of, 89

Wisdom of the Sands, 11; accepting fate, lessons in, 60; code of principles in, 206–7; editing, 172; ethical guidelines, revision of, 224; marital love, references to, 251; minorities, defence of, 45; racial discrimination, attack on, 218–19; writing of, 174–5, 260–1

women, French law on, 34

World War I: end of, 64; Lycée Saint-Louis, atmosphere at, 63–4; Saint-Maurice-de-Rémens, at, 58–9

Wright, Wilbur, 47

Wroblewski, Edouard, 54

Wroblewski, Gabriel, 52